The Building Society Industry

The Building Society Industry

MARK BOLÉAT

Deputy Secretary-General,
The Building Societies Association

London
GEORGE ALLEN & UNWIN
Boston   Sydney

George Allen & Unwin (Publishers) Ltd,
40 Museum Street, London WC1A 1LU, UK

George Allen & Unwin (Publishers) Ltd,
Park Lane, Hemel Hempstead, Herts HP2 4TE, UK

Allen & Unwin Inc.,
9 Winchester Terrace, Winchester, Mass 01890, USA

George Allen & Unwin Australia Pty Ltd,
8 Napier Street, Sydney, NSW 2060, Australia

First published in 1982

British Library Cataloguing in Publication Data

Boléat, Mark
 The building society industry.
 1. Building and loan associations – Great Britain
 I. Title
 332.3′2′0941   HG2156.G75

 ISBN 0–04–332086–4
 ISBN 0–04–332087–2 Pbk   1495015

Library of Congress Cataloging in Publication Data

Boléat, Mark.
 The building society industry.

 Bibliography: p.
 Includes index.
 1. Building and loan associations – Great Britain.
 2. Housing – Great Britain – Finance.   3. Housing –
 Finance.   I. Title.
 HG2156.G75B63   332.3′2′0941   82–6712
 ISBN 0–04–332086–4   AACR2
 ISBN 0–04–332087–2 (pbk.)

Set in 10 on 11 point Times by Northumberland Press, Ltd, Gateshead
and printed in Great Britain by Mackays of Chatham

Contents

PART TWO: POLICY

6   Building Societies and Housing Policy   79

7   The Determination and Control of House Prices   93

8   Co-Operation Between Building Societies and Local Authorities   108

9   Sources of Funds and the Stow Report   118

10 Competition for Funds and the Wilson Report   130

List of Tables

Preface

Building societies have grown spectacularly in the post-war period. They now account for 80 per cent of outstanding mortgage loans and a quarter of households are currently buying their homes with the assistance of building society loans. On the savings side, they hold nearly half of the personal sector's liquid financial assets and perform the role that in many countries is undertaken by specialist savings banks.

The growth of building societies has, as yet, not been fully recognised in the academic literature on financial institutions. This book aims to provide a comprehensive analysis of the economics of building societies and of the major policy issues with which the industry is faced.

Part I of the book is largely descriptive. An introductory chapter includes a brief history of the industry, a description of the legal framework within which societies operate, brief details of the two central bodies in the industry, The Building Societies Association and The Chartered Building Societies Institute, and an analysis of the structure of the industry. Chapters 2 and 3 analyse building society operations in the savings and mortgage markets respectively and Chapters 4 and 5 examine the financial management of societies and levels of activity.

Several major policy issues involving building societies have emerged in recent years. Some have been internal to the industry – such as prudential supervision – while others have been concerned with the relationship between building societies and government or other institutions. Part II analyses these various issues.

Unlike most other financial institutions, building societies' operations are entirely domestic – their special constitution preventing them from operating in other countries. However, this does not mean that developments in other countries can be ignored. The European Community is already having an effect on building society operations and can be expected to have more profound effects as the integration of the European economies proceeds. Chapter 15 discusses these various issues.

The final chapter examines the present state of the industry and speculates on future developments.

This book is very much an insider's view. As Deputy Secretary-General of The Building Societies Association, I have access to information not readily available to other students of the industry and I have been closely involved in many of the policy issues discussed in Part II. I hope that this involvement has not unduly influenced my objectivity.

I am grateful to my employers, The Building Societies Association, for permitting me to write this book and for allowing me to draw so freely on the Association's resources. I am indebted to two of my colleagues at the Association, Adrian Coles and Tricia Loxston, for so willingly reading through earlier drafts of the book and pointing out mistakes and inconsistencies which had eluded the author. My colleagues, Graham Pitt and Kevin

Shears, offered valuable assistance in respect of Chapters 12 and 15 and more generally I have drawn freely on the work they have done for the Association over many years. Neither my colleagues nor the Association are responsible for any remaining errors or for the various points of opinion which have been expressed.

It is said that writing a book is largely perspiration rather than inspiration. This has not been the case for this book. My secretary, Dee Kuhfuss, typed successive drafts with astonishing speed and accuracy. My deadline for completing the book coincided with Dee's departure to live and work in Germany and I am grateful to her for ensuring that the former event preceded the latter. Thanks are also due to Tricia Loxston, Sheela Gohil, Felicity Gallagher and Sue Tilton for helping to type and correct the final text.

Mark Boléat

London
November 1981

Part One

Description and Analysis

Chapter 1

An Introduction to Building Societies

A Brief History of the Building Society Industry

Building societies, together with other friendly societies, developed during the second half of the eighteenth century in response to prevailing economic and social trends including growing financial sophistication, the industrial revolution and the increasing attention being focused on self-help. The first known building society was established in Birmingham in 1775 and it is estimated that by the end of the century, between twenty and fifty had been established, predominantly in the Midlands, Lancashire and Yorkshire. The early societies were true building societies in that they built homes and were mutual. They existed to provide each member, and no one else, with a house paid for out of their funds. The members, generally artisans, numbered not more than twenty and they paid an agreed sum fortnightly or monthly into the funds of the society. When sufficient money had accumulated, land was bought and building commenced. Lots were drawn to decide the order of allocation of the houses although sometimes societies auctioned off this priority to the highest bidder. Members continued making regular payments until all the members had been housed and the society then terminated.

In the early nineteenth century societies took their first steps towards becoming savings institutions. So as to speed up the production of houses, some societies began to pay interest to people who were willing to invest but did not want a house and therefore they had to charge interest to those borrowing.

The first legislation concerned with building societies was the Regulation of Benefit Building Societies Act 1836 which gave societies their official recognition and established a 'certifying barrister' (subsequently the Chief Registrar of Friendly Societies) to register societies' rules and offer advice.

By the middle of the nineteenth century building societies had become substantially larger and a typical society had between 100 and 215 members. The trend towards becoming financial institutions continued and many societies changed from the old terminating format to become permanent societies, offering both savings and lending facilities.

In the 1850s and 1860s building societies were in dispute with the government over their exemption from stamp duty and the first steps were taken to provide a unified voice for the industry. In 1869 the *Building Societies Gazette* was established, facilitating communications within the movement, and in the same year the Building Societies Protection Association, the forerunner of the present Association, was set up.

In 1870 a Royal Commission on friendly societies was established. Building societies were within its terms of reference and came out of the report, which was finalised in 1871, fairly well. It made certain recommendations, particularly with respect to the role of the Chief Registrar (as the 'certifying barrister' had become) and the powers of societies. The report of the Royal Commission was followed by the first comprehensive Building Societies Act in 1874 and the essence of much of this Act remains in force today. The main feature of the Act was to limit building societies to building and owning land for the purposes of conducting their business. The Royal Commission's recommendations for strengthening the powers of the Chief Registrar were also implemented.

The last quarter of the nineteenth century was a time of turmoil for financial institutions generally and building societies were not unaffected. In 1892 the fairly large Portsea Island Building Society collapsed and later that year the industry was rocked by the failure of the Liberator Building Society, by far the largest in the country. An 1894 Act further strengthened the powers of the Chief Registrar and prohibited some of the more questionable practices including second mortgages and balloting for mortgages.

Comprehensive statistics on building societies became available for the first time in the 1890s. In 1895 it is estimated that there were 3,642 societies in existence with a total of 631,000 shareholders and total assets of about £45 million.

The industry grew particularly rapidly in the inter-war years, aided by low interest rates in the economy and rent restrictions which served to discourage the building of homes for rent. The number of societies declined sharply from 1,336 at the end of 1918 to 960 at the end of 1939, largely as a result of terminating societies winding up and very small societies transferring their engagements to larger units. The number of shareholders rose from 625,000 at the end of 1918 to over two million at the end of 1939 and it is estimated that there were 1½ million borrowers at the end of 1939 compared with little more than half a million at the end of 1918. The total assets of building societies increased more than tenfold in the inter-war years from £68 million in 1918 to £773 million in 1939.

However, the 1930s also saw the building society industry face a number of problems. There was fierce competition for mortgages and an attempt to introduce a code of ethics led to a division within The Building Societies Association and the formation of two separate bodies. The problems within the industry were highlighted in 1938 by the 'Borders case' which brought unfavourable publicity on the movement and led to the 1939 Building Societies Act, the main effect of which was to restrict the mortgage security which building societies could accept. The 1939 Act led to the unification of the two associations in 1940.

The immediate post-war years were relatively quiet for building societies, largely because the Labour government concentrated on building houses for rent. However, in the 1950s the rapid increase in the number of houses built for owner-occupation gave societies a much more important role and they expanded rapidly. Societies' significant role in the housing market was particularly recognised by the House Purchase and Housing Act 1959 under which the government lent building societies £100 million for on-lending to purchasers of pre-1919 houses.

The prudential supervision of the industry came under scrutiny during the

1950s, partly as a result of the liquidity problems faced by the relatively large Scottish Amicable Building Society and the dubious practices of the State Building Society. In 1959 societies were given trustee status, i.e. they were empowered to accept the investments of trustees without special authorisation under the trust deed. This 'seal of respectability' was something for which societies had long fought. The Chief Registrar was empowered to lay down conditions which a society had to meet in order to obtain trustee status but in the event these were not onerous.

The Building Societies Act 1960 empowered the Chief Registrar to pre-scribe the way in which societies should invest their liquid funds and this power was used to ensure that societies' liquid funds were both relatively liquid and completely safe. The 1960 Act also gave the Chief Registrar considerably greater powers and introduced the special advance limit which has had the effect of limiting societies' ability to lend large amounts or make loans to corporate bodies. The Building Societies Act 1962 consolidated existing legislation and remains the statute under which societies operate.

In the 1960s and 1970s the number of building societies continued to fall while the assets of the industry and its importance increased considerably. The number of societies fell from 835 at the beginning of 1950 to 726 by the end of 1960 and 273 at the end of 1980. Meanwhile, the number of borrowers increased from $1\frac{1}{2}$ million in 1951 to nearly $5\frac{1}{2}$ million in 1980.

As building societies became more important, so government took a closer interest in their activities and the mortgage rate became the focus for much political comment. In 1966 the government referred building society interest rates to the Prices and Incomes Board and following a recommendation of the Board in the following year, the Association established a committee to make recommendations on reserve and liquidity requirements. Those recommendations, the most important feature of which was to introduce a sliding scale for reserves, came into effect in 1968. In the 1970s, the political importance of building societies increased further, largely as a result of changes in the economic climate which led to substantial variations in the general level of interest rates and hence in building society rates. The industry was also blamed by some commentators for the rapid rise in house prices which occurred in the early 1970s. Relations with the government improved noticeably after the Joint Advisory Committee was established in 1973.

The Legal Framework

As the first section of this chapter has noted, building societies have been subject to special Acts of Parliament and currently they operate under the Building Societies Act 1962, statutory instruments made under that Act and also certain other statutory instruments made under other Acts including the House Purchase and Housing Act 1959 and the European Communities Act 1972.

The law provides that building societies are a special type of institution, that is, they are not companies subject to company law nor are they banks, partnerships nor co-operatives. Section 1(1) of the Building Societies Act 1962 states quite specifically that: 'The purpose for which a society may be

Table 1.1 Building Societies, General Summary, 1900–80

	1	2	3	4	5	6	7	8	Advances during year		11	12
Year	Number of societies	Number of share accounts 000's	Number of deposit accounts 000's	Number of mortgage accounts 000's	Share balances £m.	Deposit balances £m.	Mortgage balances £m.	Total assets £m.	9 Number 000's	10 Amount £m.	Average mortgage rate %	Average share rate %
1900	2,286	585					46	60		9		
1910	1,723	626					60	76		9		
1920	1,271	748			64	19	69	87		25		
1930	1,026	1,449	428	720	303	45	316	371	159	89		4.65
1940	952	2,088	771	1,503	552	142	678	756	43	21	4.76	3.27
1950	819	2,256	654	1,508	962	205	1,060	1,256	302	270	4.18	2.22
1960	726	3,910	571	2,349	2,721	222	2,647	3,166	387	560	5.89	3.37
1961	706	4,122	570	2,425	2,921	226	2,871	3,437	364	546	6.28	3.54
1962	681	4,490	579	2,510	3,265	242	3,138	3,815	378	613	6.61	3.70
1963	662	4,894	592	2,625	3,733	271	3,556	4,331	477	849	6.27	3.56
1964	635	5,284	592	2,757	4,219	293	4,092	4,863	535	1,043	6.16	3.50
1965	605	5,861	593	2,845	4,849	295	4,544	5,532	457	955	6.63	3.78
1966	576	6,563	588	2,992	5,595	299	5,219	6,306	536	1,245	6.95	4.01
1967	554	7,397	596	3,166	6,665	322	6,038	7,446	586	1,463	7.20	4.20
1968	525	8,178	619	3,334	7,453	335	6,901	8,298	595	1,590	7.46	4.37
1969	504	9,085	615	3,470	8,376	347	7,705	9,289	545	1,559	8.08	4.82

Year												
1970	481	10,265	618	3,655	9,788	382	8,752	10,819	624	1,954	8.58	4.94
1971	467	11,568	655	3,896	11,698	490	10,332	12,919	769	2,705	8.59	4.95
1972	456	12,874	675	4,126	13,821	592	12,546	15,246	893	3,630	8.26	4.88
1973	447	14,385	672	4,204	16,021	596	14,532	17,545	720	3,513	9.59	6.51
1974	416	15,856	641	4,250	18,021	633	16,030	20,094	546	2,945	11.05	7.53
1975	382	17,916	677	4,397	22,134	762	18,802	24,204	798	4,908	11.08	7.21
1976	364	19,991	712	4,609	25,760	848	22,565	28,202	913	6,183	11.06	7.02
1977	339	22,536	760	4,836	31,110	1,224	26,427	34,288	946	6,745	11.05	6.98
1978	316	24,999	781	5,108	36,186	1,254	31,598	39,538	1,184	8,808	9.55	6.46
1979	287	27,878	797	5,251	42,023	1,281	36,801	45,789	1,040	9,002	11.94	8.45
1980	273	30,640	915	5,383	48,932	1,724	42,445	53,793	937	9,506	14.94	10.37

1 The figures are based on actual returns provided by all building societies in Great Britain.
2 The figures are the aggregation of figures for societies' financial years ending between 1 February in the year in question and 31 January of the following year. (Prior to 1930 the figures are the aggregation of figures for societies' financial years ending in the calendar year in question.)
3 Before 1930 borrowers who were not also shareholders were included in the number of shareholders.
4 The number of advances includes further advances and therefore does not indicate the number of home-buyers.
5 The average mortgage rate shows the gross rate charged in the year while the average share rate indicates the net rate paid.

Source: Annual Reports of the Chief Registrar of Friendly Societies and BSA estimates for 1980.

established under this Act is that of raising, by the subscriptions of the members, a stock or fund for making advances to members out of the funds of the society upon security by way of mortgage of freehold or leasehold estate.'

Following are the most important legal constraints under which societies currently operate:

(a) Since 1 December 1981 a new society can be formed only if the founders, who must number at least ten, invest £50,000 in the society until such time as the reserves of the society reach that amount.

(b) In order to achieve trustee status (and in practice all sizeable societies have such status) a society must hold liquid assets of $7\frac{1}{2}$ per cent of its total assets and reserves, according to a sliding scale, varying from $2\frac{1}{2}$ per cent of assets not exceeding £100 million to $1\frac{1}{4}$ per cent of assets exceeding £1,000 million.

(c) Societies are mutual organisations with investing members, that is shareholders, and borrowing members. However, in practice investing members tend to regard themselves as depositors rather than owners and seek to play no part in the management of the society.

(d) The Chief Registrar of Friendly Societies is the government official responsible for ensuring that the legislation relating to building societies is observed. In certain circumstances he can make orders against particular societies and he is also responsible for the various statutory instruments which apply to societies.

(e) The Act provides for unions between two or more societies and also for one society to transfer its engagements to another. There have been many transfers of engagements in recent years.

(f) The manner in which societies can invest surplus funds, that is those funds not lent on mortgage or held in property and so on, is closely circumscribed, not so much by the requirement that a society must hold $7\frac{1}{2}$ per cent of its assets in liquid form, but rather by a statutory instrument, the Authorised Investments Order, which stipulates which investments societies are able to hold. Basically, societies can invest only in bank accounts and government and other public sector securities. The objective is to achieve 100 per cent security plus adequate liquidity.

(g) Societies can lend only on the security of freehold or leasehold estate and this sets them apart from other institutions. Moreover, by virtue of the special advances provision of the Building Societies Act, no more than 10 per cent of a society's lending in any one year can be in amounts of over £37,500 or in the form of loans to corporate bodies.

It is clear that the operations of societies are closely circumscribed. Effectively, the law limits societies to their basic functions of accepting investments from the public and making loans to home-buyers, with surplus funds having to be invested in a very narrow range of securities. Thus, societies are not permitted to hold land except for the purpose of conducting their business and the legality of a society offering additional services in the financial sphere is always open to question. Moreover, by setting building societies apart from other institutions, legislation effectively makes it impossible for a building society to be controlled by another institution or for a building society to gain control of any other commercial organisation.

It is also significant to note that the primary legislation governing building societies has been virtually unchanged since 1960 and, in fact, present day legislation is in many respects based on the 1874 Act.

The Building Societies Association

The Building Societies Association is the trade association for the building society industry. As has already been noted, the Association was founded in 1869 and was established in its present form in 1936. Over the years the Association has become increasingly important in terms of its representative status for building societies and also its more general functions. Currently over two-thirds of all building societies are members of the Association but most non-members are very small and indeed many are moribund. Societies represented in the Association account for well over 99 per cent of the total assets of the industry.

Membership of the Association is open to a building society which is:

(a) A permanent incorporated society registered in the United Kingdom.
(b) Able to produce accounts indicating active existence and covering the five years immediately preceding the application for membership.
(c) Designated for trustee status if its total assets in its latest balance sheet exceed the minimum requirement for designation.
(d) Able to comply in its latest accounts with the regulations of the Association which, broadly speaking, are the same, with the exception of size, as the requirements which a society must meet in order to achieve trustee status.

The main policy-making body of the Association is its Council which comprises thirty-five people, fifteen being elected nationally, ten being nominated by each of the ten largest societies and ten persons each being nominated by one of the regional associations affiliated to the Association. The Council and its standing committees meet monthly to discuss matters of current importance and where necessary recommendations can be made to member-societies.

Like any other trade association, one of the main functions of the Association is to inform and advise its members. Each year there are many Acts of Parliament, statutory instruments, decisions of other organisations and so on which have a bearing on the operation of societies. The Association monitors such developments and advises member-societies of the implications as necessary.

An important function of the Council of the Association is to act as a forum for discussion and policy-making. After discussing a subject, the Council can give information to societies so as to help them make their own decisions, it can advise societies as to a particular course of action or, with a two-thirds majority, it can make a recommendation to societies. The Association's recommendations are not binding but in practice they are adhered to by most societies.

One particular area in which the Association has a policy-making function is in respect of rates of interest. Since 1939, the Association has recommended to member-societies the rates of interest which they should charge to borrowers and pay to investors. This aspect of the Association's work is considered more fully in Chapter 14.

The Association has a particularly important function in explaining the work of building societies to the public and interested persons. The Association produces a series of leaflets and booklets explaining matters relating to house-purchase and investment in building societies. These are sold in bulk to member-societies and are made available free of charge to interested members of the public and bodies such as housing advisory centres and consumer advice centres. The Association also produces literature explaining the work of societies rather than the services which they offer. A regular quarterly bulletin, the *BSA Bulletin*, has become widely established as a source of statistics and authoritative comment on building society activity and on the housing market. A monthly news-sheet, *Building Society News*, provides up-to-date information on developments in the industry. The Association has also published a number of books in recent years and has sponsored conferences.

The Association is universally recognised as the representative body for building societies. Working relationships exist with a number of kindred organisations; in some cases these are on a formal basis while more frequently relations are informal, meetings being held as and when necessary and with contact being maintained at official level.

The Association is not a research body but from time to time it does commission or undertake research. For example, in 1979 the Association undertook a major market research exercise into the savings side of building society business and the results were subsequently published (*Building Societies and the Savings Market*, The Building Societies Association, 1979). Recently, the Association has been undertaking research into the possibilities of building societies operating in the other countries of the European Community.

The Association acts as the representative body for building societies in discussions with the government. The Association is frequently consulted by, and makes representations to, a number of government departments. Among the departments with which the Association has to maintain contact are the Registry of Friendly Societies, which is responsible for the prudential supervision of the industry; the Treasury, particularly for matters relating to national finance; the Bank of England, which is responsible for the implementation of monetary policy; the Department of the Environment, on housing matters; the Department of Trade; the Office of Fair Trading; and, from time to time, other government departments.

The Chartered Building Societies Institute

The Chartered Building Societies Institute (which, prior to receiving its Royal Charter in 1979, was known as The Building Societies Institute) is the professional body for building society staff. Its members comprise the individuals who work within building societies and its major function is to provide for the education and training of building society staff, in particular to arrange for professional examinations.

The first steps towards establishing training at an industry-wide level were taken in the 1920s but it was 1934 before The Building Societies Institute was established. Membership of the Institute grew rapidly and by 1941 examinations had been introduced for professional membership. The Institute received considerable impetus in the 1960s when it seemed possible that the Industrial Training Act 1964 would require that a training board for financial institutions should be established. The financial institutions were able to persuade the Government that there was no need for such an organisation, as training was already well catered for.

In addition to its responsibilities in the field of training, the Institute also offers specialised seminars for more senior staff and it produces a wide range of publications on building society practices.

The Structure of the Building Society Industry

This chapter has described the changing nature of the building society industry from a large number of very small organisations in the late nineteenth and early twentieth centuries to an ever smaller number of ever larger organisations. The number of societies declined from a peak of 3,642 in 1895 to 1,506 in 1914, 960 in 1939, 726 in 1960, 481 in 1970 and 273 in 1980. Up to the early 1950s, the number of societies declined predominantly as a result of the dissolution of societies but since that time transfers of engagements have been more important. Thus, of the 796 societies on the register at the beginning of 1953, over half (478) had transferred their engagements to other

Table 1.2 Classification of Societies by Asset Size, End-1980

Assets	Number of societies	Percentage of total	Total assets £m.	Percentage of total
Over £2,500 million	5	1.8	29,799	55.4
Over £600 million Up to £2,500 million	12	4.4	14,515	27.0
Over £140 million Up to £600 million	20	7.3	4,748	8.8
Over £35 million Up to £140 million	48	17.6	3,430	6.4
Over £2 million Up to £35 million	113	41.4	1,264	2.3
Up to £2 million	75	27.5	38	0.1
Total	273	100.0	53,793	100.0

Note: Because three of the largest five societies have financial years ending other than on 31 December 1980, the total assets of the largest five societies are £340 million (0.6 per cent of total assets) less than would be the case if figures for the end of the calendar year were shown.
Source: Building Societies in 1980 (The Building Societies Association, 1981).

societies by the end of 1980. A further fifty-two societies were involved in unions to form twenty-five new societies.

The decline in the number of societies has been accompanied by increasing concentration within the industry. The five largest societies increased their share of total assets from 39 per cent in 1930 to 55 per cent in 1980 and the market share of the 20 largest societies increased over the same period from 65 per cent to 84 per cent.

Table 1.2 shows the asset distribution of building societies at the end of 1980. It will be seen that the five largest societies accounted for 55.4 per cent of the total assets of the industry and the next twelve largest societies accounted for a further 27.0 per cent. The 188 societies with assets of under £35 million accounted for just 2.4 per cent of the industry's assets.

The decline in the number of societies has been closely linked with the growth in the number of branches. The first branches were established as long ago as the late 1840s and early 1950s although for the most part these were merely marketing and collecting agencies. The need for branches became particularly widely recognised in the 1920s. By 1938 it is estimated that there were 625 building society branches in the country, largely in Yorkshire, Lancashire and London. The number of branches began to increase fairly rapidly in the 1950s and the rate of growth accelerated sharply in the 1960s and more particularly in the 1970s. By 1955 there were 756 branches and the number increased to 1,662 in 1968, 3,009 in 1974 and 5,716 in 1980.

In terms of branch networks, building societies can basically be classified as follows:

(a) Five very large societies with substantial branch networks in all parts of the United Kingdom.
(b) A further six large societies with some significant branch representation in each region.
(c) About forty societies with branch representation throughout one or more regions.
(d) About eighty societies operating with a small number of branches in the local area only.
(e) Societies operating from a head office alone.

Table 1.3   Building Society Branches by Size of Society, End-1980

Size category of society	No. of societies	No. with branches	Branches	Branches per £10m assets	Branch staff per branch
5 largest	5	5	2,210	0.74	9.25
£600–£2,500m.	12	12	2,012	1.39	4.68
£140–£600m.	20	19	908	1.91	3.42
£35–£140m.	48	42	489	1.43	3.20
£2–£35m.	113	41	97	0.77	2.27
All over £2m	198	119	5,716	1.06	6.08

Note: Two part-time staff are counted as being equal to one full-time staff.
Source: The Building Societies Association.

In fact, of the 273 societies on the register at the end of 1980, only 119 had branches and all of these societies had assets in excess of £2 million. Table 1.3 shows the distribution of building society branches by size of society at the end of 1980.

Perhaps the most significant feature of the table is that the five largest societies, whose assets account for 55 per cent of the total assets of the industry, accounted for only 39 per cent of the total number of branches. However, the table also illustrates that these societies had an average of 9.25 full-time staff per branch compared with the average for all societies of 6.08. Thus, taken as a group, the five largest societies have a relatively small number of branches but these branches are larger than average.

Building society branches are concentrated in the south-west, East Midlands, London and the south-east. There are relatively fewer branches in Northern Ireland, Scotland and Wales. Branches are more common in large shopping centres although such centres have become increasingly saturated and branch expansion is now most noticeable in smaller shopping centres.

Chapter 2

Building Societies and the Savings Market

The Importance of the Savings Market to Building Societies

Building societies are basically simple organisations with just two functions – to provide a home for savings and to make loans to house-purchasers. The importance of these functions can be illustrated by examining the aggregate balance sheet for building societies. At the end of 1980, shares and deposits accounted for 94.2 per cent of the total liabilities of societies. Taxation and other liabilities, primarily the tax liability on investors' interest, represented a further 2.3 per cent of the total and reserves accounted for almost all the remainder. Thus, by far the most important source of building society funds is receipts from investors.

Similarly, the bulk of building society expenditure is in respect of shares and deposits. Share, deposit and loan interest (of which loan interest is a very small fraction) account for some 70 per cent of societies' expenditure and tax liability on this interest accounts for a further 20 per cent.

It is apparent that the attraction of savings is essential to the operation of building societies. In this respect societies are different from banks whose activities are also concerned with providing a money transmission service and whose expenditure on deposit interest is therefore proportionately less important than it is for building societies.

The Nature of Personal Saving

Before examining in detail societies' activities in the savings market, it is necessary to understand the nature of personal saving. It is sometimes suggested that the savings which building societies attract are part of the difference between the expenditure of households and their income. Furthermore, it is frequently suggested, if only implicitly, that the savings market is a fixed size and if building societies attract a greater amount of savings, other institutions necessarily attract a smaller amount. In reality, the savings market is more complex.

This can be illustrated by Table 2.1 which shows personal sector income, expenditure and saving for 1980.

It will be seen that wages and salaries, which most people associate with income, totalled £115,047 million but that other sources of personal income were equal to over £80,000 million, resulting in personal income before

Table 2.1 Personal Sector, Income, Expenditure and Saving, 1980

	£m.
Wages and salaries	115,047
+ Forces pay	2,425
+ Employers' contributions to national insurance and pension funds	17,258
+ Grants from government	25,473
+ Other personal income	38,644
= Personal income before tax	198,847
− UK taxes on income	25,956
− National insurance, etc., contributions	13,977
− Net transfers abroad	327
= Personal disposable income	158,587
− Consumer expenditure	134,594
= Saving	23,993

Source: *Financial Statistics*, September 1981, Table 10.1.

tax of £198,847 million. After deduction of tax, national insurance contributions and net transfers abroad, the figure for personal disposable income was £158,587 million. It is estimated that consumer expenditure totalled £134,594 million and the difference between that and personal disposable income represents the saving of the personal sector, which in 1980 was equal to £23,993 million.

It is necessary to stress that this amount does not represent the market within which building societies have to compete. The saving of the personal sector is only one of the sources of the personal sector's funds available for investment. This is illustrated in Table 2.2 which shows a modified presentation of the sources and uses of funds account for the personal sector for 1980.

Table 2.2 Personal Sector, Sources and Uses of Funds, 1980

Sources of funds	£m.	Uses of funds	£m.
Saving	23,993	Taxes on capital and transfers	1,025
Capital transfers	1,324	Investment in fixed assets and stocks	7,895
Borrowing for house-purchase	7,083	Acquisition of liquid assets	16,284
Other borrowing	3,340	Acquisition of public sector securities	2,394
Accruals and unidentified	881	Acquisition of life assurance and superannuation funds	10,758
Sales of company securities, etc.	1,735		
Total	38,356	Total	38,356

Source: *Financial Statistics*, September 1981, Table 10.2.

It will be seen that the total sources were £38,356 million, of which saving, that is the difference between the personal sector's disposable income and consumer expenditure, represented little more than half. Most of the remainder was accounted for by borrowing. Sales of company securities are also significant.

It is this total sum of £38,356 million which represents the savings market within which building societies competed in 1980. However, again it is necessary to stress that this amount is not a given sum outside of the influence of financial institutions. It will be noted that loans for house-purchase account for a significant amount of the sources of funds of the personal sector. Thus, when a building society makes a loan, it increases the funds of the personal sector and some of these funds may come back to building societies in the form of deposits. Building societies can also directly increase the size of their market through raising their interest rates. Given societies' current balances, a 1 per cent increase in the net share rate will, other things being equal, lead to a £32 million a month increase in interest credited to investors' accounts and therefore in personal incomes. Clearly, this cannot be at the expense of other financial institutions and, to this extent, higher interest rates in themselves increase the market within which building societies operate.

Table 2.2 does, however, usefully illustrate the competition which building societies face in attracting funds. After individuals have satisfied their consumer needs they have two options. They can either acquire fixed assets (largely houses) or they can acquire financial assets. The final figure in the uses of funds column, acquisition of life assurance and superannuation funds, does not for the most part represent voluntary saving of the personal sector but rather reflects compulsory pension and life insurance schemes.

In 1980, the personal sector borrowed £5,715 million and deposited with building societies £7,175 million, thus it increased its net investment in building societies by £1,460 million. Had building societies elected to lend an extra £300 million in 1980 then this would have increased the total sources of funds by this amount and this additional sum would have been available for consumer expenditure or for investment in the various financial assets or fixed assets.

It is important to realise that such figures are net and of course a building society loan does not necessarily create capital funds which might be used for investment in other financial institutions or the purchase of a house. A building society loan on a secondhand dwelling will result in the vendor receiving a capital sum. The vendor may choose to spend this on consumer goods, in which case building society lending indirectly finances consumer expenditure.

However, the major point remains that building societies, while they do compete strongly with other institutions in order to attract personal savings, are not operating in a narrowly defined, closed market. Because societies' activities are almost entirely with the personal sector, their operations basically involve intermediating between those individuals who wish to invest and those who wish to borrow. It is possible for the volume of building society activity to rise or fall substantially without there being significant effects on other financial institutions or indeed on the economy generally.

There has, in fact, been a significant increase in personal sector intermediation in relation to whole economy. Between 1958 and 1962, total sources and uses of funds for the personal sector were equal to 9.9 per cent of GDP but since that time there has been a steady increase with the proportion reaching 17.1 per cent in 1979. Loans for house-purchase more than doubled as a percentage of GDP between 1958 and 1979 and correspondingly acquisition of liquid assets as a proportion of GDP also more than doubled.

This is not just a case of the personal sector as a whole increasing its saving; it also reflects a greater number of individuals saving *and* borrowing, for the most part the savings of some individuals compensating for the borrowings of others. In some cases, individuals may, seemingly paradoxically, have both large savings and large borrowings; thus an individual may simultaneously have a £10,000 mortgage account with a building society and a £10,000 savings account with the same society. If he used his savings to pay off his mortgage then the net saving of the personal sector is unaffected, as is the financial position of the building society, but the extent of financial intermediation within the personal sector is reduced by £10,000.

The Growth of Building Societies' Share of the Savings Market

The savings market in which building societies operate is not easy to define. For the most part, building societies' competitors are banks and other financial institutions offering short-term accounts but there is also some competition with longer term investments such as government securities and even with the acquisition of real assets such as houses. In order to examine societies' developing market share, it is therefore necessary to look at several variables and not just one.

Table 2.3 reproduces from the Wilson Committee report (*Report of the Committee to Review the Functioning of Financial Institutions*, Cmnd 7937, HMSO, 1980) a table showing the balance sheet of the personal sector for selected years between 1957 and 1978.

Table 2.3   Balance Sheet of the Personal Sector, 1957–78

	Amounts outstanding at end of year; £ billion					
	1957	*1962*	*1967*	*1972*	*1977*	*1978*
Assets						
Physical assets	21.0	35.9	65.2	124.7	243.2	297.6
of which:						
dwellings	*12.6*	*22.5*	*38.2*	*82.2*	*150.0*	*188.7*
Liquid assets	13.7	18.1	26.4	40.9	73.9	85.1
of which:						
cash and bank deposits	*4.9*	*6.5*	*10.5*	*16.2*	*28.0*	*32.2*
national savings	*6.2*	*7.6*	*8.3*	*9.8*	*13.6*	*15.7*
building society shares and						
deposits	*2.2*	*3.5*	*6.9*	*14.2*	*31.7*	*36.6*
Stocks and shares	15.5	26.6	32.9	52.1	53.1	53.1
of which:						
British government securities	*3.6*	*3.7*	*3.9*	*3.9*	*10.5*	*8.8*
listed UK ordinary shares	*6.3*	*14.4*	*17.8*	*31.7*	*23.1*	*23.2*

Table 2.3 – *cont.*

	Amounts outstanding at end of year; £ billion					
	1957	*1962*	*1967*	*1972*	*1977*	*1978*
Loans and debtors	3.9	5.1	5.2	5.5	8.8	9.7
Equity in life assurance and pension funds	6.5	10.1	16.2	28.1	51.6	59.6
Total assets	60.7	95.8	145.9	251.3	430.6	505.1
Liabilities						
Loans for house purchase	3.5	5.3	8.4	15.9	33.2	38.6
Other debts	3.5	6.1	7.3	11.8	16.8	19.5
Total liabilities	7.0	11.4	15.7	27.7	50.0	58.1
Net wealth	53.7	84.4	130.2	223.6	380.6	447.0

Source: Roe, A., *The Financial Interdependence of the Economy, 1957–66* (Chapman & Hall, 1971); Central Statistical Office. (There are discontinuities in some of the series between 1962 and 1967.)

Table 2.3 shows that the personal sector holdings of building society shares and deposits increased from £2.2 billion in 1957 to £36.6 billion in 1978. Table 2.4 translates the actual figures in Table 2.3 into building society shares of the various aggregates.

Table 2.4   Building Society Deposits and Personal Sector Wealth, 1957–78

Year	Building society shares and deposits as proportion of		
	Net wealth %	Financial assets %	Liquid assets %
1957	4.1	5.5	16.1
1962	4.1	5.8	19.3
1967	5.3	8.6	26.1
1972	6.4	11.2	34.7
1977	8.3	16.9	42.9
1978	8.2	17.6	43.0

Source: Table 2.3.

The table shows that building society shares and deposits as a proportion of net wealth doubled from 4.1 per cent in 1957 to 8.2 per cent in 1978. As building society shares and deposits are used almost entirely to finance house-purchase, it is also significant to note that the share of net wealth accounted for by dwellings increased very sharply from 23.5 per cent in 1957 to 42.2 per cent in 1978.

Building society shares and deposits increased much more rapidly as a pro-portion of financial assets, from 5.5 per cent in 1957 to 17.6 per cent in 1978. Table 2.3 also shows that equity in life assurance and pension funds has been taking an increasing share of financial assets while British government securities and UK ordinary shares in particular have been taking a declining share. This reflects another important trend in the economy, that is that individuals rather than investing directly in government securities and equities now do so through the intermediaries of life assurance and pension funds.

The growth of building societies is perhaps best illustrated when the market for liquid assets is examined because, as has been indicated, building society shares and deposits compete most strongly with bank deposits and other liquid instruments. Table 2.4 shows that societies' share of this market increased from 16.1 per cent in 1957 to 43.0 per cent in 1978.

It is helpful at this stage to examine the market for short-term financial assets in more detail. Table 2.5 shows market shares for the various short-term financial instruments since 1966. It should be noted that this table covers the household sector rather than the whole personal sector (which includes unincorporated business), hence the proportions are slightly different from those in Tables 2.3 and 2.4.

Table 2.5   Shares of Short-Term Household Financial Assets, 1966–80

Year	Building societies %	Banks %	National savings %	Notes and coins %	Other %
1966	24	30	34	9	3
1967	26	31	32	9	2
1968	28	32	30	8	2
1969	30	31	28	9	2
1970	32	31	26	9	2
1971	34	30	26	8	2
1972	35	31	24	8	1
1973	35	34	22	8	1
1974	35	36	19	8	1
1975	39	33	19	9	1
1976	41	31	18	9	–
1977	44	28	18	9	–
1978	44	28	18	9	–
1979	43	31	17	8	1
1980	43	32	17	8	–

Notes:
1   1979 and 1980 figures are for the personal sector.
2   National savings includes trustee savings banks.
Source: Economic Trends, January 1978; Financial Statistics, February 1981 and September 1981.

It will be seen that building societies have increased their market share largely at the expense of national savings rather than the banks. As recently as 1966, national savings, which includes in Table 2.5 the savings banks, accounted for 34 per cent of household short-term financial assets but the proportion has fallen steadily to reach only 17 per cent in 1980. The banks' share has tended to fluctuate, reaching a peak of 36 per cent in 1974 falling to 28 per cent in 1977 and then rising to 32 per cent at the end of 1980.

The Capital Structure of Building Societies

This section describes the various types of account offered by building societies and changes in the capital structure over the years. Traditionally, building societies have raised the vast bulk of their funds by means of ordinary share accounts or paid-up share accounts as they are sometimes called. For all practical purposes, such accounts can be considered as deposits and indeed they are frequently referred to as such although this is not strictly correct. Money can be paid into ordinary share accounts at any time and fairly substantial withdrawals can be made without notice. The entire account can usually be withdrawn within a few days of notice being given. Transactions are recorded in a passbook so the investor is always aware of exactly how much is in his account. It is sometimes stated that ordinary share accounts are used by some people as bank accounts but this is true to only a very limited degree. An ordinary share account is as effective as a bank account if the investor uses his account solely as a means of obtaining cash and depositing his savings. A building society cannot operate a money transmission service and does not issue cheque books. However, a society will, on request, make a cheque payable to a third party although in this case the cheque is drawn on the building society and not on the individual's account within that society.

At the beginning of 1974, ordinary shares accounted for over 90 per cent of share and deposit balances with building societies. However, early in 1974 societies faced an outflow of funds and many responded by marketing term shares which offered a fairly substantial differential, perhaps 1 or 1½ per cent, over the ordinary share rate. In May 1974, term shares accounted for just 2.4 per cent of all investment balances but there was a rapid growth throughout the year and by the end of 1975 they accounted for 7.2 per cent of balances. Since that time, term shares have further increased their share of the total and by the end of 1980 they accounted for 14.7 per cent of building society share and deposit balances. Meanwhile, ordinary share balances had fallen to under 80 per cent of the total.

The nature of term shares has also changed considerably since 1974. Initially, most term shares were for two year periods but gradually terms have been lengthened such that most new issues are now for five years and some longer issues have also been made. Term shares have also become more flexible with many societies offering schemes in which the differential above the ordinary share rate varies according to the initial contracted term. Once that term has been achieved the shares continue to earn the higher, and sometimes rising, rate of interest and are subject to withdrawal at three or six months' notice. A more recent development has been to allow a withdrawal facility in exchange for a substantial interest rate penalty. Indeed, most new term share issues are of this type and therefore the extent to which societies' capital structure is made more long-term is reduced. Nevertheless, term shares have had the effect of reducing the proportion of societies' shares and deposits which can be withdrawn on demand. In 1974 perhaps 95 per cent of shares and deposits could be withdrawn within one month. At the end of June 1978 that proportion was 88.7 per cent and it has since fallen slowly but steadily to reach 83.0 per cent at the end of December 1980.

Correspondingly, a significant proportion, now over 5 per cent, of building society share and deposit balances cannot be withdrawn within two years.

Regular saving shares or subscription shares, as they are sometimes known, accounted for 3 per cent of building society share and deposit balances at the end of 1980. Societies offer an attractive preferential rate of interest on these, typically 1¼ per cent above the ordinary share rate, in order to encourage regular monthly savings. These accounts provide only a small proportion of building society balances but they are particularly popular with young couples saving the deposit for their first home. Societies normally allow the entire balance on such accounts to be withdrawn on demand and some societies also allow partial withdrawals.

Building societies offer Save-As-You-Earn accounts as a special form of regular savings which pay a tax-free bonus to those who contract to save a regular sum for at least five years. This scheme is most attractive to higher rate taxpayers but over the years it has tended to become less attractive for various reasons and balances within the scheme now account for only 0.5 per cent of total share and deposit balances.

Building societies also offer deposit accounts, usually at a slightly lower rate of interest than is paid on ordinary share accounts. Depositors are not shareholders in a society but rather are creditors. In return for the lower rate of interest, they have a preferential claim on the assets in the unlikely event of a society being wound up. Demand for deposits from individuals is negligible but companies, trusts and other institutions find the deposit account attractive. It is institutions which now account for the great bulk of deposit money which altogether comprises 3 per cent of total share and deposit balances held with building societies.

A recent innovation in the capital structure of societies has been high interest notice or penalty accounts which offer up to an additional 1 per cent interest in exchange either for a period of notice of between one and three months before a withdrawal or an interest penalty on withdrawals. These accounts came onto the market in 1980 and 1981 and were vigorously promoted. They accounted for most of the net receipts during 1981.

Table 2.6 shows the estimated distribution of share and deposit balances as at end-June 1981.

Table 2.6   Share and Deposit Balances, June 1981

Type of account	Percentage of total
Ordinary shares and deposits	74.4
High interest accounts	4.4
Term accounts	15.7
Regular savings	3.0
SAYE	0.5
Other	2.0
Total	100.0

Source: The Building Societies Association.

Interest Rates and Tax on Shares and Deposits

Interest rates payable on shares and deposits are all variable (although a small number of societies do offer fixed rate investments for relatively short periods such as one year) and tend to be geared to the ordinary share rate of societies. Thus, personal deposits normally attract a rate of interest of $\frac{1}{4}$ per cent less and regular savings shares $1\frac{1}{4}$ per cent more. Term shares are currently attracting a differential of up to 2 per cent and high interest accounts up to 1 per cent over the ordinary share rate. It is important to note, especially in respect of term shares, that the rates of interest can be changed at very short notice and an investor in a term share is not guaranteed a fixed rate of interest for his stated term but rather a fixed differential over the ordinary share rate. Because the rate of interest on all shares and deposits can be moved together, liability management is considerably facilitated.

Tax on interest on building society shares and deposits is paid in accordance with special arrangements set out in section 343 of the Income and Corporation Taxes Act 1970. The arrangements apply to amounts of up to £20,000 (£40,000 for joint accounts) held, broadly speaking, by individuals. Through the arrangements, the Inland Revenue is required to collect as much tax as it would if each investor were taxed separately. Under the arrangements, a composite rate of tax is calculated which represents the average liability of building society investors to the basic rate of tax. In the current financial year (1981/82), the composite rate is 25.5 per cent compared with the basic rate of 30 per cent and thus societies pay tax of 25.5 per cent on the interest they pay to investors (grossed-up at the basic rate of tax). Those investors liable to the investment income surcharge or to the higher rates of tax are separately assessed while investors not liable to the basic rate are not able to claim a refund.

It has been alleged that the income tax arrangements give building societies a competitive advantage. This point is examined in more detail in Chapter 13.

Building Society Investors

It has been noted that building societies have been taking a growing share of the personal savings market. It follows that they have been increasing their market penetration and the proportion of adults with building society accounts has grown markedly. This is illustrated in Table 2.7 which shows the growth of building society accounts and estimates of the percentage of the adult population holding accounts since 1930.

The earliest period for which market research data is available is 1953/54 when a survey conducted by Oxford University showed that 4 per cent of adults had a building society account. Table 2.7 shows that that proportion increased to 11 per cent by 1965, 22 per cent by 1972 and 48 per cent by 1980. In terms of numbers, this 48 per cent represented over 20 million individuals. It will be seen that the number of share accounts is considerably in excess of the number of individuals who are building society investors, this largely being explained by investors who have accounts with more than one society.

Table 2.7   Building Society Accounts, 1930–80

Year	Share accounts	Deposit accounts	Percentage of adult population holding building society accounts
	(000's)	*(000's)*	
1930	1,449	428	
1940	2,088	771	
1950	2,256	654	
1960	3,910	571	
1965	5,861	593	11
1968	8,178	619	15
1970	10,265	618	17
1971	11,568	655	20
1972	12,874	675	22
1973	14,385	672	24
1974	15,856	641	24
1975	17,916	677	28
1976	19,991	712	34
1977	22,536	760	36
1978	24,999	781	41
1979	27,878	797	43
1980	30,640	915	48

Sources: Figures for share and deposit accounts are taken from the Annual Reports of the Chief Registrar of Friendly Societies. The figures in the final column are based on market research exercises conducted for the Stock Exchange (1965), The Building Societies Association (1968) and the BMRB Target Group Index (1970 onwards).

Building society investors come from all age groups and social grades. In 1978 and 1979, The Building Societies Association commissioned a comprehensive market research exercise on building society investors and the results (*Building Societies and the Savings Market*, The Building Societies Association, 1979) provide the basis for most of the remainder of this section. Table 2.8 shows the profile of building society investors.

The table shows that the number of investors is split equally between men and women although because there are more women than men in the population building societies have a higher market penetration amongst men. As far as age groups are concerned, building society market penetration is highest in the 25–34 age group but a consistently high penetration is achieved for all age groups. As far as social grade is concerned, building societies, not surprisingly, have a much higher market penetration amongst higher social grades. However, it is significant that over half of building society investors are in the CZDE grades and market penetration in these grades is very high compared with that of other institutions.

This market research data can be combined with other information to analyse in more detail the holders of building society shares and deposits. Table 2.9 shows an analysis of share and deposit balances by size of account as at the end of 1980.

This data is obtained from direct returns from building societies rather than

Table 2.8   Profile of Building Society Investors, 1978/79

	All adults %	Building society investors %	Non-building society investors %
Sex			
Men	48	50 (45)	46
Women	52	50 (41)	54
Age			
16–19 years	8	6 (34)	9
20–24 years	9	9 (47)	8
25–34 years	19	23 (52)	16
35–44 years	16	16 (42)	17
45–54 years	15	14 (39)	16
55–64 years	14	14 (42)	14
65 years or more	19	18 (40)	20
Social grade			
A B	13	18 (61)	9
C1	23	30 (55)	18
C2	33	31 (41)	33
D E	31	21 (28)	40
All adults	100	100 (43)	100

Notes:
1 Figures in brackets show the proportion of each demographic sub-group with a building society account. Thus 61 per cent of all A Bs have a building society account (although only 18 per cent of all building society investors are A Bs).
2 The social grade classification is very broadly as follows:
A B – upper middle and middle class
C1 – lower middle class
C2 – skilled working class
D – semi and unskilled working class
E – state pensioners, lowest grade manual
  Source: *Building Societies and the Saving Market* (The Building Societies Association, 1979).

from the market research but does serve to show that although building societies have a larger number of small accounts, the bulk of share and deposit balances are in fact held in large accounts. Thus, well over 50 per cent of accounts are of less than £500 yet these accounted for under 5 per cent of balances. By contrast, the 7.6 per cent of accounts of more than £5,000 accounted for 47.9 per cent of total balances.

If the market research data is combined with comparable figures to those in Table 2.9 for the end of 1978, it is possible to analyse investors by various characteristics such as tenure and age. Table 2.10 analyses investors by tenure as at the end of 1978 but it must be stressed that the figures are tentative and for this reason they have been rounded.

By far the most significant feature of this table is that half of the balances invested with building societies are held by those owning outright and more than a quarter are held by those buying on mortgage. It is evident that the money invested in building societies is not held by those wishing to become

Table 2.9   Share and Deposit Balances by Size of Account, End-1980

Size category	Balances held £m.	%	Number of accounts 000's	%
Up to £100	276	0.6	11,938	34.5
Over £100 up to £500	1,852	3.7	6,991	20.2
Over £500 up to £1,000	3,198	6.5	4,293	12.4
Over £1,000 up to £2,000	6,166	12.4	4,286	12.4
Over £2,000 up to £5,000	14,321	28.9	4,420	12.8
Over £5,000 up to £10,000	13,531	27.3	1,917	5.5
£10,000 and over	10,211	20.6	729	2.1
Total	49,555	100.0	34,574	100.0

Notes:
1 The figures are based on returns provided by 11 societies which accounted for 71.7 per cent of share and deposit balances at the end of 1980.
2 The figures exclude SAYE accounts.
3 Many investors have more than one account and the figures for numbers of accounts should not be taken to indicate the numbers of investors.
Source: Building Societies in 1980 (The Building Societies Association, 1981).

Table 2.10   Analysis of Building Society Investors by Tenure, End-1978

Tenure	Investors Millions	Percentage of total	Amount invested £m.	Percentage of total	Average investment £
Owning outright	4.9	27.0	18,500	50.3	3,780
Owning on mortgage	7.8	43.3	10,100	27.4	1,290
Council renting	3.8	21.0	4,400	12.0	1,160
Private renting	1.1	6.3	2,700	7.3	2,440
Rent-free	0.4	2.4	1,100	2.9	2,670
All	18.0	100.0	36,800	100.0	2,040

Source: The Building Societies Association.

owner-occupiers but rather, for the most part, is held by existing owner-occupiers. The reason for this can be explained with the assistance of Table 2.11 which shows investment in building societies by age of investor.

This table shows that investors over the age of 55 accounted for 55.1 per cent of the share and deposit balances held with societies. Investors in the first-time buying age group, that is, between 20 and 24, accounted for only 4.4 per cent of balances. Thus, it is clear that building societies attract savings from elderly, existing owner-occupiers and use these to make loans to young, new owner-occupiers. This very much reflects the typical life cycle. Young couples tend to build up only small amounts of savings, using these for major items of expenditure such as cars, holidays and houses. After the age of 40,

Table 2.11   Investment in Building Societies by Age of Investor, End-1978

Age band	Investors		Amount invested		Average invest- ment £
	Millions	Percentage of total	£m.	Percentage of total	
16–19	1.1	6.3	300	0.8	280
20–4	1.7	9.5	1,600	4.4	950
25–34	4.2	23.2	4,500	12.3	1,070
35–44	2.9	15.9	4,700	12.7	1,610
45–54	2.5	13.7	5,800	15.8	2,320
55–64	2.4	13.6	9,100	24.8	3,800
65+	3.2	17.9	10,800	29.3	3,370
All	18.0	100.0	36,800	100.0	2,040

Source: The Building Societies Association.

earnings tend to reach a peak and expenditures might well fall as children leave home and mortgages are paid off. Savings balances are therefore built up in anticipation of retirement. Perhaps more importantly is that inheritances are most likely to be received between the ages of 40 and 60 and by the time many people reach retirement age they would expect to have a fairly substantial volume of financial assets which can be used to earn interest to provide for their retirement.

Receipts, Withdrawals and Interest Credited

So far, this chapter has been concerned with balances and investors and now it is necessary to turn to the dynamics of shares and deposits. The net increase in the savings balances held with societies each year conceals a substantial volume of receipts, withdrawals and interest payments. Table 2.12 shows the major figures for building society shares and deposits for the period 1955–80.

It will be seen that the net receipts of £3,816 million recorded in 1980 reflected receipts of £22,183 million and withdrawals of £18,367 million. In addition, interest credited to investors' accounts was £3,343 million and this accounted for a major part of the increase in savings balances of £7,159 million.

It is the growth of building society shares and deposits which provides the funds available to finance the net increase in mortgage lending and it is necessary to examine in detail the factors that determine this growth. Three separate variables merit analysing:

(a) Interest credited to investors' accounts
(b) Small savings
(c) Large savings

Table 2.12   Building Society Shares and Deposits, 1955–80

Year	Receipts £m.	Withdrawals £m.	Net receipts £m.	Interest credited £m.	Increase in savings £m.	Savings held at end-year £m.
1955	436	279	157	37	194	1,956
1960	584	422	162	43	205	2,945
1965	1,363	815	548	103	651	5,167
1970	3,080	1,867	1,213	277	1,490	10,142
1971	4,091	2,391	1,700	334	2,034	12,176
1972	5,296	3,495	1,801	392	2,193	14,369
1973	6,053	4,541	1,512	650	2,162	16,531
1974	6,370	5,205	1,165	828	1,993	18,524
1975	9,037	5,846	3,191	981	4,172	22,696
1976	10,250	7,972	2,278	1,127	3,405	26,101
1977	14,325	9,603	4,722	1,377	6,099	32,200
1978	15,858	12,548	3,310	1,512	4,822	37,022
1979	19,045	15,530	3,515	2,254	5,769	42,791
1980	22,183	18,367	3,816	3,343	7,159	49,950

Source: A Compendium of Building Society Statistics, 3rd edition, The Building Societies Association, 1980; *BSA Bulletin*.

The importance of interest credited to investors' accounts is often not fully appreciated. Investors are given the option of having interest paid to them, generally six monthly, or allowing it to be added to their accounts in which case of course interest will be earned on that interest. Over the years there has tended to be an increase in the proportion of investors preferring interest

Table 2.13   Building Society Interest, 1955–80

Year	Average share rate %	Interest credited £m.	Interest paid out £m.	Interest credited/ total interest %	Interest credited/ increase in savings balances %
1955–9	3.21	227	122	65.0	23.2
1960–4	3.53	289	310	48.2	16.3
1965–9	4.24	751	582	56.3	18.2
1970–4	5.76	2,481	1,305	65.5	25.1
1975–9	7.22	7,251	3,103	70.0	29.9
1975	7.21	981	458	68.2	23.5
1976	7.02	1,127	533	67.9	33.1
1977	6.98	1,377	605	69.5	22.6
1978	6.46	1,512	616	71.1	31.4
1979	8.45	2,254	892	71.7	39.1
1980	10.37	3,343	1,235	73.0	46.7

Source: A Compendium of Building Society Statistics, 3rd edition, The Building Societies Association, 1980; *BSA Bulletin*.

to be credited but, more importantly, the general rise in interest rates has increased the volume of interest credited such that it now provides a very substantial proportion of the increase in savings balances each year. This is illustrated in Table 2.13.

Table 2.13 shows that there was a fall in the proportion of total interest credited between 1955–9 and 1960–4 during which time the average proportion was 48.2 per cent but since then there has been a steady increase, with the proportion reaching 73.0 per cent in 1980. What is more significant, however, is the contribution which interest credited has made to the increase in savings balances. In 1960–4, that proportion was 16.3 per cent whereas in 1975–9 it averaged 29.9 per cent and by 1980 it had reached 46.7 per cent. The first column of the table, showing the average share rate, explains this development. In 1955–9 the average rate was 3.21 per cent whereas in 1975–9 it was 7.22 per cent and in 1980 it was an unprecedented 10.37 per cent.

In September 1981 interest credited was averaging £272 million per month and was increasing by about £2 million a month in line with the increase in savings balances. Account has to be taken of the effect on interest credited of a change in interest rates. For example, the ordinary share rate recommended by the Association increased from 8.5 per cent to 9.75 per cent on 1 November 1981 and this had the effect of increasing interest credited by £40 million a month.

Net receipts of new savings are complicated to analyse because they reflect a number of factors such as:

(a) A typical difference between monthly income and expenditure for the average household.
(b) Withdrawals to finance major items of expenditure such as cars or houses.
(c) Receipts of large capital sums received by investors, for example, through an inheritance or on the sale of a house.
(d) Withdrawals in favour of alternative forms of investment.

There is no necessary link between these various types of transaction and for this reason net receipts of shares and deposits are best analysed by disaggregating the statistics as far as possible. The Building Societies Association has for some years collected figures showing receipts and withdrawals by size band, and figures showing net receipts by size band were published in the Stow Report (*Mortgage Finance in the 1980s*, The Building Societies Association, 1980). Table 2.14 reproduces the size band figures for 1977 and 1978.

Table 2.14 shows that small money exhibits a seasonal pattern, with peaks generally occurring in January and October and troughs in June (because of holiday expenditure) and December (because of Christmas expenditure). There is a secular upward movement in the volume of net receipts of small money and this component of total net receipts does not appear to be interest-sensitive.

The medium size band is influenced by the natural tendency for people to invest modest sums and withdraw sizeable sums to finance major items of expenditure. Thus, many households will normally pay into their account surplus cash which they have available but will only make a withdrawal when

Table 2.14 Building Society Net Receipts by Size Band and Interest Rate Competitiveness, 1977–8

Month	Net receipts				Interest rate competitiveness
	Up to £500 £m.	£501– £2,000 £m.	Over £2,000 £m.	Total £m.	%
1977 Jan.	180	−61	−6	113	−1.92
Feb.	150	−25	100	225	0.12
Mar.	129	−61	158	226	1.42
Apr.	137	48	314	499	3.01
May	118	51	366	535	3.06
June	73	9	246	328	2.81
July	118	15	211	344	2.51
Aug.	100	1	225	326	3.25
Sep.	152	29	306	487	4.04
Oct.	182	40	393	615	5.14
Nov.	132	29	417	578	3.89
Dec.	135	30	281	446	2.31
1978 Jan.	204	− 1	162	365	2.89
Feb.	190	− 1	149	338	1.62
Mar.	169	−12	135	292	1.62
Apr.	163	− 3	175	335	0.82
May	122	−24	114	212	−0.78
June	101	−29	75	147	−1.54
July	166	−49	82	199	−0.02
Aug.	133	−39	105	199	0.63
Sep.	189	−16	172	345	0.71
Oct.	216	− 6	153	363	−0.35
Nov.	158	—	103	261	−1.96
Dec.	128	13	113	254	−0.37

Note: Interest rate competitiveness is the difference between the BSA recommended ordinary share rate grossed-up at the basic rate of tax and the local authority three month deposit rate, a good proxy for those rates which compete with building society rates.
Source: The Building Societies Association.

a substantial item of expenditure needs to be financed. Such items include holidays, motor cars and house purchase. Some consumer durables also come into this category. The medium size band is also affected by new issues or extensions of national savings certificates which have tended to have a maximum holding of between £1,000 and £5,000.

Net receipts of large sums are, not surprisingly, interest rate sensitive. The table shows the correlation between net receipts in the £2,000 + category and societies' interest rate competitiveness. Statistical analysis shows that a 1 per cent change in the differential between the building society grossed-up share rate and competing interest rates causes an eventual £60 million a month change in building society net receipts.

It is necessary to analyse in more detail the source of the large net receipts which building societies attract. Some 85 per cent of building society lending is on the security of secondhand houses. A building society loan thus becomes a receipt in the hands of the vendor. There may possibly be several other transactions but at the end of the day the loan must be received by someone who is selling a house and not purchasing another with the assistance of a building society loan. That person might be an elderly owner-occupier moving down-market, purchasing his new property with cash and using the remaining proceeds from the sale of his previous property to provide him with income. Alternatively, the recipient may be the beneficiary of an estate.

The point which was made earlier in this chapter is that building society lending itself creates capital sums which societies can then seek to attract as deposits. Whether or not they are successful in so doing depends of course on the relative competitiveness of the interest rates which they are offering compared with those offered by other institutions.

The Stow Report attempted to quantify this effect and concluded that the amount of money released through the proceeds of house sales in 1979 was some £4,500 million and that this amount can be expected to increase in line with house prices. In the past, societies seem to have been successful in attracting up to one third of the proceeds of house sales. The Stow Report concluded that this factor, together with mortgage repayments and interest credited to accounts, meant that building societies were self-financing to the extent of about two thirds of their total lending activities.

Chapter 3

Building Societies and the Housing Market

The Housing Stock

At the end of 1980 there were 21,025,000 houses in Great Britain. This number represents a 50 per cent increase on the stock at the end of 1950 of 13,912,000. In the 1950s and 1960s it was fashionable to talk of the housing shortage and certainly in the 1950s there was a considerable shortage of houses. In 1951 in England and Wales there were 730,000 more households than houses but in the early 1970s the number of houses overtook the number of households and by 1976 there were over half a million more houses than households. This does not mean that there is a surplus of housing but rather that there is no longer an absolute shortage of housing which necessitates a very high level of new building.

The housing stock has primarily grown through construction but offsetting new house-building have been losses, largely as a result of slum clearance. Slum clearance was at a particularly high level between 1956 and 1974 when it was fashionable to redevelop whole areas rather than attempting to rehabilitate the existing stock. Since 1974 there has been a change in emphasis towards rehabilitation and moreover there has been a smaller number of slums requiring demolition.

This factor, together with the growing surplus of houses over households, has led to a decline in the rate of new house-building from over 350,000 a year at the end of the 1960s to nearer 200,000 a year by the end of the 1970s. Table 3.1 shows how the Great Britain housing stock grew between 1950 and 1980.

Notwithstanding a very high level of new house-building in the 1950s and 1960s, a high proportion of the existing housing stock remains fairly old. No less than 30 per cent of the housing stock at the end of 1980 was built before the end of the First World War and only little more than half has been built since the end of the Second World War. Old housing is not necessarily poor housing and much pre-1919 housing has been renovated to bring it up to modern day standards. Indeed, arguably the pre-1919 houses are more soundly built and more attractive to consumers than many modern dwellings. Nevertheless, a fair proportion of the pre-1919 housing stock is in a serious state of disrepair and will either have to be rehabilitated or replaced in the near future.

More so than most other countries, Britain has a high proportion of detached and semi-detached houses and a relatively small proportion of flats.

Table 3.1   The Growth of the Housing Stock, Great Britain, 000's 1950–80

	Gains		Losses			
Period	New construction	Other	Slum clearance	Other	Net gain in period	Stock at end of period
1950						13,912
1951–5*	283.8	10.1	31.4	15.7	246.8	15,146
1956–60*	290.0	10.8	66.9	20.3	213.6	16,215
1961–5*	331.8	7.5	77.5	27.2	234.6	17,387
1966–70*	384.2	5.5	90.5	30.5	268.7	18,731
1971	350.6	7.6	95.3	27.1	235.8	18,999
1972	319.3	10.3	88.8	27.0	213.8	19,213
1973	294.1	12.2	83.3	20.4	202.6	19,415
1974	269.5	11.8	55.1	14.0	212.2	19,627
1975	313.0	10.2	63.0	17.6	242.6	19,870
1976	315.2	9.4	58.0	12.8	253.8	20,124
1977	302.7	8.8	47.5	12.2	251.8	20,375
1978	279.2	11.7	38.8	11.0	241.1	20,617
1979	234.9	12.4	37.0	11.0	199.2	20,816
1980	233.0	11.5	31.8	8.8	203.9	21,025

* Annual averages
Source: Housing and Construction Statistics.

Nearly half of all dwellings in Britain are detached or semi-detached and less than a quarter are flats. As far as the owner-occupied stock is concerned, there is an even smaller proportion of flats, 6 per cent, while three-quarters of dwellings are detached or semi-detached.

Housing Tenure

Table 3.2 shows the distribution of the housing stock by tenure at the end of 1980.

Table 3.2   Distribution of the Housing Stock by Tenure, Great Britain, End-1980

Tenure	Number of dwellings	Percentage of total
Owner-occupied	11,653,000	55.4
Local authority rented	6,633,000	31.6
Private rented and other	2,739,000	13.0
Total	21,025,000	100.0

Source: Housing and Construction Statistics.

The table shows that 55.4 per cent of houses were owner-occupied, 31.6 per cent were rented from local authorities or new town corporations and the remaining 13.0 per cent were either private rented or held in some other form of tenure. The proportion of owner-occupation in Britain is lower than in other English-speaking countries such as the United States, Canada and Australia, but higher than on the continent of Europe. However, one distinguishing feature of housing tenure in Britain is the rapid growth in the proportion of owner-occupied houses, which is illustrated in Table 3.3.

Table 3.3   The Growth of Owner-Occupation, Great Britain, 1914–80

End year	Percentage of owner-occupied houses	End year	Percentage of owner-occupied houses
1914	10.6	1972	51.5
1950	29.5	1973	52.3
1961	43.0	1974	52.7
1965	46.6	1975	53.0
1966	47.2	1976	53.3
1967	48.0	1977	53.6
1968	48.8	1978	54.1
1969	49.4	1979	54.6
1970	50.0	1980	55.4
1971	50.5		

Sources: *Housing and Construction Statistics*; Department of the Environment.

In order to understand the growth of owner-occupation, it is necessary to analyse the environment within which the other two sectors operate. In most countries there is a reasonably healthy private rented sector of housing which provides much-needed mobility, particularly for young households. In some countries, for example Switzerland and West Germany, most families rent houses throughout their lives and do not in fact become owner-occupiers. In Britain, until the First World War, about 90 per cent of houses were rented from private landlords. With the outbreak of war, rent control was introduced as a temporary measure but it has been maintained to this day. Successive Rent Acts have made life difficult for private landlords, in particular by preventing them from drawing up contracts with tenants which allow the landlord to recover possession at the end of a stated period or for any other reason. Furthermore, the private rented sector receives no tax or subsidy advantages and therefore is not able to compete effectively with either council housing or with owner-occupation. The result has been a very sharp decline in the proportion of privately rented houses and this decline is expected to continue. As dwellings suitable for owner-occupation become vacant, for example on the death of a tenant, then generally they are sold for owner-occupation rather than maintained as dwellings to be let. A fairly high proportion of the private rented sector which remains is, in fact, not suitable for owner-occupation.

The private rented and other sector also includes houses rented as part of a contract of employment, for example in respect of the armed forces. The scope for a reduction of this form of private renting is therefore limited.

By international standards, Britain has a very high proportion of houses owned by local authorities and new town corporations. For the most part, this stock is relatively new and tenants are chosen basically by means tests. Local authority rented housing is not really part of the market and is not normally available on demand although, increasingly, difficult-to-let properties are made available outside of the normal arrangements. For the tenant, local authority rented housing has the advantage of being cheap but inevitably it suffers from the accompanying disadvantages, that is access is limited and so is mobility. Local authority rented housing is not generally available to young couples without children nor are tenants allowed much choice with respect to the area or the type of property.

These factors have contributed to a very high demand for owner-occupation and most households now seek to become owner-occupiers as soon as they are established. This applies to single person households as well as to married couples. The proportion of owner-occupied houses has risen very sharply from no more than 10.6 per cent in 1914 to 29.5 per cent in 1950 and 55.4 per cent in 1980. Arguably, this growth of owner-occupation reflects not so much an innate desire for the owner-occupied form of tenure but rather the lack of suitable alternatives for many households. Even established council tenants enjoying low rents often seek to become owner-occupiers because it is only in this way that they can exercise a reasonable degree of choice in respect of their housing.

Table 3.3 has shown that the proportion of owner-occupied houses has nearly doubled since 1950. However, seemingly paradoxically, the majority of new houses since the war have been built by local authorities for renting rather than for the private market. This is illustrated in Table 3.4.

Table 3.4　Housebuilding Completions, Great Britain, 1945–80

Period	Private sector 000's	%	Public sector 000's	%	Total 000's
1945–9*	26.2	21.0	98.5	79.0	124.7
1950–4*	47.6	18.3	212.4	81.7	260.0
1955–9*	128.6	43.8	165.3	56.2	293.9
1960–4*	182.8	58.1	131.6	41.9	314.4
1965–9*	204.7	52.4	185.9	47.6	390.6
1970	170.3	48.6	180.1	51.4	350.4
1971	191.6	54.7	158.9	45.3	350.5
1972	196.5	61.5	122.8	38.5	319.3
1973	186.6	63.4	107.5	36.6	294.1
1974	140.9	52.3	128.6	47.7	269.5
1975	150.8	48.2	162.3	51.8	313.0
1976	152.2	48.3	163.0	51.7	315.2
1977	140.8	46.4	162.5	53.6	303.3
1978	149.0	53.3	130.7	46.7	279.8
1979	140.3	57.4	104.0	42.6	244.3
1980	125.9	54.1	106.7	45.9	232.6

* Annual averages.

Sources: Economic Trends Annual Supplement 1981 Edition; Housing and Construction Statistics.

Table 3.4 shows in particular that house-building in the ten years immediately following the end of the Second World War was predominantly for local authorities. Since 1955, a slight majority of new houses have been for owner-occupation but it was only in 1972 and 1973 and since 1979 that that proportion has been significant.

The owner-occupied stock has grown not only because of new building but also because of transfers of houses from the local authority rented sector and more importantly from the private rented sector. There has also been a limited amount of gains through conversions while on the other hand there have been losses to the stock, primarily through slum clearance. These trends are illustrated in Table 3.5.

Table 3.5   Growth of the Owner-Occupied Housing Stock, 1971–80

Year	1 Net increase in stock	2 Com- pletions of new houses	3 Con- version gains	4 Slum clear- ance losses	5 Other losses	6 Council house sales	7 Local auth- ority acquisi- tions	8 Gains from private rented sector
	000's	000's	000's	000's	000's	000's	000's	000's
1971	242	192	2	23	3	21	2	55
1972	292	197	2	22	4	62	–	57
1973	264	187	3	20	3	42	–	55
1974	186	141	2	14	3	6	2	56
1975	189	151	3	16	1	3	7	56
1976	195	152	1	17	1	6	3	57
1977	194	140	1	12	1	12	2	56
1978	231	149	1	9	2	31	2	63
1979	226	140	1	8	2	42	2	55
1980	278	126	1	6	2	80	2	81

Note: The relationship between the figures in this table is as follows: (figures in column) 1−2−3+4+5−6+7=8.

Sources: *Housing and Construction Statistics*; *Housing Policy Technical Volume*; BSA estimates.

Table 3.5 shows that between 50,000 and 80,000 privately rented houses a year have moved into the owner-occupied sector; a highly variable number of former council houses have also joined the owner-occupied stock. The sale of council houses is a major political issue and this is reflected in the variability of the figures. The present government is committed to a vigorous policy of selling and thus the owner-occupied stock seems likely to grow quite significantly as a result of this factor in the coming years. On the other hand, the number of privately rented houses available for transfer to owner-occupation is declining and this will compensate to some extent for the effects of increased council house sales.

The demand for owner-occupation remains strong and there is a considerable unsatisfied demand for this form of tenure. Provided that there are no supply side constraints, the proportion of owner-occupied houses looks set to continue to rise. The most reliable evidence on public attitudes towards housing tenure is a survey conducted in 1975 by the British Market Research Bureau for the National Economic Development Office. Table 3.6 shows respondents' ideal housing tenure in two years' time.

Table 3.6 Ideal Housing Tenure in Two Years' Time (1975)

Preferred tenure	Age category, % 16–19	20–44	45–54	55+	Total	Present tenure %
Owner-occupation	65	78	71	55	69	52
Council renting	15	15	20	31	21	32
Private renting	14	3	7	10	8	13
Don't know	7	2	2	2	3	4

Source: BRMB, *Housing Consumer Survey* (NEDO, 1977).

Table 3.6 shows that 69 per cent of all households considered owner-occupation to be their ideal tenure and for those in the 20–44 age group, the proportion was as high as 78 per cent. 40 per cent of local authority tenants and 36 per cent of private tenants expressed owner-occupation as being their ideal form of tenure in two years' time.

The survey did not confine itself to preferences but rather also asked respondents which tenure they expected to be in in ten years' time. Table 3.7 shows the results.

Table 3.7 Expected Tenure in Ten Years' Time (1975)

Expected tenure	Age category, % 16–19	20–4	25–34	35–44	45–54	55–64	65+	Total
Owner-occupied	76	81	77	70	60	49	41	62
Council renting	9	12	14	22	28	37	36	25
Private renting	5	1	3	5	6	8	15	6
Don't know	9	6	7	4	5	6	9	6

Source: BMRB, *Housing Consumer Survey* (NEDO, 1977).

The table shows that 62 per cent of households expected to be owner-occupiers in ten years' time and for those in the 20–4 age group, the proportion was as high as 81 per cent. 25 per cent of all council tenants expected to be owner-occupiers within ten years.

With owner-occupation now being accepted as the main form of tenure for the majority of young households, the proportion of owner-occupied houses can be expected to rise simply for demographic reasons. Tables 3.6 and 3.7 have shown that preference for, and expectation of, owner-occupation is least among the higher age groups, simply because most families not now owner-occupiers in these age groups do not think they will be able to achieve owner-occupation. On the other hand, once people are owner-occupiers they very seldom leave that tenure except possibly to move into some form of sheltered housing late in life.

House Purchase Finance

In most countries, finance for house purchase is provided by a variety of institutions, including commercial banks, savings banks and specialist institutions such as building societies. Britain is exceptional in that building societies have dominated the house-purchase finance market. Table 3.8 shows the distribution of loans for house-purchase outstanding as at end-1980 and the distribution of net advances in 1980.

Table 3.8   Loans for House Purchase, 1980

Institution	Net advances during year		Balances outstanding at end of year	
	£m.	%	£m.	%
Building societies	5,722	80.7	42,708	82.1
Local authorities	440	6.2	3,641	7.0
Insurance companies	255	3.6	2,082	4.0
Banks	520	7.3	2,940	5.7
Savings banks	93	1.3	115	0.2
Other public sector	60	0.8	536	1.0
Total	7,090	100.0	52,022	100.0

Source: Financial Statistics, July 1981, Supplementary Table E.

Table 3.8 shows that building societies accounted for 82.1 per cent of loans outstanding with local authorities, insurance companies and banks accounting for most of the remainder.

Another distinguishing feature of housing finance in Britain has been that the market share of the major lending institutions has been very variable. Building societies' share of net advances has varied between as little as 62.9 per cent in 1974 and as much as 95.7 per cent in 1977 and 1978. Local authorities' share has varied between a high point of 23.5 per cent in 1974 and a low point in 1978 when advances made were actually exceeded by repayments of existing loans. Bank lending has also been very variable, reaching a peak of 12.4 per cent of the market in 1972 and falling to under 2 per cent in 1975 and 1976. Insurance company net lending has been slightly more stable but even that has varied between almost nothing in 1972 and 5.1 per cent in 1974. In order to understand these trends, the various institutions other than building societies need to be studied in a little detail.

Traditionally, the British banks have not been involved in the mortgage market, except to provide bridging finance, that is, to make a short-term loan to a borrower to tide him over until he can obtain a building society loan. The banks have done a very limited amount of more normal mortgage lending but generally this has been for terms of no more than ten years. Much of their lending has been to their own staff. However, in recent years all of the major clearing banks, together with other British and foreign banks, have announced intentions of entering the mortgage market in a more vigorous way with longer term loans. The high level of net advances by the banks in 1980 reflects this trend and the banks seem likely to take a higher share of the mortgage market in the coming years. Indeed, provisional estimates for 1981 suggest that bank net advances for house-purchase will total £2,200 million, 24 per cent of the total.

Compared with their counterparts in other countries, British savings banks are exceptional in that they have not lent for house-purchase on any significant scale. In fact, until recently the only function of the savings banks was the collection of savings which were then handed over to the government. The savings banks are now moving into the private sector and obviously mortgage lending is an attractive market for them. Table 3.8 shows a significant level of savings bank net advances in 1980 and a much higher level of lending can be expected in future years.

Local authorities make mortgage loans in pursuance of their statutory housing duties. Some authorities have confined their lending to cases which come within their overall housing strategy while others have seen an extensive home loans programme similar to those offered by building societies as being an objective in its own right. Local authority lending ran at fairly modest levels until the early 1970s. In 1973 and 1974, the high level of interest rates in the economy led to a considerable cutback of building society lending. Because local authorities pool their debt and because some of the debt is long-term, their interest rates tend to lag behind those of building societies and other financial institutions. Thus, in 1973 and 1974, local authorities were able to lend at lower rates than building societies and moreover the shortage of building society funds meant that there was a strong demand for their home loans. The government, anxious to avoid the building society interest rate rising, was happy to acquiesce in an expansion of local authority lending and by 1974 the authorities accounted for no less than 23.5 per cent of the mortgage market. A momentum had been built up which was difficult to reverse and in 1975, as building society lending recovered, local authority lending increased even further, although their market share fell back.

By 1975 the government was under pressure to bring public expenditure under tighter control and local authority lending was cut back in pursuance of this objective. Building societies were asked to step in to fill the gap and this they duly did. (This aspect of building societies' work is considered in more detail in Chapter 8.)

The apparent sharp increase in local authority lending in 1980 reflects the sale of council houses. Normally, when a local authority sells a house, all that happens is that the debt is transferred from being a debt in respect of rented housing to being a mortgage debt. No money actually passes hands. However, the volume of loans for house-purchase does rise to the extent that the volume of outstanding debt for council housing falls. The sharp rise in local authority lending for house-purchase in 1980 does not therefore reflect building society-type lending but rather is a result of the increased level of sale of council houses. This can be expected to continue for some time although eventually of course repayments resulting from the sales will also increase and net lending can be expected to fall.

Building Society Lending Policy

It was established earlier in this chapter that many households seek to become owner-occupiers at a comparatively young age. Obviously, such households have only a limited amount of savings and as their incomes are not at peak level they are able to afford only relatively modest houses. However, as incomes increase, households tend to move up-market, perhaps two or three times. The housing finance system has had to adapt to this market situation and building societies must therefore be ready to assist young first-time buyers with limited capital or income and also to help people move up-market later on in their lives.

More so than their counterparts in many other countries, building societies are prepared to make high percentage loans, assisted by an indemnity scheme guarantee operated with the major insurance companies. Currently, the scheme permits 100 per cent loans on properties valued up to £20,000; 95 per cent loans on properties valued up to £26,316 and 90 per cent loans for properties up to £33,332. For properties valued above this amount, societies' rules normally permit them to lend only 80 per cent of valuation or purchase price, whichever is the lower.

The amount that a building society is willing to lend to a prospective house-purchaser depends on the value of the property and on the ability of the purchaser to repay the loan required. As a rule of thumb, societies are normally prepared to lend up to $2\frac{1}{2}$ times an applicant's gross annual earnings. If there is to be a joint mortgage, the multiple may be up to $2\frac{1}{2}$ times the gross annual income of the higher income earner plus once the income of the other earner. Additional earnings such as commission and overtime may be taken into account, depending on their permanency and regularity.

Normally, mortgages are granted for twenty or twenty-five year terms although, exceptionally, longer terms are permitted. However, when interest rates are at a very high level only a very small advantage is to be gained from a longer mortgage term. For example, when the mortgage rate is 8.5 per cent, £10,000 over twenty years would cost £88.10 per month whereas over thirty-five years the cost is reduced quite significantly to £75.20 a month. The comparative figures for a mortgage of 15 per cent are £133.20 and £126.00. Moreover, the longer the initial period of the loan, the less the flexibility for extending the term of the loan in the event of an increase in interest rates.

Building societies lend on almost all types of property provided they are structurally sound and either have the basic amenities (hot and cold water, an inside toilet and a fixed bath or shower) or will have these amenities installed immediately after purchase. Problems may possibly arise in the following areas:

(a) Properties with a short life. Most societies require the expected life of the property to be at least thirty years.
(b) Leasehold properties. Societies will require that the lease should run for twenty or thirty years after the mortgage will have been fully paid off.
(c) Converted flats. Most societies will lend on converted flats as long as

the conversion is structurally sound and the lease makes adequate provision for the maintenance and repair of the common parts of the building.

The problem that house-purchasers in Britain have faced has not
been that a building society has been unwilling to grant them a loan but
rather that the societies have been unable to because of lack of funds.
Characteristically, the mortgage rate has been held at below a market clearing
level with the result that there has been a considerable unsatisfied demand
for mortgage funds. Societies have rationed the available funds through
restricting the number of loans and also the amount of individual loans.
In allocating their funds, societies have given preference to their investing
members and young people are frequently advised to open a savings account
with a building society if they hope for a mortgage at some time in the future.
However, over the past year or so there has been a significant change in
this situation, largely because of the entry of the banks into the mortgage
market. In future, mortgages seem likely to be available on demand to those
willing and able to pay the market price.

The Process of House-Purchase

Potential house-buyers are generally advised to consult a building society
before taking any steps to purchase a house. The society may be able to
give an indication of how much can be borrowed and the potential house-
purchaser can set his sights accordingly. In fact, it seems that many households do not consult a building society until fairly late in the process, perhaps
because they are well aware of their chances of obtaining a mortgage of the
size they require.

Purchasing a new house offers a number of advantages to the home-
buyer:

(a) The sale of the house cannot fall through because of the 'chain' problem,
    that is, a vendor of a secondhand house may have to pull out of the
    transaction if his own subsequent purchase fails to go through.
(b) Many house-building companies negotiate block mortgage arrangements
    with societies whereby societies guarantee to make funds available to any
    purchaser of a new house provided he meets the usual status requirements.
    Therefore it may be easier to obtain a mortgage loan on a new house
    than on an existing house.
(c) House-builders are in the business of selling houses and employ expert
    staff who can assist the home-buyer in going through the rather com-
    plicated process of house-purchase.

New houses have an intrinsic value in themselves to many house-buyers and
a brand new virgin house may well attract a higher price than an identical
but slightly used house next door.

Purchasers of new houses also have the advantage of being protected by
the National House-Building Council. In 1966 The Building Societies
Association recommended to its member-societies that they should make
loans to purchasers of newly built houses only if the houses have been con-

structed by a builder registered with the NHBC except where the construction has been supervised by an architect or qualified surveyor employed
solely by the purchaser. The houses of registered builders are periodically
inspected during the course of construction and they must be built to defined
standards of quality in respect of such matters as insulation, wood preserva-
tion, storage space and electrical safety. Provided that the house-purchaser
enters into the house purchaser's agreement, he immediately has protection
against the builder going bankrupt where, after exchange of contracts, the
purchaser has lost his deposit or has to meet the cost of remedying a faulty
building. More importantly, in the first two years, the builder will at his
own expense put right any defects which may arise as a result of his failure
to comply with the Council's minimum standards and, from the end of the
second year to the end of the tenth year, the NHBC insurance policy provides cover against major damage due to any defect in the load-bearing
structure. Largely because of the Association's recommendation, nearly all
new houses are now constructed by registered builders and have NHBC
cover.

Over 80 per cent of house-buyers purchase secondhand houses rather than
new dwellings. The main reason for this is simply that the supply of secondhand houses coming onto the market is much greater than the supply of
new houses. Some home-buyers prefer existing houses rather than the
attraction of a new, previously unlived-in house, primarily because it is existing houses which are more conveniently situated in respect of public services
and so on.

House-purchasers can seek dwellings either through using the services of
an estate agent or by looking at newspaper advertisements. Estate agents
charge no fee to those purchasing and are able to supply details of houses
on their books to any potential buyer.

Once an offer to purchase has been made, it is then essential that the house-
purchaser, if he has not already done so, secures the necessary finance
to complete the purchase. The building society, or indeed any other lender,
will value the property and a fee for this will be charged to the purchaser.
Building societies point out that a valuation is not a structural survey and
advise potential buyers to commission a full independent structural survey
if they wish to be satisfied that the house is structurally sound and worth
the price that they are being asked to pay.

The legal formalities in the house-purchase process are normally handled
by a solicitor although some house-buyers prefer to do the legal work themselves. The whole process, from deciding on the property to be purchased
to completion, is likely to take three or four months although sometimes
transactions can be completed very much more quickly.

The Mortgage loan

Contrary to popular usage, building societies and other lenders do not 'give
mortgages'. Rather, they provide loans to home-buyers and it is the home-
buyers who give the mortgage to the building society, the mortgage being
a legal charge on the property. The mortgage deed is the legal contract between
the society and the borrower and comprises:

(a) The names of the parties to the contract, that is, the borrower and the building society.
(b) A statement of the amount of the loan being made and an acknowledgement by the borrower of receipt of the loan.
(c) A promise by the borrower to repay the loan with interest on the terms stipulated.
(d) The legal charge of the property to the society until such time as the loan is repaid.
(e) Promises by the borrower concerning such matters as insurance premiums, repairs and letting the property.

Most borrowers elect to take out annuity loans by which the loan is repaid by equal instalments of principal and interest over the stated term. Initially most of the repayments are interest and only in later years do capital repayments become significant. Currently, interest on annuity loans is charged on what is known as an annual rest basis, that is interest in the first year is charged on the initial loan for the period up to the end of the society's financial year and in subsequent years interest is charged on the debt outstanding at the beginning of the society's financial year. The effect of this arrangement is that the 'true' rate of interest is slightly higher than the stated nominal rate.

The alternative way of repaying loans is to link the loan to an endowment assurance plan. During the life of the loan, the borrower pays interest only to the building society but simultaneously he pays a monthly premium to an insurance company. At the end of the period of the mortgage, the proceeds of the endowment policy are used to repay the building society loan and normally there will also be a bonus for the home-buyer. In recent years, about one quarter of all mortgage loans have been on the endowment basis. Societies normally charge a quarter or half per cent higher rate of interest on endowment loans.

Mortgage interest on the first £25,000 of a loan qualifies for income tax relief at the borrower's highest marginal tax rate. Such relief is normally granted through the tax system. Instead of claiming tax relief on mortgage interest, borrowers can elect to use the government's option mortgage scheme. The purchaser takes advantage of a subsidy from the government which is paid directly to the society on behalf of the borrower. The subsidy scale is maintained such that it is broadly equivalent to the tax relief which a basic rate taxpayer would qualify for. Generally speaking, it pays a borrower to opt for this scheme only if he is unable to obtain tax relief at the basic rate on all of his mortgage interest. (It might be added that given the current low tax threshold there are few potential house-buyers who are not earning enough to pay tax yet who are earning sufficient to qualify for a mortgage.)

In the event of an increase in the mortgage rate, it may be possible for annuity (but not endowment) borrowers to extend the term of the loan rather than to make higher repayments. However, as has already been noted, when interest rates are at a high level the benefits of doing this are limited. Nevertheless, in hardship cases and when there are sharp increases in the mortgage rate, some societies are prepared to allow mortgage debts to rise with interest effectively being capitalised.

The Distribution of Building Society Loans

So far this chapter has analysed the housing stock, the house-purchase finance market, building society lending policies and the process of house-purchase. This section of the chapter analyses the distribution of building society mortgage loans in 1980 and thereby illustrates some of the points made earlier in the chapter. The data for this section is drawn almost exclusively from the 5 per cent sample survey of building society mortgages which the Department of the Environment, in conjunction with The Building Societies Association, has conducted in its present form since 1968. The sample survey yields a wide range of information in respect of the characteristics of building society borrowers, the characteristics of the houses they purchase and the nature of the loans granted by societies.

Before analysing the pattern of building society lending in 1980, it is helpful to list those factors which help determine this pattern:

(a) The distribution of houses coming onto the market. There is no reason to expect an exact correlation between the housing stock and the houses coming onto the market. For example, all new houses come onto the market each year whereas only a fraction of existing houses are sold in any one year. Thus, although new houses account for little more than 1 per cent of the total housing stock in a year, they are responsible for some 16 per cent of houses being sold. More generally, there is evidence to suggest that smaller, cheaper houses, typically bought by first-time buyers, turn over more rapidly than expensive houses.

(b) The number and nature of potential buyers in an area. In regions where there is already a high level of owner-occupation, such as the south-east of England, it follows that the number of potential first-time buyers is comparatively small. Conversely, where owner-occupation is at a low level, as in Scotland and the north of England, there is a higher number of potential first-time buyers.

(c) The availability of building society loans and general economic conditions. If the demand for building society loans is greatly in excess of the supply, then this might be expected to have an effect on the average percentage advance and possibly also on the characteristics of borrowers obtaining loans. Thus, the most marginal potential buyers might be squeezed out.

(d) The activities of other lenders. Local authority lending for house-purchase was at very high levels in 1974 and 1975. This lending was concentrated at the lower end of the housing market and therefore the demand for building society loans on poorer quality housing was reduced. As local authority lending fell off in 1976 and 1977, so building society lending on pre-1919 houses increased sharply. It seems probable that over the last few years the growth of bank lending, primarily at the top end of the market, has led to a reduction in the demand facing building societies for loans on more expensive dwellings.

Table 3.9 shows the regional distribution of building society loans in 1980 together with details of the private housing stock at the beginning of that year and private housing completions during the year.

Table 3.9 Regional Distribution of Loans, Housing Stock and House Completions, 1980

Region	Number of loans 000's	Percentage of total	Value of loans £m.	Percentage of total	Owner-occupied housing stock (end-1979) 000's	Percentage of total	Owner-occupied stock as percentage of total	Private houses completed 000's	Percentage of total
Greater London	58	9	977	11	1,336	11	49	4	3
South West	56	8	751	8	1,057	9	63	15	12
East Anglia	27	4	336	4	419	4	58	8	6
South East	150	22	2,288	26	2,345	20	62	31	24
Northern	34	5	378	4	547	5	46	5	4
Yorks. and Humber	64	10	684	8	1,017	9	55	9	7
North West	75	11	879	10	1,434	12	59	12	9
East Midlands	56	8	628	7	829	7	57	10	8
West Midlands	65	10	804	9	1,063	9	56	13	10
Wales	28	4	329	4	630	5	59	6	4
Scotland	51	8	680	8	698	6	35	12	9
Northern Ireland	11	2	151	2	244	2	49	4	3
United Kingdom	675	100	8,887	100	11,619	100	54	128	100

Sources: BSA Bulletin No. 26; Housing and Construction Statistics.

It will be seen that there is a fairly close correlation between the number and value of building society loans going to the various regions and the size of the housing stock in each region. Perhaps the most significant variation is in respect of the south-eastern region which had 20 per cent of the housing stock but accounted for 26 per cent of the value of loans. To some extent this can be explained by house prices being higher in the south-east than in other regions but another factor is that the housing stock probably turns over more rapidly in the south-east as is evidenced by the fact that nearly a third of new houses completed in 1980 were in that region.

Building societies lend to finance the purchase of houses in all price ranges. During 1980, for example, societies financed the purchases of some houses costing under £5,000 and others costing above £60,000. 48 per cent of all houses mortgaged to societies in 1980 cost less than £20,000. 70 per cent of first-time buyers were able to purchase houses costing under this amount; not surprisingly, former owner-occupiers tended to purchase more expensive houses.

Several years ago it was fashionable to argue that building societies preferred to concentrate their lending on houses such as inter-war, semi-detached houses. This has never been true although admittedly building society lending has tended to move down-market in recent years. Table 3.10 shows the distribution of building society loans by age and type of dwelling in 1980.

Table 3.10 Distribution of Loans by Age and Type of Dwelling, 1980

Type of dwelling	Percentage of total number of loans granted					
	Pre-1919	1919–39	1940–60	Post-1960	New	Total
Bungalow	–	1	1	4	2	9
Detached	3	3	1	7	6	20
Semi-detached	4	9	4	11	4	32
Terraced	16	5	1	6	2	30
Purpose-built flat	2	1	–	3	1	7
Converted flat	2	–	–	–	–	2
Total	28	18	8	31	15	100

Source: *BSA Bulletin* No. 26.

It will be seen that over a quarter of all loans were on pre-1919 houses and, perhaps surprisingly, societies gave more loans on pre-1919 terraced houses than they did on inter-war semi-detached houses. Table 3.10 also shows that the detached houses and bungalows on which building societies lend tend to be comparatively new while terraced houses tend to be older.

There are substantial variations in respect of the distribution of houses and these are very much reflected in the pattern of building society lending. For example, while nationally 9 per cent of all building society loans were on bungalows, the proportion ranged from a high of 32 per cent in Northern Ireland to as low as 1 per cent in the Greater London area. The special characteristics of London housing are particularly evident. Thus, 36 per cent of all building society loans in Greater London were on flats compared with the national average of 9 per cent. Only 6 per cent of loans in London were on detached houses or bungalows compared with the national average of 29 per cent. Scotland also stands out as having a very high proportion of loans on flats and, correspondingly, a low proportion on detached and semi-detached houses.

Building societies lend both to those purchasing their first homes and people moving up-market. The housing market is unified and some 85 per cent of first-time buyers purchase existing houses which, for the most part, means houses from people moving. Not all owner-occupiers moving are moving up-market of course. Some may be moving because of their jobs and some may even be trading down-market, for example on retirement. In recent years, the proportion of building society loans going to first-time buyers has tended to decline for reasons which will be explained later in this chapter. However, around half of all loans have gone to those buying for the first time and of these a fairly high proportion have been new households of one form or another. Again, there are substantial regional variations in the origins of building society borrowers.

In 1980 47 per cent of all borrowers were first-time buyers with the proportion ranging from a low of 42 per cent in the south-east and south-west (where the high level of owner-occupation means that there are comparatively few potential first-time buyers) to a high of 58 per cent in Greater London (where the opposite situation obtains). Over half of first-time buyers were new households but in some ways this figure is misleading because many of those formerly privately renting may have been doing so for only a very limited period of time. However, significantly 24 per cent of all building society borrowers in Greater London in 1980 were previously renting privately. Partly this reflects high house prices in London which means that people are not able to purchase at such an early age as is common in other parts of the country.

As building society lending covers the whole spectrum of houses on the market, not surprisingly it also covers a very wide spectrum of house purchasers. Sometimes there is a tendency to compare average earnings with average house prices and thereby come to the conclusion that no one can afford to buy houses but in reality the position is very different. In most parts of the country houses can be bought by people with below average earnings and in recent years some 40 per cent of building society borrowers have been earning below national average earnings. In 1980, 26 per cent of all borrowers were earning less than £6,000 a year while for first-time buyers the proportion was 28 per cent.

Because house prices are relatively low in relation to incomes in many parts of the country, first-time buyers are often able to purchase their homes at a very early age. In 1980, 36 per cent of first-time buyers were under the age of 25 although, perhaps equally significantly, 7 per cent were above the age of 45. Not surprisingly, people moving tend to be older than first-time buyers.

Trends in Building Society Lending

The previous section showed a snapshot of building society lending in 1980. The pattern of building society lending is not constant. It varies with changes in building society practices and changes in market conditions. This section illustrates the major trends in building society lending in recent years.

One of the most significant trends in the pattern of building society lending has been the falling proportion of loans going to first-time buyers and correspondingly the rising proportion going to owner-occupiers moving. This is illustrated in Table 3.11

Table 3.11 Building Society Loans to First-Time Buyers and Former Owner-Occupiers, 1969–80

Year	First-time buyers		Former owner-occupiers		Total
	Number of loans 000's	Percentage of total	Number of loans 000's	Percentage of total	number of loans 000's
1969	290	63.0	170	37.0	460
1970	329	61.0	211	39.0	540
1971	394	60.4	259	39.6	653
1972	394	57.9	287	42.1	681
1973	283	51.9	262	48.1	545
1974	220	50.8	213	49.2	433
1975	306	47.0	345	53.0	651
1976	352	49.2	363	50.8	715
1977	355	48.2	382	51.8	737
1978	379	47.3	423	52.7	802
1979	324	45.3	391	54.7	715
1980	318	47.0	358	53.0	675

Source: BSA Bulletin.

Table 3.11 shows that in 1969, 63.0 per cent of all loans went to first-time buyers whereas by 1980, 11 years later, the proportion had fallen to 47.0 per cent. However, the number of loans going to first-time buyers has not declined but rather has tended to fluctuate erratically, with high points being reached in 1971 and 1972 and more recently in 1978.

The declining proportion of loans going to first-time buyers is not explained by potential first-time buyers finding greater difficulty entering the housing market but rather, very simply, by the fact that there are fewer potential first-time buyers. People can be first-time buyers only once and the higher the proportion of owner-occupation in the country, the smaller the number of potential first-time buyers amongst existing households. Taking the extreme case, if there was a zero level of owner-occupation then 100 per cent of loans would go to first-time buyers. At the other extreme, if there was a stable number of households and if all households were owner-occupiers and bought four houses during their lifetimes then 25 per cent of loans would go to first-time buyers. In fact, the decline in the proportion of loans going to first-time buyers matches very closely the rise in the ratio of owner-occupied to non owner-occupied houses.

This trend suggests that a higher proportion of first-time buyers are new households and thereby younger households rather than existing households moving from other tenures. Between 1971 and 1980 the proportion of first-time buyers under the age of 25 increased from 75 per cent to 80 per cent and the proportion who were new householders increased from 33 per cent to 54 per cent.

The second major trend in building society lending has been the declining proportion of loans going to purchasers of new houses. However, notwithstanding this trend, the proportion of new houses financed by building societies has risen sharply. This is illustrated in Table 3.12.

Table 3.12   Building Society Loans on New Houses and Houses Completed, 1958–80

Year	Building society loans on new houses 000's	Number of private houses completed 000's	Loans as percentage of completions
1958	78	128	61
1959	99	151	66
1960	105	169	62
1961	103	178	58
1962	102	175	58
1963	112	175	64
1964	139	218	64
1965	132	214	62
1966	146	205	71
1967	147	200	74
1968	155	222	70
1969	128	182	70
1970	133	170	78
1971	165	192	86
1972	164	197	83
1973	142	187	76
1974	102	141	72
1975	121	151	80
1976	129	152	85
1977	122	141	87
1978	134	149	90
1979	117	138	85
1980	94	126	75

Sources: A Compendium of Building Society Statistics, 3rd edition (The Building Societies Association, 1980), Table A9 and *Economic Trends*.

It will be seen that the number of loans on new houses as a percentage of completions of new houses has fluctuated sharply, this largely being explained by the fact that the time when new houses are purchased does not necessarily correspond with when they are completed. Thus, in a very active market, houses will be sold at quite an early stage in the construction process while when the market is depressed houses may be completed and left unsold for some considerable time. However, the trend in the final column of the table is very clear. Between 1958 and the mid-1960s little more than 60 per cent of new houses were financed by building societies whereas in more recent years the proportion has been over 80 per cent.

The rise in the proportion of new houses financed by building societies has, as has already been noted, been accompanied by a decline in the proportion of loans going on new houses; this figure has fallen from a peak of 35 per cent in 1965 to only 16 per cent in the late 1970s. The decline in the proportion of loans going to first-time buyers was explained by the rise in the number of existing owner-occupiers compared with the number of potential first-time buyers. Similarly, the fall in the proportion of loans going on new houses can be explained by the rise in the owner-occupied housing stock together with a decline in the number of private houses completed. In 1968 the number of new houses completed was equal to 2.6 per cent of the stock outstanding at the beginning of the year whereas in 1980 the proportion was as low as 1.2 per cent. There is a very clear inverse relationship between the number of private houses completed as a proportion of the existing stock and the proportion of building society loans going on new houses.

The third major trend in the pattern of building society lending has been the increase in the proportion of loans going on pre-1919 houses. This is illustrated in Table 3.13.

Table 3.13 Building Society Lending on Pre-1919 Houses, 1970–80

Year	Number of loans 000's	Proportion of total %
1970	90	16.7
1971	119	18.2
1972	131	19.2
1973	99	18.1
1974	81	18.7
1975	125	19.2
1976	164	22.9
1977	188	23.5
1978	192	24.0
1979	172	24.0
1980	189	28.0

Source: 5 per cent sample survey of building society mortgage completions.

It will be seen that the proportion has risen from 16.7 per cent in 1970 to 28.0 per cent in 1980. Table 3.13 also shows the number of loans on pre-1919 houses and, while this has varied in line with the variations in the overall level of lending, there has been a very definite upward trend. Obviously, the number of pre-1919 houses has not increased (although theoretically it is possible for the number of owner-occupied pre-1919 houses to increase) and thus the rising proportion of building society loans going on this type of property must be explained by other factors. Two such factors can be identified:

(a) In recent years there has been a change in emphasis in government policy away from redevelopment towards rehabilitation and there has probably been a significant increase in the number of pre-1919 houses which societies are prepared to mortgage.
(b) Since 1975, societies have been working closely with local authorities. The nature of the support scheme is described in more detail in Chapter 8 but at present it is sufficient to say that this increase in co-operation together with the reduction in local authority lending from 1975 probably explains a major part of the increased building society lending on older houses.

Chapter 4

The Financial Management of Building Societies

The previous two chapters have been concerned with the two major functions of building societies:

(a) Attracting savings from the public.
(b) Lending money to finance house purchase.

This chapter is concerned with the overall financial management of building societies and thereby explains the relationships between the savings and lending functions.

Balance Sheets: An Overview

Table 4.1 shows the aggregate balance sheet for building societies at the end of 1980.

Table 4.1 Building Society Assets and Liabilities, End-1980

Liabilities	£m.	%	Assets	£m.	%
Shares	48,932	91.0	Mortgages	42,445	78.9
Deposits	1,724	3.2	Cash & investments	10,600	19.7
Loans	21	–	Office premises	621	1.2
Taxation and other			Other assets	127	0.2
liabilities	1,228	2.3			
General reserves	1,888	3.5			
Total	53,793	100.0	Total	53,793	100.0

Source: Building Societies in 1980 (The Building Societies Association, 1981).

Table 4.1 shows the very simple nature of the balance sheet of building societies compared with that of other financial institutions. There are five basic items on the liabilities side of the balance sheet with shares accounting for over 90 per cent of the total. The assets side of the balance sheet has four basic items with mortgages accounting for nearly 80 per cent. Moreover, there has been no significant change in the composition of the balance sheet in recent years. Indeed, the balance sheet of the average building society is now little different from the position fifty years ago.

The most significant trend has been the increase in the share of liabilities accounted for by shares and the corresponding decline in holdings of deposits. A second trend has been the decline in reserves as a proportion of total assets. The remainder of this section of this chapter briefly describes the components of the balance sheet and explains the changes in trends.

The nature of shares and deposits was described in detail in Chapter 2 and therefore only a brief summary is necessary at this stage. Depositors are creditors of a society rather than shareholders and in the unlikely event of a society being wound up they have preferential claim on the assets of the society. Because building societies have demonstrated an exceptionally good record for safety, the proportion of liabilities in the form of deposits has declined sharply and correspondingly the proportion held in the form of shares has increased. Currently, a high proportion of deposits is held by companies not able to take advantage of the composite rate tax arrangement. For most purposes, shares and deposits can be analysed together as being equal to investors' balances.

Table 4.1 shows that societies had loans of £21 million outstanding as at the end of 1980. £3 million of this was accounted for by government loans. There have been two occasions in the past twenty-five years when government has loaned money to building societies:

(a) Under the House Purchase and Housing Act 1959 the government loaned £100 million to building societies for on-lending to purchasers of pre-1919 houses. The entire amount was taken up between 1959 and 1961 since which time the loans have been gradually repaid. At their peak, in the fourth quarter of 1961, these loans accounted for 2.6 per cent of the total liabilities of all building societies. The £3 million outstanding at the end of 1980 is the residue of these loans.
(b) In 1974 the government made loans of £500 million to building societies in exchange for societies agreeing not to increase their rates of interest. The loans were made on the basis that they would be repaid in accordance with a mathematical formula when net receipts rose above a certain level. When the loans were taken up, loans outstanding from the 1959 arrangement were equal to 0.2 per cent of the liabilities of building societies and the new £500 million loans put this proportion up to 2.6 per cent again. The loans were almost entirely repaid by the end of the first quarter of 1975.

The remaining £18 million was in respect of a loan raised by one society from a bank.

The item in the balance sheet for taxation and other liabilities largely reflects the fact that most societies draw up their balance sheets on 31 December while tax payments have to be made in January and February. This item also includes a small amount of other liabilities similar to those which any commercial organisation must incur.

Reserves conventionally appear on the liabilities side of the balance sheet and they are equal to the difference between the total assets of a society and all of its liabilities. The nature of reserves is explained in more detail later in this chapter.

Societies' mortgage lending was explained in detail in Chapter 3. It is sufficient at this stage to note that mortgages account for some 80 per cent of all building society assets and that proportion has varied only slightly in recent years, reaching a low point of 77.1 per cent in 1977 and a high point of 82.2 per cent in 1973. Cash and investments usually account for about 20 per cent of building society assets.

The remaining building society assets are their office premises and other assets such as computers and motor cars. There has been a steady increase in the proportion of assets held in this form since 1949. At the end of 1980 office premises accounted for 1.2 per cent of total assets and all other assets for 0.2 per cent. Although these assets are a relatively small proportion of the total, they are important because, unlike mortgages and cash and investments, they are not interest-earning. On the other hand, office premises do appreciate and, to some extent, the rise in the proportion of total assets accounted for by other assets is explained not by increased expenditure on office premises but rather by the revaluation of those premises. In such a case total assets will increase by the same amount as the increase in other assets although of course the proportion of other assets to total assets will rise.

Liquidity

The laws and regulations governing the way a building society may invest its liquid funds are fairly straightforward although somewhat indirect. Under the Building Societies Act 1962 a society need not have any liquid funds. However, section 58(1) of the Act requires that a society shall invest those liquid funds which it does hold only in classes of investments which have been authorised for this purpose by an order made by the Chief Registrar. The Registrar made his first order under this section in 1962 and the current relevant statutory instrument is the Building Societies (Authorised Investments) (No. 2) Order 1977 (Statutory Instrument 1977 No. 2052) as amended by the Building Societies (Authorised Investments) (Amendment) Order 1979 (Statutory Instrument 1979 No. 1301).

In addition to this order, the Designation for Trustee Investment Regulations are also relevant in that they require a society to have liquid funds of at least $7\frac{1}{2}$ per cent of its total assets. However, in practice, societies do not run their liquidity ratios this low as it would be prudentially unwise. Therefore it is the Authorised Investments Order which is the most important regulation concerning the way societies invest their surplus funds.

Paragraph 3 of this Order lays down that investments may be made only within part I of the schedule to the Order until the book value of the investments already held falling in that part amount to $7\frac{1}{2}$ per cent or more of the book value of the society's total assets at the end of the preceding year. If the investments in part I amount to at least $7\frac{1}{2}$ per cent, investments may then be made in part II. If the total value of investments in parts I and II combined amount to 15 per cent or more of the book value of the society's total assets at the end of the preceding financial year, investments may then be made in part III.

Very broadly speaking, part I investments are short-term government and government-guaranteed securities, part II investments are medium-term government and government-guaranteed securities and part III investments are long-term government and government-guaranteed securities. There is also a list of authorised banks in which societies can hold money. Funds kept in cash or in current accounts or on temporary loan to a bank are deemed to be investments within part I.

The Authorised Investments Order does circumscribe the way in which societies can invest surplus funds and has the effect of ensuring that it is difficult for societies to incur losses through their management of liquid funds, that is a society should not be put in the position of having to sell securities at a loss in order, for example, to meet a sudden increase in withdrawals. However, the Order is open to question in a number of respects. For example, although there is a requirement that $7\frac{1}{2}$ per cent of assets should be held in short-term securities, there is no requirement to have liquid assets which can be transformed into cash immediately.

In determining their policies with respect to liquidity, societies need to have regard to a number of factors in addition to the requirements set out above. These factors include:

(a) The need to have funds available to meet withdrawals. In recent years, the ratio of withdrawals to receipts has varied from as low as 64.7 per cent in 1975 to as high as 82.4 per cent in 1979. If interest rates suddenly move against building societies there might be a surge of withdrawals and societies must have funds available to meet such demand. Building societies therefore always need to keep a large reserve of very liquid funds so as to meet withdrawals.

(b) The need to finance known items of expenditure. Most of the expenditure which building societies incur is regular. That is, each month they have to pay out wages and salaries and so on. However, there are two major irregular items of expenditure:

   (i) Building societies make most of their tax payments (that is tax on investors' interest and corporation tax) in the first two months of the calendar year. When interest rates are at a high level these tax payments can be equal to as much as 1 per cent of the total assets of building societies. Obviously societies must have liquid assets available to make these payments.

   (ii) Most interest is credited to investors' accounts but a fairly sizeable amount is paid out. The peak months for paying out interest are December, January, June and July. Societies can readily predict how much interest they will be required to pay out and again must have liquid funds available for this purpose.

(c) Stabilisation of mortgage lending. Building society liquid assets act as a buffer which enable fluctuations in the inflow of savings to be partially absorbed. Thus, if there is suddenly a large increase in the inflow of savings, liquid assets are built up and conversely if the inflow of savings falls off liquid assets are run down so as to enable the volume of lending to be maintained. This is a particularly important part of building society operations and is explained in more detail in Chapter 5.

(d) Meeting mortgage commitments. House purchase is a fairly lengthy process and on average two to three months will elapse between a building society formally promising the offer of a loan to a borrower and the money being taken up. A society must ensure that it has access to funds to meet advances. Thus, if building societies face an outflow of funds they can react by stopping all new commitments immediately but this still leaves them having to find the funds to finance loan commitments already made. Part of loan commitments are in fact financed by repayments of existing loans but nevertheless a society prudentially should have funds available to meet about 40 per cent of its outstanding loan commitments. In recent years loan commitments have varied between 3.5 and 6 per cent of total assets and thus an amount equal to between 2 per cent and 4 per cent of total assets must be kept in liquid form available to meet these commitments.

(e) Earning income. Liquid assets (except cash and bank current accounts), like mortgage assets, are interest-earning and in determining its policy with respect to liquidity a society needs to have regard to relative yields. Societies do not seek to maximise profits and for this reason do not necessarily invest in liquid funds when the yield is higher than on mortgages and vice-versa. However, a society will always seek to obtain the maximum possible yield from those funds which it does keep in liquid form. Like any other institution, a society also has to secure a balance between liquidity and yield. A society with a high ratio of liquid assets to total assets can afford to sacrifice some liquidity in order to obtain a better yield whereas a society with only a low liquidity ratio might need to keep its assets in more liquid form and thereby accept a lower yield.

In recent years, interest rates in Britain have become more unstable and societies have suffered greater fluctuations in net receipts of new savings. This has tended to mean higher average liquidity ratios and, as importantly, a tendency to hold liquid assets in more liquid form. In practice, societies' holdings of British government securities and local authority long-term debt, which form by far the greatest proportion of liquid assets, are regarded as long-term investments and are seldom reduced in absolute terms. Changes in the volume of liquid assets are largely accounted for by changes in holdings of short-term assets. These trends are illustrated in Table 4.2.

Table 4.2 shows very clearly that the volume of holdings of British government securities has never declined whereas holdings of short-term assets and, to a lesser extent, local authority long-term debt, have fluctuated markedly. Thus, in 1977 holdings of short-term assets rose by no less than 66 per cent before falling back in 1978.

Building societies are huge financial institutions and their holdings of government debt in particular form a significant proportion of the total. At the end of 1980 societies accounted for 15.37 per cent of government debt with maturity of up to five years. The figure compares with a proportion of 10.64 per cent at the end of 1975.

The most significant long-term trend with respect to the composition of societies' liquid assets has been the shortening maturity. Of the total of government securities held by societies the proportion with five years to maturity rose from 62.8 per cent in 1973 to 94.4 per cent in 1978 although

Table 4.2 Composition of Liquidity by Type of Asset 1976–80 (End-Year) (Holdings at Book Value)

	1976 £m.	%	1977 £m.	%	1978 £m.	%	1979 £m.	%	1980 £m.	%
Short-term assets	1,500	29.1	2,485	38.1	2,139	29.4	2,470	29.8	3,952	37.5
British government securities	2,075	40.1	2,755	36.8	3,163	43.4	4,027	48.6	4,959	47.0
Local authority long-term debt	1,580	30.6	2,234	29.9	1,982	27.2	1,783	21.5	1,635	15.5
Total	5,159	100.0	7,477	100.0	7,285	100.0	8,280	100.0	10,546	100.0

Note: The differences between the totals and the sums of the three components are accounted for by very small holdings of overseas government debt.

Source: Financial Statistics, Table 8.7.

subsequently it has fallen back to 81.8 per cent at the end of 1980 – probably because some societies purchased longer dated securities in the hope of making a capital gain as interest rates fell.

Reserves

The Authorisation Regulations (and also the Designation for Trustee Status Regulations) require societies to hold a certain level of 'reserves', that is the difference between total assets and all liabilities. The Regulations provide that a society should hold reserves of not less than:

2.5 per cent of its assets not less than £100 million, plus
2 per cent of its assets exceeding £100 million but not exceeding £500 million, plus
1.5 per cent of its assets exceeding £500 million but not exceeding £1,000 million, plus
1.25 per cent of its assets exceeding £1,000 million.

The Authorisation Regulations now require a society to have minimum reserves of £50,000 or a combination of reserves and deferred shares (basically capital provided by the founders of the society) of that amount.

Thus, as a society grows, it need maintain a lower reserve ratio and small societies need to hold significantly larger reserve ratios than larger societies. This is illustrated in Table 4.3.

Table 4.3   Reserve Requirements by Size of Society

Size of society total assets £m.	Minimum reserve ratio %	Minimum reserves £m.
10	2.50	0.25
100	2.50	2.50
300	2.17	6.50
500	2.10	10.50
750	1.90	14.25
1,000	1.80	18.00
2,000	1.53	30.50
5,000	1.36	68.00
10,000	1.31	130.50

Table 4.3 shows that a society with total assets of £100 million has to maintain a reserve ratio of 2.50 per cent while for societies with assets of £1,000 million the required ratio is 1.80 per cent and for a society with £10,000 million total assets, the ratio falls to 1.31 per cent.

The reserve ratio requirements set out above were introduced following the publication of the Hardie Committee Report (*The Report of the Enquiry into Building Society Reserves and Liquidity to The Building Societies Association*, The Building Societies Association, 1967,) which in turn was established as a result of the Prices and Incomes Board Report (*Rate of*

Interest on Building Society Mortgages, National Board for Prices and Incomes, Report No. 22, Cmnd 3136, HMSO, 1966). The Hardie Committee considered in detail why building societies need to hold reserves. It set out three reasons:

(a) Societies need fixed assets, that is, premises and other equipment, in order to carry on their activities. Fixed assets have accounted for about 1 per cent of building society assets.
(b) To meet mortgage losses. However, as the Hardie Committee noted, mortgage losses have been very low and it would require a depression of the kind experienced in the 1920s and 1930s before significant mortgage losses could be made.
(c) To meet losses on investments. The Hardie Committee considered that the risk of loss on investments was very small, largely because of the strict regulations relating to the assets in which building societies can invest.

These considerations led the Hardie Committee to suggest a fairly modest requirement for reserves.

The reserves of building societies can be likened to the savings of a household. The increase in a household's savings between one year and the next is equal to the difference between its total income and its total expenditure. If the household wishes to maintain a given ratio of savings to its total assets then the faster the income of the household grows, the greater will be the need to save so as to maintain a constant ratio of savings to assets. So it is with building societies. Societies have to maintain the minimum ratios set out above and obviously the faster growing their assets, the greater the volume of additional reserves they need to make each year.

The precise relationship between a building society's initial reserve ratio, its growth rate and the net surplus needed to maintain that growth rate, can be presented in algebraic form:

$$S = \frac{GR}{0.5G + 100}$$

where S = annual surplus expressed as a percentage of mean assets in
        the year
      G = percentage rate of growth of total assets
      R = reserve ratio at beginning of financial year

This formula can be used to show the surplus that societies would have required in 1980 to maintain the end-1979 reserve ratio of 3.58 per cent for varying growth rates. The figures are shown in Table 4.4.

The point has been made that the addition to societies' reserves each year is equal to the difference between their income and expenditure. Table 4.5 shows income and expenditure for the years 1979 and 1980 and how the amount added to reserves in each of those two years was made up.

It will be seen for example that in 1980 societies' normal income was £7,100 million while normal expenditure was £6,914 million, leaving an excess of normal income over normal expenditure of £186 million. To this must be added exceptional items such as investment profits and in 1980 these

Table 4.4   Surplus Needed to Maintain End-1979 Reserve Ratio in 1980

Growth rate %	Net surplus required £ per £100 mean assets
10	0.34
12	0.41
14	0.47
16	0.53
18	0.59
20	0.65

Table 4.5   Building Societies: Income and Expenditure, 1979–80

	1979 £m.	£ per £100 mean assets	1980 £m.	£ per £100 mean assets
Normal Income				
Mortgage interest	4,082	9.57	5,912	11.89
Investment and bank interest	800	1.87	1,072	2.16
Commission	79	0.19	93	0.19
Rents	11	0.03	13	0.03
Other (net)	5	0.01	10	0.02
	4,977	11.67	7,100	14.29
Normal Expenditure				
Management expenses	449	1.05	579	1.16
Share, deposit and loan interest	3,396	7.97	4,851	9.76
Income tax on share and deposit interest	925	2.17	1,372	2.76
Corporation tax	81	0.19	112	0.23
	4,851	11.37	6,914	13.91
Normal income less normal expenditure	127	0.30	186	0.37
Investment profits and other exceptional or non-recurrent income (net)	38	0.09	62	0.12
Added to general reserves	164	0.39	247	0.50

Source: *Building Societies in 1980* (The Building Societies Association, 1981) and *Annual Report of the Chief Registrar, 1979* (HMSO, 1980).

amounted to £62 million, resulting in a total amount added to general reserves of £247 million. Reserves at end-1979 were £1,641 million and thus reserves at end-1980 were equal to this amount plus £247 million, £1,888 million. Table 4.6 shows how general reserves were built up between 1975 and 1980.

The amount added to reserves has fluctuated considerably from year to year. The figure was highest, at £287 million, in 1977 but fell sharply in 1978 and 1979. It is more relevant to compare the amount added to reserves each year with the average total assets during the year because the higher total assets are, the greater the addition to reserves needed to maintain a given

Table 4.6 Building Societies: Reserves, 1975–80

Year	Amount added to reserves						Total amount added to reserves		Reserves at end-year £m.	Reserve ratio at end-year %
	Normal income less normal expenditure £m.	£ per £100 mean assets		Exceptional income £m.	£ per £100 mean assets		£m.	£ per £100 mean assets		
1975	78	0.35		22	0.10		100	0.45	790	3.26
1976	144	0.55		43	0.16		187	0.71	977	3.46
1977	192	0.62		95	0.30		287	0.92	1,264	3.69
1978	142	0.38		70	0.19		212	0.57	1,477	3.73
1979	127	0.30		38	0.09		164	0.39	1,641	3.58
1980	186	0.37		62	0.12		247	0.50	1,888	3.51

Sources: *Building Societies in 1980* (The Building Societies Association, 1981) and Annual Reports of the Chief Registrar of Friendly Societies.

reserve ratio. Table 4.6 shows even greater variations in the amount added to reserves per £100 mean assets. Again, a peak was achieved in 1977 of 0.92 whereas the 1979 figure was 0.39.

One of the main reasons for the fluctuations in the amounts added to reserves in recent years has been the greater instability of interest rates which has had two important effects on societies:

(a) Societies have changed their interest rates more frequently and sometimes this can have unavoidable effects on reserves, for example, if an increase in the mortgage rate lags behind an increase in the investment rate.
(b) Investment profits contribute significantly to societies' reserves and the amount of such profits is heavily dependent on the trend of interest rates.

Another factor affecting the amount added to reserves is the composite rate of income tax. Frequently this has not been fixed until well into societies' financial years and in recent years the rate has changed markedly from year to year. This worked to the advantage of societies in 1977 when there was an unexpected reduction in the composite rate at the end of the calendar year but worked against societies in 1979 when there was a considerable increase in the composite rate for which societies were not able to compensate by changing their rates of interest.

Table 4.3 showed the minimum reserve requirements for societies by size. In practice, societies generally have held reserves well above the required minima. However, over time there has been a steady decline in the ratio of reserves to total assets. At the end of the Second World War, the average reserve ratio was 6.4 per cent but since that time it has fallen steadily, reaching a low point of 3.26 per cent in 1975 before recovering slightly to 3.73 per cent at the end of 1978 and then falling back to 3.50 per cent at the end of 1980.

The smaller societies do tend to maintain higher reserve ratios than the larger societies. This is illustrated in Table 4.7.

Table 4.7   Building Society Reserves, End-1980

Size classification of societies	Reserves £m.	Total assets £m.	Reserve ratio %
5 largest (assets over £2,500 million)	936	29,799	3.14
Assets £600m.–£2,500m.	534	14,515	3.68
Assets £140m.–£600m.	201	4,748	4.23
Assets £35m.–£140m.	150	3,430	4.37
Assets £2m.–£35m.	64	1,264	5.10
All societies	1,888	53,789	3.51

Source: The Building Societies Association.

It will be seen that the average reserve ratio for the five largest societies was 3.14 per cent while that for the societies with assets of between £2 million and £35 million was 5.10 per cent.

Income and Expenditure

Table 4.5 showed the income and expenditure for building societies for the years 1979 and 1980. It is now necessary to examine in more detail the various components of income and expenditure and in particular management expenses.

The basic components of income and expenditure are very few, matching the small number of components on either side of the balance sheet. On the income side, all but a very small amount of income is in the form of mortgage interest and investment and bank interest. The amount of mortgage interest per £100 of assets for an individual society depends on the proportion of its total assets in the form of mortgages and the average yield on its mortgage portfolio. In fact, most societies maintain mortgage portfolios of between 77 and 82 per cent of total assets and there are not significant changes over time. A change in the mortgage rate will of course have an immediate and direct effect on mortgage interest received. It should be noted at this stage that published figures for mortgage interest generally include payments received from the government under the option mortgage scheme which was described in Chapter 3.

Investment and bank interest forms an important proportion of total income. What is particularly significant is that when building societies change their interest rates then although mortgage interest and share, deposit and loan interest change, there will be no immediate change in investment and bank interest. Thus, a decline in building society interest rates is likely to mean that investment and bank interest will generate a higher proportion of total income and vice versa.

The published figures for commission are not entirely satisfactory because for some societies, commission paid out is netted against commission received. For the most part, the commission figures are in respect of property insurance and, to a lesser extent, life insurance policies arranged in conjunction with mortgages.

Rents provide a small amount of additional income. Such rents are usually in respect of surplus accommodation either in building society head offices or in their branches.

Share, deposit and loan interest together with income tax payable on that interest is responsible for most building society expenditure. A change in building society interest rates would lead to an immediate and direct change in the amount of share, deposit and loan interest and also in the income tax payable on that interest. Building societies discharge basic rate tax liability on investors' interest under what are known as the Income Tax Arrangements. Each year a composite rate is fixed by reference to a periodic statistical investigation and an annual analysis of trends in tax rates, incomes and personal allowances and the intention is that the Inland Revenue should secure from building societies collectively the same amount as would be received if each individual investor were assessed separately at the basic rate. The composite rate can change significantly from year to year, especially if the basic rate of income tax changes.

Before considering in slightly more detail management expenses, it should be noted at this stage that corporation tax is generally included under the heading of 'normal expenditure'. In fact, the amount of corporation tax is equal to 40 per cent of the excess of societies' normal income over their normal expenditure. Thus, in 1980, the corporation tax payment of £112 million was equal to 40 per cent of societies' total income (£7,100 million) less their normal expenditure excluding corporation tax (£6,802 million), that is 40 per cent of £298 million, i.e. £119 million but after allowing for special factors the amount actually charged was £112 million.

Management expenses in 1980 were equal to £579 million or £1.16 per £100 of total assets. Table 4.8 shows the composition of management expenses in 1979 and 1980.

Table 4.8   Composition of Management Expenses, 1979–80

Component	1979		1980	
	£m.	£ per £100 mean assets	£m.	£ per £100 mean assets
Directors' emoluments	5.0	0.01	6	0.01
Staff	231.0	0.54	298	0.60
Office expenses	110.0	0.26	142	0.28
Advertising	28.7	0.07	37	0.07
Commission and agency fees	37.5	0.09	41	0.08
Depreciation	27.8	0.07	37	0.07
Other expenses	9.3	0.02	17	0.03
Total	449.3	1.05	579	1.16

Sources: Annual Report of the Chief Registrar, 1979 (HMSO, 1980) and *Building Societies in 1980* (The Building Societies Association, 1981).

It will be seen that approximately half of management expenses are in the form of staff expenses. These include not only wages and salaries but also National Insurance contributions and so on. Directors' emoluments account for a very small proportion of total management expenses and even then the figures are inflated by including salaries paid to executive directors.

Office expenses account for approximately a quarter of all management expenses. The nature of their business means that building societies have to handle considerable volumes of correspondence and paperwork and this factor, together with the obvious high expenses of running a large number of branches, accounts for the figure for office expenses.

Advertising has been growing in recent years but still accounts for no more than 7 per cent of total management expenses. The figure for 1980 of £37 million includes not only television, radio and press advertising but also such items as showcards and in some cases, sponsorship.

It was noted earlier that some societies net out commission received and commission paid. Therefore, the figure for commission and agency fees paid out is perhaps not a true reflection of the total amount of commission which societies pay. Commission is payable by societies to those who introduce investment business. Agency fees are paid to appointed agents of societies in return for the services which they offer.

In recent years the ratio of management expenses to mean assets has increased quite considerably. Between 1920 and 1969, the ratio was fairly constant at between 0.60 and 0.65. Since then it has risen rapidly to reach 1.16 in 1980. The reasons for this increase were set out by The Building Societies Association in evidence to the Wilson Committee and the evidence has subsequently been reprinted by the Association (*Studies in Building Society Activity 1974–79*, The Building Societies Association, 1980). The main problem that societies face in this respect is one common to all financial institutions. Their expenses increase at least in line with inflation while their total assets are not directly linked to inflation, in particular, because the general level of short-term interest rates on which societies' fortunes so heavily depend is not directly related to the rate of inflation and in recent years short-term rates of interest have been negative by substantial amounts in real terms. There is a close correlation between the rate of inflation and the rate of increase in the management expense ratio. Thus, the biggest increase in the management expense ratio in recent years, from 0.77 to 0.89 in 1975, was accompanied by the unprecedented annual inflation rate of 24 per cent. As inflation declined between 1975 and 1978, so the management expense ratio increased more modestly. The acceleration of inflation in 1979 and 1980 resulted in substantial increases in the average management expense ratio.

The management expense ratio is frequently used as a measure of efficiency over time or between societies but it is extremely unsatisfactory in this respect. A more meaningful indication of management costs over time is perhaps gained by examining the growth of management expenses in relation to the number of accounts in real terms. Table 4.9 shows the position.

Table 4.9   Management Expenses per Member, 1970–80

Year	Manage-ment expenses	Number of shareholders and borrowers	Average cost per shareholder and borrower	Average cost per shareholder and borrower in 1980 prices	
					Index
	£m.	000's	£	£	1970=100
1970	68	13,919	5.17	18.65	100
1971	85	15,464	5.81	19.16	103
1972	102	17,000	6.31	19.41	104
1973	119	18,589	6.68	18.83	101
1974	145	20,106	7.50	18.23	98
1975	197	22,313	9.27	18.14	97
1976	237	24,600	10.12	16.99	91
1977	297	27,372	11.42	16.56	89
1978	363	30,106	12.65	16.93	91
1979	449	32,129	14.43	17.03	91
1980	579	36,023	16.99	16.99	91

Notes:
1 The average costs have been calculated on the mean number of shareholders and borrowers during the year.
2 The average costs per shareholder and borrower at 1980 prices have been calculated by reference to changes in the retail prices index.
Sources: Annual Reports of the Chief Registrar of Friendly Societies, BSA estimates and *Economic Trends*, March 1981, Table 42.

It will be seen that there has been a significant, albeit erratic, reduction in the real costs per shareholder and borrower since 1972. To a significant extent this can probably be attributed to computerisation.

Chapter 5

Rates of Interest and Levels of Activity

The Importance of Interest Rates

The previous three chapters have established the importance of interest rates to the operations of building societies. Chapter 2 demonstrated that the inflow of funds into building societies depends on the competitiveness of the interest rates offered by building societies as against those offered by competing institutions. Chapter 3 described the lending function of societies and noted that interest rates on building society loans are variable. Chapter 4 described the financial management of societies and emphasised the importance of interest in the income and expenditure account. Table 4.5 showed that mortgage interest accounted for 83.3 per cent of societies' normal income in 1980 and investment and bank interest accounted for a further 15.1 per cent. Interest on shares, deposits and loans was responsible for 70.2 per cent of normal expenditure and income tax on that interest for a further 19.8 per cent. Interest rates are therefore at the heart of building society operations and it is the difference between the interest which they pay and that which they receive which enables societies to function and to grow.

The Variable Rate Mortgage

In Britain, it is taken for granted that the rate of interest on existing mortgage loans is variable. However, this situation has not obtained in many other countries, where a fixed rate of interest has been more normal. It is therefore necessary to examine the importance of the variable rate mortgage for building societies in Britain.

Chapter 3 established that, for the most part, the savings which building societies attract are short-term. Notwithstanding the growth of term shares in recent years, 80 per cent of building society liabilities have a residual maturity of less than one month and in fact most can be withdrawn theoretically at no notice. It follows that when there is a significant change in short-term rates of interest then the inflow of funds into building societies is directly affected. A decline in interest rates will make building societies more competitive and hence lead to a greater inflow of funds while an increase in the general level of interest rates will have the opposite effect.

Significant changes in competing interest rates must cause building societies to adjust the rates of interest they pay to investors. Thus, if the general level of interest rates increases by, say, 5 per cent then if societies do not follow suit they would suffer a severe outflow of funds causing liquidity problems and possible insolvency. Because their liabilities are short-term, when interest rates change societies have to change their rates not just in respect of new savings but also in respect of existing savings which could otherwise be withdrawn. It follows that if the rate of interest on all societies' liabilities is increased then this causes a considerable increase in expenditure which can be matched only if additional income can be achieved from the assets side of the balance sheet. Interest on bank deposits and investments cannot in fact be changed unilaterally by societies but they are in a position, through use of the variable rate mortgage, to increase the rate of interest charged to all existing borrowers and hence pay for any increase in the rate paid to investors.

The fact that building societies can change rates of interest on both sides of their balance sheets simultaneously is of crucial importance to their success. The conventional wisdom is that borrowing short and lending long is inherently dangerous. *Prima facie*, there are good grounds for saying this. If, for example, a financial institution has £100 million of deposits at a rate of interest of 10 per cent which are withdrawable at one month's notice and lends that £100 million at a rate of 12 per cent over a fixed twenty-five year period then clearly that institution is very vulnerable if the general level of interest rates rises by, say, 5 per cent. The institution is faced with a choice of losing its deposits and therefore becoming insolvent, or paying a higher rate of interest on its deposits which it is not then able to recover on the fixed rate loans.

The variable rate mortgage means, in effect, that building societies are lending short-term in that the rate of interest on their loans can be varied at very short notice. Equally important is the fact that because rates of interest can be changed simultaneously on both sides of the balance sheet, the margin between the borrowing and lending rate can be kept very small because societies have the knowledge that it will always be adequate. This is in contrast to financial institutions which lend predominantly at fixed rates of interest. They have to allow for the fact that the cost of the money they are attracting might rise in relation to the yield on their loans and therefore must operate on a wider margin to be able to finance this.

This crucial point can be illustrated by comparing societies with their American equivalents, savings and loan associations. The latter have been forced to lend at fixed rates and by 1981 had run into serious difficulty as their loan portfolio was yielding under 11 per cent while their new money was costing them 15 per cent. The industry lost $5,000 million during the year.

The Use of Liquidity to Stabilise Lending

In fact, building societies do not respond to every change in interest rates by varying their own rates. Primarily, this is because of the effect on existing borrowers. It is quite acceptable to increase the price of any service to someone being offered it for the first time but it is a different matter to increase that price after the commodity has been purchased. If a borrower takes out a loan at a rate of interest of, say, 8 per cent, he might anticipate that that rate could increase modestly but he could not reasonably be expected to anticipate an increase of 10 per cent within a year. Moreover, increases of such magnitudes would threaten the financial viability of lending institutions if borrowers could not afford the additional repayments. Societies therefore try to steer a middle course, increasing interest rates only as a last resort. It follows that the inflow of funds into societies is very variable as societies' competitiveness changes and, in the normal course of events, this could be expected to lead to variations of equal magnitude in the volume of lending.

However, societies adopt a stabilisation policy so as to maintain lending at as stable a level as possible notwithstanding fluctuations in the inflow of new savings. When societies become more competitive so they build up their liquid assets and increase their lending only modestly. When societies become less competitive the liquid funds so built up can be run down so as to enable lending to be maintained. The way that societies have followed this principle in recent years is illustrated in Table 5.1 which shows societies' sources and uses of funds from 1973 to the third quarter of 1981.

The most significant figures are in column 9 which shows the increase in societies' holdings of cash and investments. It will be seen that in years of an exceptionally high inflow of funds, cash and investments have been increased. For example, in 1975 the record increase in shares and deposits led to an increase in cash and investment holdings of £1,269 million. More noticeably, the even higher level of the increase of savings balances in 1977 led to only a modest increase in mortgage balances outstanding and an increase of £2,318 million in cash and investments. In 1978, by contrast, the inflow of shares and deposits declined significantly and societies actually ran down their cash and investment holdings so enabling the increase in mortgage balances to continue rising.

The Interest Rate Decision

However, there does come a time when liquidity is no longer adequate to compensate for the effects of changes in competing interest rates and societies have to consider setting new interest rates. The triggering point for a change in interest rates is generally a sharp actual or anticipated change in net receipts of shares and deposits. To take one example, the increase in minimum lending rate to 17 per cent on 15 November 1979 caused an immediate outflow of funds from societies, something which cannot be tolerated for more than a very short period and within a week new building society interest rates had been set. At the other extreme, at the end of 1977 societies were enjoying an unprecedented inflow of funds which was more than adequate for their needs and hence there was a reduction in interest rates at the beginning of 1978.

Societies do not act autonomously in changing interest rates. Most societies follow recommendations made by the Council of The Building Societies Association. Even if the levels of rates recommended by the Council are not followed to the letter, the sizes of changes in the rates almost inevitably are.

In setting a new rate structure, the starting point has to be the demand for mortgage loans as this is the reason for attracting savings. The demand for mortgages is not something that can be scientifically measured but it is possible to make reasonable estimates. Having established such a figure,

Table 5.1 Building Societies: Sources and Uses of Funds (Cash Transactions), 1973-81

Period	Sources of funds						Uses of Funds		Cash and Investments				
	1 Shares and deposits-principal £m.	2 Interest credited accrued £m.	3 Govern-ment loans £m.	4 Other liabilities £m.	5 Reserves £m.	6 Total sources and uses £m.	7 Mort-gages £m.	8 Other assets £m.	9 Total £m.	10 Cash and bank balances £m.	11 Local authority invest-ments £m.	12 British govern-ment securities £m.	13 Other £m.
1973	1,512	705	-3	109		2,323	1,999	44	280	189	16	62	13
1974	1,165	880	326	209		2,580	1,490	61	1,029	152	718	61	106
1975	3,191	1,014	-335	205		4,075	2,768	38	1,269	24	564	641	40
1976	2,278	1,192	-3	300		3,767	3,618	151	-2	-3	-186	172	9
1977	4,722	1,425	-7	409		6,549	4,100	131	2,318	292	1,044	680	302
1978	3,310	1,616	-4	63		4,985	5,115	143	-273	46	-454	382	-247
1979	3,515	2,467	-3	416		6,395	5,271	168	956	1	74	822	59
1980	3,816	3,602	-3	740		8,155	5,722	229	2,204	724	462	873	145
1979Q.1	817	446	-1	-50		1,212	1,267	40	-95	-353	23	167	68
Q.2	825	567		218		1,610	1,352	41	217	8	-72	276	5
Q.3	980	728	-1	233		1,940	1,413	43	484	105	225	169	-15
Q.4	893	726	-1	15		1,633	1,239	44	350	241	-102	210	1
1980Q.1	659	818	-1	-348		1,128	1,242	45	-159	-386	90	192	-55
Q.2	730	825	-1	452		2,006	1,257	52	697	110	397	116	74
Q.3	1,127	900	-1	466		2,492	1,511	61	920	399	93	408	20
Q.4	1,300	1,059		170		2,529	1,712	71	746	601	-118	157	106
1981Q.1	1,081	853	-1	-652		1,281	1,562	79	-360	-417	-346	581	-178
Q.2	1,103	817		615		2,465	1,810	90	565	92	122	325	26
Q.3	868	858		494		2,220	1,562		568				

Source: BSA Bulletin, October 1981.

it is then necessary to calculate the increase in share and deposit balances needed to fund this level of lending. Mortgage repayments finance a considerable proportion of lending and the level of such repayments corresponding to the desired level of lending is a fairly simple matter to calculate. However, as societies grow, it is necessary for them to increase their liquidity holdings if a constant liquidity ratio is to be maintained. In the long term, societies seem to aim for an 18 per cent liquidity ratio and therefore it is reasonable to assume that the inflow of funds they require should be sufficient to maintain this ratio as well as funding the desired level of lending. The resultant figure is equal to the required increase in savings balances. From this figure is deducted the volume of interest credited (which in turn depends on the rate of interest so the process is something of a circular one) and the level of net receipts is a residual. The interest rate that societies need to achieve such a level of net receipts can be estimated quite simply by reference to competing interest rates.

By this process a share rate emerges. The mortgage rate is calculated simply on a cost-plus basis, that is added to the share rate is the income tax liability, management expenses, the desired surplus and the corporation tax on that surplus.

Needless to say, the process is not quite as mechanistic as is suggested in the preceding analysis. Frequently, an increase in competing interest rates has been so great that societies could not hope to fully match it without imposing intolerable burdens on existing borrowers. In such a case, as in November 1979, the calculation starts from what the maximum mortgage rate could possibly be and the appropriate share rate is worked out from this. Depending on circumstances, societies might also find it necessary to remain slightly uncompetitive and to use their liquid resources or alternatively to remain slightly more competitive so as to build up liquid funds. Generally speaking, societies make no attempt to follow other interest rates one hundred per cent and hence on an increase in rates they do not fully regain their competitiveness and on a decrease they tend to maintain a slightly more than competitive position.

Societies are also able to vary the margin on which they operate. On occasions they might feel it appropriate to narrow the margin so as to protect existing borrowers. On other occasions they might prefer to widen the margin so as to help build up reserves which might then be released at a later time should the need arise.

Table 5.2 shows the rates of interest recommended by the Council of The Building Societies Association from 1973 to 1981.

Changes in Interest Rates in 1979, 1980 and 1981

The principles outlined so far in this chapter can be illustrated by describing in detail the events surrounding the recent changes in the rates of interest recommended by the The Building Societies Association; those announced in July 1979, November 1979, December 1980 and March and October 1981. In November 1978, societies had increased the recommended mortgage rate from 9.75 per cent to 11.75 per cent and the ordinary share rate from 6.70

Table 5.2 BSA Recommended Rates of Interest, 1973–81

Year	Date of recommendation	New mortgages		Ordinary shares		
		Effective date	Rate	Effective date	Rate	Gross equivalent
			%		%	%
1973	12 January			1.2.73	5.60	
	16 March			1.4.73	6.30	9.00
	4 April	4.4.73	9.50	1.5.73	6.75	9.64
	14 August	14.8.73	10.00			
	14 September	14.9.73	11.00	1.10.73	7.50	10.71
1975	24 April			1.6.75	7.00	10.77
1976	9 April	9.4.76	10.50	1.5.76	6.50	10.00
	8 October	8.10.76	12.25	1.11.76	7.80	12.00
1977	15 April	15.4.77	11.25	1.5.77	7.00	10.61
	10 June	10.6.77	10.50	1.7.77	6.70	10.15
	23 September	23.9.77	9.50	1.11.77	6.00	9.09
1978	13 January	13.1.78	8.50	1.2.78	5.50	8.33
	9 June	9.6.78	9.75	1.7.78	6.70	10.00
	10 November	10.11.78	11.75	1.12.78	8.00	11.94
1979	13 July	1.1.80	12.50	1.8.79	8.75	12.50
	22 November	22.11.79	15.00	1.12.79	10.50	15.00
1980	12 December	12.12.80	14.00	1.1.81	9.25	13.21
1981	13 March	13.3.81	13.00	1.4.81	8.50	12.14
	9 October	9.10.81	15.00	1.11.81	9.75	13.93

Source: *BSA Bulletin*, October 1981.

per cent to 8 per cent. This was in response to the increase in minimum lending rate on 9 November 1978 from 10 per cent to 12.50 per cent. When MLR had been increased, the general expectation was that interest rates would fall during 1979 and for this reason societies did not attempt fully to match the rise in competing interest rates. The grossed-up recommended BSA share rate, at 11.94 per cent, was a little below what societies would have regarded as being a reasonable competitive level.

Societies began 1979 in an unfavourable position. Not only was the recommended share rate a little below a reasonable competitive level but the liquidity ratio had been run down by 3 per cent during 1978 and there was little scope for a further fall. Also, house prices had risen by some 28 per cent during 1978 and even though the average advance had not risen nearly as rapidly, a given volume of money could finance significantly fewer loans.

Contrary to earlier expectations, MLR did not fall during the early months of 1979. Indeed, when the new Conservative government came to power, one of its first actions in its Budget on 12 June was to increase MLR from 12 per cent to 14 per cent. Simultaneously, the government announced an increase in VAT from 8 per cent to 15 per cent and this led to an immediate spending spree. The result was that net receipts fell from £322 million in May to £146 million in June and although much of this decline was seasonal, it was not a reduction which societies could view with equanimity.

The Association's Council met on 13 July and had to take the following factors into account when deciding whether to make a recommendation on interest rates:

(a) The share rate was significantly uncompetitive and funds were moving away from societies.
(b) The high M L R was expected to last for a few months but the next move in interest rates was expected to be downwards.
(c) In the Budget, the basic rate of income tax was reduced from 33 per cent to 30 per cent and it was expected that this would lead to a fall in the composite rate of tax which societies pay on their investors' interest. In effect, societies had a windfall profit which could be used to narrow the margin between the investment and the mortgage rate for some time.

On this occasion, the Council of the Association took a somewhat unusual decision. A modest increase in the share rate from 8 per cent to 8.75 per cent (11.43 per cent to 12.50 per cent gross equivalents) was recommended with effect from 1 August. This left societies in a slightly less competitive position than they had been prior to the increase in M L R. However, societies were banking on a reduction in short-term interest rates in the not-too-distant future such that the share rate would become competitive. On a cost-plus basis, the appropriate mortgage rate for an 8.75 per cent share rate was 12.50 per cent and this was recommended. However, partly because of the anticipated reduction in societies' composite rate of tax, the new mortgage rate was deferred until 1 January 1980. There was a widespread expectation at the time that the general level of interest rates would fall such that a new recommendation could be made prior to the end of the year and that the 12.50 per cent would not become effective.

In the event, these hopes were to be unfulfilled. In the late autumn, the failure of the money supply to respond to the measures which had been taken by the government brought about a significant upward movement of market interest rates. On 15 November, the government increased M L R by an unprecedented three percentage points to the equally unprecedented level of 17 per cent. The commercial banks followed suit and societies were left in a very uncompetitive position which was reflected in a record outflow of funds in the week following the government's announcement. Such was the outflow of funds that a special meeting of the Council was called on 22 November, a week after the increase in M L R had taken place. On this occasion there was no question of societies being able to move their share rate to a competitive position because this would have meant an intolerably high mortgage rate, bearing in mind that some borrowers had taken out loans at 8.5 per cent at the beginning of 1978. The question for societies to face on this occasion therefore was to decide the maximum mortgage rate that borrowers could be expected to bear and what was the minimum rate that would be necessary to give societies a reasonable inflow. It did not take the Council long to recommend that the ordinary share rate should be increased to 10.50 per cent. (15 per cent gross equivalent) and that the mortgage rate should be increased to 15 per cent. The increase in the share rate did no more than restore societies' competitive position to the unsatisfactory level that it had been a month earlier and at the time it was forecast that net receipts of only £300 million a month would be attracted whereas societies required a figure of nearer £550 million a month to meet the estimated level of mortgage demand.

Perhaps surprisingly, this unprecedented increase in building society mortgage rates, affecting some five million households, was accepted with little comment or criticism. For the average existing borrower with a £7,000 loan, the increase in mortgage repayments, which for most borrowers became effective on 1 January 1980, was from about £73 a month to over £90 a month. For those taking out £20,000 loans, the increase was from £209 a month to £258 a month. However, tax relief did of course cushion some of these increases.

The general expectation was that the 17 per cent MLR would not be sustained for long and societies publicly expressed the view that they were banking on reductions in competing interest rates to make their position more competitive and that such reductions could therefore not be expected to be accompanied by a reduction in building society rates. As has happened so frequently, the expectations were unfounded and the 17 per cent MLR was maintained until 3 July 1980 when a token reduction to 16 per cent was made. The banks followed suit and this did increase societies' competitiveness such that by October net inflow was at the very high level of £520 million. During the year societies had also been able to build up their lending levels such that monthly net new commitments topped £1,000 million for the first time, also in October. Liquidity ratios had also been increased by about one per cent in seasonally adjusted terms since the beginning of the year.

On 24 November, the government announced a reduction in MLR from 16 per cent to 14 per cent. This reduction was not justified by the money supply figures which still showed an adverse growth but the government felt confident that the situation would soon be rectified and it was also concerned with the continuing and deepening recession in industry. However, in the same package, the Chancellor of the Exchequer announced that the government intended to take £1.5 billion from the personal sector during the remainder of the 1980/81 financial year through the issue of a new index-linked national savings certificate available to people aged 60 and above. The Chancellor also indicated that the government would seek to take £3 billion from the personal sector through national savings in 1981/82.

Thus, when the Council of the Association met on 12 December 1980 it had to consider not only the increased interest rate competitiveness of societies as against other institutions but also the effect of non-interest competition from the government. A third vital factor which came into the calculation was the composite rate of tax. The point has been made that in 1979/80 societies were able to enjoy a reduction in the composite rate of tax from 22.5 per cent to 21 per cent. For 1980/81, the abolition of the 25 per cent lower rate tax band caused the composite rate to return to 22.5 per cent. Societies made no attempt to recover this additional tax either from their investors or from their borrowers and therefore the effect was a considerable squeezing of margins. The Building Societies Association forecast that the average reserve ratio would fall during 1979 from 3.58 per cent to 3.50 per cent. However, far more threatening for societies was the likely composite rate for 1981/82. The early indications were that the rate would be as high as 26 per cent and with the interest rate structure that they were currently operating, this would have put most societies into a deficit position.

Societies were therefore in an exceptionally difficult position. Their interest rate competitiveness was good but against this was the unknown effect of the government's competing on non-interest grounds. Anything other than a modest reduction in building society interest rates to investors would therefore be potentially dangerous. However, such was the need to widen operating margins in order to accommodate the expected composite rate of tax for 1981/82 that a fairly substantial reduction had to be made in the share rate in order to allow any reduction at all in the mortgage rate. The choice was therefore between having a comfortable operating margin but risking either an unduly low share rate or a virtually insignificant reduction in the mortgage rate or accepting a fairly narrow working margin so as to allow a significant 1 per cent reduction in the mortgage rate and a reasonably competitive share rate. The second option was chosen and the recommended mortgage rate was reduced from 15 per cent to 14 per cent and the share rate from 10.50 per cent to 9.25 per cent.

Market-determined interest rates fell during the first two months of 1981 and these were officially recognised by the Chancellor in his Budget speech on 10 March when he announced a 2 per cent reduction in minimum lending rate to 12 per cent. Other administered rates of interest were reduced on the same day. On 13 March, three days after the reduction in M L R, the Council of the Association had its usual monthly meeting and responded to the reduction in other interest rates promptly by announcing a reduction in building society rates with effect from 1 April. Again, this decision was more complicated than usual because although market interest rates had fallen, the government had simultaneously announced its intention of introducing a new national savings certificate and extending the eligibility for the purchase of existing index-linked national savings certificates to those in the 50–60 age group. These factors meant that the reduction in building society rates was perhaps slightly less than would otherwise have been the case.

In the event, the recommended ordinary share rate was reduced from 9.25 per cent (gross equivalent 13.21 per cent) to 8.50 per cent (gross equivalent 12.14 per cent). Other recommended investment rates were also reduced by 0.75 percentage points. The recommended mortgage rate was reduced from 14 per cent to 13 per cent.

It was a general expectation that interest rates would continue declining throughout 1981. However, in July market interest rates rose substantially and there was speculation that the bank base rates would have to be increased but the authorities resisted this pressure.

On 20 August, the Bank of England discontinued its practice of posting a minimum lending rate. This was part of a longer term strategy of switching the emphasis of monetary policy towards open market operations. Early in September there was no suggestion that interest rates would need to rise, partly because of the depth of the UK recession. However, on 14 September 1981 the Bank of England seemingly went back on its stated policy by forcing discount houses to borrow from the Bank at a rate of interest which signalled a 1 per cent increase on previously established market rates and a 2 per cent increase on existing administered rates of interest. The authorities justified this move by referring to the fairly substantial fall in the value of sterling, the rapid increase in bank lending and the civil servants' strike which had served to obscure the money supply figures. The banks immediately responded with a

2 per cent increase in base lending rates. However, the market was not satisfied and market interest rates continued to rise with the result that the banks had to put up their base rates a further 2 per cent on 1 October.

Thus, when it met early in October, the Association's Council was faced with an increase of 4 per cent in base lending rates and an increase in deposit rates of 5 to 5.5 per cent. Normally these factors would signal a fairly substantial increase in building society rates. However, against this was the fact that net inflow in September had been reasonably high, mortgage demand was weak, largely because of the economic recession, and, as importantly, the banks had become well established in the mortgage market and had increased their rates to only 15 or 15.5 per cent. Moreover, there was nervousness at a substantial increase in building society rates because the general economic situation meant that this could pose severe problems for some borrowers.

The Association's Council decided to recommend only a modest increase in building society rates. The recommended ordinary share rate was increased from 8.50 per cent to 9.75 per cent (13.93 per cent gross equivalent). Correspondingly, the mortgage rate was increased from 13 per cent to 15 per cent.

Part Two

Policy

Chapter 6

Building Societies
and Housing Policy

Chapter 3 of this book illustrated the importance of building societies in the housing market. The chapter noted that over half of all households are owner-occupiers and that building societies have in recent years provided between 80 per cent and 95 per cent of the institutional funds for house-purchase. It is therefore obvious that housing policy is very relevant to building societies and moreover that building societies are relevant when the government is considering and implementing housing policy.

However, until comparatively recently housing policy rather by-passed building societies and societies themselves showed no great interest in policy making or implementation. Perhaps two main reasons can be deduced for this situation:

(a) Not unnaturally, government must be primarily concerned with the public sector of housing which is more directly under its control, rather than the private sector.
(b) In the post-war period, building societies have not been in a position whereby they could meet the demand for mortgage funds and hence there has been less need for them to be aware of and to attempt to influence housing market activity.

However, in recent years the substantial growth of owner-occupation together with the increasing politicisation of housing policy has meant that societies have become more involved in the policy-making process and also in the implementation of specific housing policy measures.

This chapter begins with a brief description of the development of housing policy, in particular with respect to owner-occupation, up to 1970 and then considers in more detail policy developments during the 1970s.

A Brief History of Housing Policy up to 1970

The first chapter of this book noted that building societies had their origins in the late eighteenth century and that the industrial revolution, causing as it did a shift of population from rural areas to the towns, played a part in the development of the building society industry. However, throughout the nineteenth century, owner-occupation remained a minority form of tenure and it is estimated that at the outbreak of the First World War only about

10 per cent of houses were owner-occupied with the remainder being rented from private landlords. The limited amount of housing legislation that had been enacted during the nineteenth century was primarily concerned with housing conditions rather than tenure.

One immediate consequence of the First World War was the enactment of the Rent and Mortgage Interest Restriction Act 1915. This fixed rents, gave tenants security against eviction and prevented increases in interest rates on mortgages and the calling in of mortgages. It was intended to be a temporary measure but of course rent restrictions have remained in force ever since and have contributed to the decline in the stock of rented housing.

During the First World War, The Building Societies Association set up a committee to consider the provision of new housing after the war ended. Perhaps surprisingly, the committee was primarily concerned with examining ways in which the private sector could be encouraged to build houses for letting. It should be noted that at this time much of societies' money was loaned to landlords rather than to owner-occupiers. The committee suggested that building costs would be high in relation to the value of property. Among the recommendations made by the committee were that builders or purchasers should be relieved of charges for making streets and sewers, that houses erected under approved conditions should be exempt from rates for a period of years and that subsidies should be paid to builders equal to the difference between cost and economic value.

The government also established a number of committees to look at various aspects of housing. The Carmichael Committee examined ways in which the provision of building materials could be accelerated. The Tudor Walters Committee examined house design and recommended that the design of housing should allow for improvement in living standards over the next fifty or so years. The Committee said that families would require more space, more privacy and the provision of individual rooms for separate activities. A minimum area of 900–50 square feet was proposed as well as three bedrooms and a bathroom. The Committee's report had a major influence on housing design in the post-war period.

The first post-war legislation was the Housing and Town Planning Act 1919 (the Addison Act). This required local authorities to assess the needs of their districts and to implement plans for the provision of houses required. The broad aim was to build 500,000 houses a year over a period of three years. The Exchequer and the local authorities would meet any deficit caused by a difference between the cost of the new dwellings and the level of rents which were to be based on the level of controlled rents. The Housing (Additional Powers) Act 1919 introduced subsidies for private building. The Housing Act 1923 extended subsidies for private builders and 43 per cent of houses built for private owners between the end of the First World War and 1930 were built with subsidy. The subsidy was mainly in the form of a £75 capital sum. The 1923 Act also fixed annual subsidies for local authority houses.

The outbreak of the Second World War saw a further extension of rent control and the cessation of house-building. As during the First World War, a number of government committees published reports on various aspects of housing and planning. Shortly before the end of the war, the government published a White Paper *Housing* (Cmnd 6609) which set out three objectives:

(a) A separate dwelling for each family which wanted to have one.
(b) The rapid completion of post-war slum clearance and overcrowding programmes.
(c) The progressive improvement in the conditions of housing.

Housing was physically rationed in the immediate post-war period and new building was almost entirely by local authorities for rent. The first major post-war legislation was the Housing Act 1949 which removed from local authorities the requirement to provide houses for the 'working classes' only. Thus local authorities were seen, for the first time, as having a much wider role in housing. The 1949 Act also introduced improvement grants payable at the discretion of the local authority to owner-occupiers.

Between 1952 and 1954 building controls were eased and private house-building expanded rapidly during the remainder of the 1950s. The Housing (Repairs and Rents) Act 1954 aimed to deal with obsolete and obsolescent houses through slum clearance, an increase in improvements and encouragement of repairs and maintenance. The Housing Subsidies Act 1956 marked the first attempt to reduce local authority involvement in housing. The subsidy for housing to meet normal needs was reduced substantially and the government was given power to abolish it completely as indeed it subsequently did.

The Rent Act 1957 was the first major attempt to reverse the effects of forty years of rent regulation in Britain. The Act freed from rent control the better privately owned houses and permitted rents to rise on other dwellings, subject to a ceiling. All new tenancies were released from rent control. For various reasons the Rent Act did not have its desired effect in increasing the quality and quantity of provision of rented housing. Rather, landlords, perhaps fearing the reimposition of controls, took what opportunities they could to sell with vacant possession. The position of sitting tenants was safeguarded by an amending Act, the Landlord and Tenant (Temporary Provision) Act 1958.

The House Purchase and Housing Act 1959 saw the first direct involvement of building societies in a government housing programme. One of the main objectives of the Act was to encourage owner-occupation through the provision of government loans to building societies for on-lending on older, cheaper property. The loans were to be made in respect of houses built prior to 1919 with values up to £2,500. £100 million was advanced over the next few years to societies under the provisions of the Act and some £3 million is still outstanding. The House Purchase and Housing Act is also significant in that it introduced the concept of trustee status for building societies. The second objective of the 1959 Act was to increase the improvement of older houses. Mandatory grants were introduced for the provision of certain facilities.

In 1963 the White Paper *Housing* (Cmnd 2050) called for increased house-building and greater attempts to deal with slums and obsolescent housing. This was followed by the Housing Act 1964 and again building societies were heavily involved in implementing some of the provisions of the Act. The Act established the Housing Corporation with funds to loan to housing associations building cost rent and co-ownership schemes. The Housing Corporation was initially allocated £100 million with which to make loans and building societies indicated that they would be prepared to advance another

£200 million. The Act also gave local authorities power to declare general improvement areas.

The late 1960s also saw a major step forward in respect of the provision of new houses for owner-occupation. The National House-Builders' Registration Council had existed since the 1930s and although it was essentially a creature of the building industry, its aim was to provide protection to purchasers of new houses. In the mid-1960s, following discussions with the government, building societies and local authorities decided that they would make loans for the purchase of new houses, subject to a limited number of exceptions, only where the houses had been constructed by a builder registered with the NHBRC (which has subsequently changed its name to the National House Building Council – NHBC). NHBC requirements relate to workmanship, standards of construction and facilities. The vast majority of new houses for owner-occupation are now built by builders registered with the Council.

The Housing Subsidies Act 1967, which was primarily concerned with the subsidy system for local authority housing, provided for the option mortgage scheme which came into effect in April 1968. This enables house-purchasers to forego tax relief and instead obtain a subsidy which is achieved by the borrower paying a lower rate to the building society with the government making up the difference. The intention was to benefit low-income borrowers who could not obtain full tax relief.

The Establishment of the Joint Advisory Committee

The early 1970s were significant not only for major legislation but also for important developments in the housing market. Concern at the level of unemployment led the government to expand the economy and this factor, together with several other factors which are examined in more detail in the following chapter, led to a marked increase in house prices in 1972 and 1973. During 1973 the sharp increase in the general level of interest rates led to a rise in The Building Societies Association recommended mortgage rate from 8.5 per cent to 11 per cent. The rise in house prices and the increases in the mortgage rate brought the owner-occupied sector of housing into the political arena in a major way for the first time and contacts between the Association and the government became more numerous. The eventual result was that in October 1973 a Memorandum of Agreement on Building Society Mortgage Finance was drawn up between the then Conservative government and The Building Societies Association. The Memorandum set out as the joint objectives of government and building societies:

(a) To continue to support the growth of owner-occupation.
(b) To produce and maintain a flow of mortgage funds to enable the house-building industry to plan for a high and stable level of house-building for sale.
(c) To contribute towards the stabilisation of house prices.
(d) To maintain an orderly housing market in which, subject to (c) above, sufficient mortgage funds are available to allow purchasers to exercise a reasonable choice of owning the sort of house they want.

The Memorandum said that these objectives 'are likely to be most readily achieved by a system based on a more flexible approach to changes in the rate paid to investors but, as far as possible, with the minimum frequency of consequential adjustments to the mortgage rate'. In fact this policy has not been implemented nor has government sought to encourage societies to implement it.

The Memorandum provided for the government and the Association to establish a Joint Advisory Committee on building society mortgage finance. The Committee would meet monthly and would have the functions of:

(a) Providing the Council of the Association with a forecast, normally for a period of one year ahead and which would be reviewed periodically, of the investment receipts required to realise the objectives set out in the Memorandum.
(b) Providing the Council of the Association with an agreed analysis and review of the current situation with particular reference to changes in interest rates in the economy generally, the inflow and outflow of building society funds, advances to first-time purchasers, housing starts and completions and house prices.

In fact, the Committee has performed neither of these two functions but rather has developed into the main regular source of contact between representatives of the Association and Government. In the late 1970s the Committee was primarily concerned with attempts to stabilise house prices, a subject which is discussed in detail in the following chapter.

The Labour Government 1974–9 and the Housing Policy Review

In 1973 the Government published a White Paper *Widening the Choice: The Next Steps in Housing* (Cmnd 5280) and a second White Paper *Better Homes: The Next Priorities* (Cmnd 5339) set out measures to implement such a policy. A Bill was published early in 1974 and it was largely taken over by the incoming Labour government. The main thrust of the Housing Act 1974 was to change the policy of dealing with poor housing from one of clearance to one of rehabilitation. In its first year of office, the Labour government enacted two other significant pieces of housing legislation. The Rent Act 1974 extended security of tenure to furnished tenancies. The Housing Rents and Subsidies Act 1975 made considerable amendments to the housing Finance Act 1972 and had the objective of making financial provisions for housing pending a complete review of housing finance for all sectors.

In the housing field, the 1974–9 Labour government is perhaps best remembered for its review of Housing finance. In 1974 the then Secretary of State for the Environment (Mr Anthony Crosland) announced that he had set up a searching and far-reaching inquiry into housing finance to be carried out, for the most part internally, by the Department of the Environment. The stated aim was to go back to first principles and to overcome the 'ad hocery' which had characterised policy. The review was subsequently widened to cover housing policy generally rather than just housing finance.

In March 1976 The Building Societies Association submitted evidence to the review. This marked the first occasion on which the Association chose to comment on housing policies generally rather than on those matters purely concerned with building societies. The Association's evidence (published in *The Housing Policy Review and the Role of Building Societies*, The Building Societies Association, 1978) made the following principal points:

(a) Surveys show conclusively that the vast majority of households in Britain want to own their own homes and that the desire for owner-occupation is particularly pronounced amongst the young.

(b) There are no strong grounds for calling tax relief on mortgage interest a subsidy. Increases in tax relief do not represent a significant call on public funds because they are largely automatically balanced by increased tax revenue from interest paid by building societies to investors.

(c) Even if tax relief is considered to be a subsidy, owner-occupiers receive considerably less support from public funds than council tenants.

(d) If it is government policy to redistribute income then this can best be achieved by use of the tax and social security systems. Attempting to re-distribute income through housing policy is both arbitrary and damaging.

(e) The housing market is unique in that the durable nature of dwellings means that the secondhand sector is dominant and the ability of house-holds to enter the market largely depends on cheaper houses at the bottom end of the market being vacated by those moving up-market. Measures aimed at helping people at the bottom of the market or in the council sector at the expense of those further up-market seem likely to be counter-productive.

(f) In general terms, increased government intervention in the housing market is not desirable. The way to help more people become owner-occupiers is through making more houses available for owner-occupation through the concentration of new building in the private sector and the sale of council houses. An adequate supply of mortgage funds is also required and this can best be achieved by the government's giving support to building societies in trying to maintain a proper interest rate structure and also by the government's making every effort to manage the economy such that there are not violent swings in short-term interest rates.

(g) Council tenants should be permitted to buy their homes.

Publication of the results of the review was delayed primarily, it is believed, because of differences within government about attitudes towards subsidies. Eventually a Green Paper *Housing Policy* (Cmnd 6851) was published in June 1977. The Green Paper was accompanied by a three-part technical volume which makes available a comprehensive range of economic and statistical information on all aspects of housing and housing finance. As is so often the case, it is the technical work which accompanied the Green Paper which has retained its usefulness long after the Green Paper itself has been forgotten.

The main conclusion of the Green Paper was that housing should be seen as an 'area needs' issue rather than as a national problem. Building societies were seen as being instrumental in meeting those needs. The Green Paper noted that there had been a very substantial improvement in housing conditions since the war. In 1951 there were 750,000 more households than houses in England and

Wales but by 1976 this had been transformed into an excess of 500,000 houses over households. The quality of the housing stock had also increased considerably with the number of households living in sub-standard or over-crowded conditions falling from 10 million in 1951 to 2.7 million in 1976.

The Green Paper noted that there had been a substantial increase in the proportion of owner-occupiers, particularly in the under-30 and 30–44 age groups. It was also pointed out that there was a considerable overlap between socio-economic groups in respect of housing tenure. The Green Paper included a lengthy discussion of housing subsidies but eventually put forward only modest proposals. It was felt that major changes would severely disrupt household budgets. Tax relief on mortgage interest was described as an integral part of housing policy, the continuation of which was vital to the growth of home-ownership.

The Consultative Document argued that the key to the success of the proposals put forward lay in the development of effective local housing strategies and that local authorities would need to develop relationships with other bodies including building societies.

The technical volume made tentative projections of the numbers of new houses required. It suggested an underlying level of demand for 135,000 private houses a year in the mid-1970s rising to 170,000 a year in the early 1980s and 195,000 a year by the mid 1980s. A fall-off in the number of new public sector houses from 161,000 in 1976 to 125,000 in 1981 and 105,000 in 1986 was also projected.

A significant feature of the Green Paper was the government's stated view that it welcomed the trend towards home-ownership 'because it gives people the kind of home they want'. The government also stated that it was not opposed to sales of council houses 'provided that they can be made without impairing an authority's ability to deal with pressing housing needs or to maintain a housing stock of adequate quality for renting'.

The Green Paper contained a long section dealing with home-ownership. It stated:

A preference for home ownership is sometimes explained on the grounds that potential home-owners believe that it will bring them financial advantage. A far more likely reason for the secular trend towards home ownership is the sense of greater personal independence that it brings. For most people owning one's own home is a basic and natural desire, which for more and more people is becoming attainable.

Building societies' dominant role in providing finance for home-ownership was noted and it was described as 'probably unique among countries where home ownership is the largest tenure, and places their operations at the centre of housing policy'.

The Green Paper saw the terms on which mortgage loans were made as being one obstacle to the continued growth of owner-occupation. Possible measures to improve the situation were set out as:

(a) Low start mortgages.
(b) Building societies making greater use of insurance company guarantees for higher percentage loans.

(c) More building society lending on unmodernised properties and conversions.
(d) Closer co-operation between building societies and local authorities.
(e) A government-financed savings bonus and loan scheme for first-time buyers.

With respect to the provision of mortgages, the Green Paper expressed the hope that building societies could achieve a greater degree of stability in their lending by using liquidity more vigorously than had hitherto been the case; by keeping their interest rates paid to investors more in line with the market; by adopting a more flexible relationship between the rate paid to investors and that charged to borrowers; and by being prepared to raise short-term loans in the money markets. The view was expressed that in order to meet the demand for home-ownership societies might have to supplement their traditional sources of finance through raising funds from other financial institutions, in particular, the life and pension funds.

The Green paper recognised the need for private rented housing but put forward only modest proposals, including making improvement grants more readily available and making marginal changes to the Rents Acts, to improve the situation.

With regard to the public sector, the Green Paper commented on three major trends:

(a) The growth of owner-occupied housing could narrow the social make-up of the public rented sector unless tenants could be offered more varied housing opportunities and a greater degree of personal independence.
(b) The continued contraction of the private rented sector meant that the public sector would have to take over many of its functions.
(c) The demand for public sector housing from small, particularly elderly, households and from the disabled and other groups would continue to grow.

The government said that local authorities would be given greater freedom in spending their housing allocations and it announced that a new subsidy system would be introduced.

Reaction to the Green Paper was mixed. Generally it was regarded as a pragmatic document and therefore inevitably it disappointed many of those who had been calling for radical reform. However, the publication of the technical volume did much to improve the quality of the housing debate and in particular 'the numbers game', with parties outbidding each other in an attempt to build more houses regardless of whether they were needed seems to have died a natural death. In December 1977 The Building Societies Association formally welcomed the Green Paper 'as marking a great step forward in the field of housing policy'. The Green Paper was described as being realistic in respect of its analysis and conclusions and it was noted that the aspirations of people had been recognised. The Association made the following more detailed comments on the Green Paper:

(a) The demand for owner-occupation had been underestimated.
(b) The Green Paper's suggestion that building society lending policies

prevented the full demand for owner-occupation from being realised was rejected. The Association argued that it was the volume of mortgage money rather than the terms on which money is lent which was the key factor.

(c) There had been a considerable increase in building society lending on older property but defects in the improvement grant system prevented societies playing their full role in this area.

(d) The desirability of stabilising, as far as possible, mortgage lending was accepted but the suggestions put forward by the government in this respect were unlikely to be effective.

(e) The recognition in the Green Paper that a greater proportion of new building needed to be in the private sector and that more council houses should be sold was welcomed but the Association considered that the government had not gone sufficiently far in this respect.

(f) The government's commitment to maintain tax relief on mortgage interest was welcomed.

Major legislation was not necessary to implement the modest proposals set out in the Green Paper. However, the Home Purchase Assistance and Housing Corporation Guarantee Act 1978 provided for the proposed bonus and loan scheme for first-time buyers. This came into operation on 1 December 1978 and provides modest benefits (an interest-free loan up to £600 and a cash bonus of up to £110) for those saving under the scheme for a period of two years. In fact, so modest are the benefits that take-up has been minimal and the overall effect of the scheme can best be described as negligible.

The 1979 Conservative Government and the Sale of Council Houses

One of the main planks of the Conservative Party's campaign in the May 1979 election was the sale of council houses. The Conservatives promised to give council tenants the legal right to buy their homes at substantial discounts of up to 50 per cent of market value. Almost immediately after gaining power, the government took what administrative action it could to make it easier for local authorities to sell homes to sitting tenants. The right to buy was implemented through the Housing Act 1980. However, this Act was concerned with much more than the sale of council houses and indeed much of it was based on a Housing Bill published in late 1978 by the then Labour government. In addition to measures relating to the sale of council houses, the Act made the following important provisions:

(a) Public sector tenants were formally given security of tenure, something which in essence they have had for a considerable time, and a number of other minor improvements were made to their rights.

(b) The new concept of shorthhold tenancy was introduced in the private rented sector. This tenancy allows landlords to let at a fair rent for a fixed term of between one and five years with the right to regain possession.

(c) The concept of assured tenancies was also introduced. These can be operated only by approved bodies and tenants have the right to renew their tenancy but rents can be fixed at market levels.

(d) The provisions relating to improvement grants were modified in such a way as to make it easier for owner-occupiers to apply for grants and for building societies to loan to purchasers improving their homes with grant aid.

(e) Provision was made for a scheme by which local authorities could guarantee building society mortgages.

(f) The requirements for switching into and out of the option mortgage scheme were eased.

However, these points were of relatively minor importance compared with the main thrust of the government's policy, that is, the expansion of owner-occupation. Before considering in detail the question of council house sales, it is important to note that the present Conservative government sees a considerably reduced need for public sector housing in total and this has been reflected in a sharp decline in public sector house-building and subsidies as well as in a vigorous policy of selling council houses. The decline in the importance of public sector house-building is illustrated in Table 6.1.

Table 6.1   Housing Completions, 1973–83

Year	Private sector 000's	Public sector 000's	Total 000's	Public sector/ total %
1973	187	108	294	37
1974	141	129	270	48
1975	151	162	313	52
1976	152	163	315	52
1977	141	162	303	53
1978	149	131	280	47
1979	140	104	244	43
1980	126	107	233	46
1981	120	85	205	41
1982	140	50	190	26
1983	150	40	190	21

Sources: Figures for 1973–80 are taken from *Housing and Construction Statistics*. Figures for 1981–3 are forecasts published in May 1981 by the Joint Forecasting Committee of the Building and Civil Engineering ED Cs.

It will be seen that between 1974 and 1978, completions in the public sector were equal to about half of all completions. The proportion fell to 46 per cent in 1980 and is forecast to fall to 21 per cent in 1983. Table 6.1 also shows a distinct relationship between the proportion of building in the public sector and the government in power. The election of the Labour government in 1974 saw a steady increase in the proportion of new housing accounted for by the public sector while the election of the Conservative government in 1979 marked a considerable downturn. However, it seems likely that this downturn, albeit in a milder form, would have occurred anyway.

The sale of council houses has always been a party political issue and the volume of sales can be directly related to the political parties in power in local and central government. This is illustrated in Table 6.2 which shows council house sales in England and Wales for the period 1970–80.

Table 6.2   Sales of Council and New Town Houses, England and Wales, 1970–80

Period	Sales of council houses	Sales of new town houses	Total sales
1970	6,816	551	7,367
1971	17,214	3,438	20,652
1972	45,878	16,079	61,957
1973	34,334	7,497	41,831
1974	4,657	715	5,372
1975	2,723	227	2,950
1976	6,090	84	6,174
1977	13,020	367	13,387
1978	30,045	574	30,619
1979	41,660	813	42,473
1980	80,440	4,266	84,706

Source: *Housing and Construction Statistics.*

It will be seen that in the early 1970s when the then Conservative government was encouraging the sale of council houses, sales reached 62,000 in 1972. The election of the Labour government in 1974 led to a sharp downturn in sales, the number falling to under 3,000 in 1975. There was however a modest upturn between 1976 and 1978, partly as a result of the activities of Conservative controlled local councils. Sales increased markedly in 1979 and 1980 following the election of the Conservative government.

One justification for the sale of local authority housing is that there is a substantial unmet demand for owner-occupation which cannot be met unless local authority houses are sold. The market research survey conducted by the British Market Research Bureau for the National Economic Development Office (*Housing Consumer Survey*, NEDO, 1977) showed that in 1975 69 per cent of all households considered owner-occupation to be their ideal housing tenure in two years' time and 62 per cent expected to be owner-occupiers in ten years' time. Indeed, 25 per cent of all local authority tenants expected to be owner-occupiers within ten years. Given the decline in the number of new houses being built, it is impossible that these aspirations can be met simply by the natural turnover of the housing stock. If people's aspirations are to be met then the sale of council houses is a necessary pre-requisite.

The sale of council houses has also been justified on financial grounds. This is a very technical issue and one on which there has been considerable debate. The question that has to be answered is whether the revenue which can be achieved from the sale of a council house is greater than the present value of the future stream of rents less expenditure on repairs, management and maintenance. Any such calculation necessarily requires taking views about future levels of rents and interest payments and it is impossible to come to any definitive conclusion. However, there are few who would argue that the justification for the sale of council houses rests on the financial question.

Perhaps a more convincing argument is the need to have a social mix in housing estates. Local authority housing has tended to be allocated on the basis of housing need and, almost by definition, those in need tend to be elderly, the poor and large families. It follows that, initially, local authority dwellings are allocated to people in these categories. As people cease to be poor they tend to move out of local authority housing as this does not enable them to exercise the sort of choice in their housing that they require. Thus increasingly local authority housing is being occupied by old people and poor families who cannot afford owner-occupation. This trend can be expected to continue. However, if houses in council estates can be sold then it is possible that a better social balance will be preserved in those estates.

The main argument used by those who oppose the sale of council houses is that the better houses are likely to be sold and this makes it less likely that existing local authority tenants will be able to obtain the sort of houses which they want, that is, houses with gardens. Initially, many local authority tenants start in a fairly poor flat and hope to obtain a better dwelling, perhaps as their family size increases, or as dwellings become available as existing tenants move out or die. Another argument which is advanced is that piecemeal disposal of properties on an estate can lead to management problems. Certainly there are problems in the case of flats and it seems unlikely that many flats will be sold.

A further argument advanced against the sale of local authority houses is that it reduces the local authority's housing stock and that this is improper at a time when waiting lists are so long. It is obviously true that the sale of a local authority house does reduce a local authority's stock but of course the overall stock of housing is unchanged. The relevance of sales to the size of waiting lists is a factor which is relevant only in the long term. Given that a person buying a local authority house would otherwise have remained as a tenant then the sale can have no implications for the waiting list. However, if the house is resold after, say, five years then it would not be available to someone from a waiting list whereas had the person remained a local authority tenant and moved out, which is unlikely except on death, then it could have been so available.

In practice, the debate about the sale of council houses has not been conducted at such a sophisticated level. Rather, Conservative politicians have argued strongly for sales on grounds of principle while Labour politicians have tended to oppose sales although significantly the Labour government's Green Paper *Housing Policy* was not as antipathetic to sales as might have been expected given the stated view of the Labour Party in the past.

The Conservative Party set out its policy with respect to the sale of local authority houses in the *Conservative Manifesto 1979*:

Many families who live on Council estates and in new towns would like to buy their own homes but either cannot afford to or are prevented by the local authority or the Labour Government. The time has come to end these restrictions. In the first session of the next Parliament we shall therefore give Council and new town tenants the legal right to buy their homes, while recognising the special circumstances of rural areas and sheltered housing for the elderly. Subject to safeguards over re-sale, the terms we propose would allow a discount on market values reflecting the fact that Council tenants effectively have security of tenure. Our discounts will range from 33 per cent after three years, rising with length of tenancy to a maximum of 50 per cent after 20 years. We shall also ensure that 100 per cent mortgages are available for the purchase of Council and new town houses. We shall introduce a right for these tenants to obtain limited price options on their homes so they know in advance the price at which they can buy, while they save the money to do so.

As far as possible, we will extend these rights to housing association tenants. At the very least, we shall give these associations the power to sell to their tenants.

This policy was given effect through the Housing Act 1980 which achieved the Royal Assent on 8 August 1980. Chapter 1 of the Act is concerned with this 'right to buy'.

Broadly speaking, tenants of local authorities and also certain housing associations, the Commission for the New Towns, development corporations, the Housing Corporation and the Development Board for Rural Wales were given the legal right to purchase their homes if they have been tenants for more than three years. There are limited exceptions including tied tenants, tenants in temporary accommodation awaiting development, tenants in homeless family temporary accommodation, tenants in dwellings especially for the old and the handicapped and tenants of charitable housing associations.

The purchase price payable by a tenant exercising this right is equal to the market value of his property less a discount. For tenants of between three and four years' standing the discount is 33 per cent and if the period of tenancy is four years or more then there is an additional 1 per cent discount for each year by which the period exceeds three years. However, the maximum is 50 per cent. There is another limit on the discount inasmuch as the discounted price cannot be less than the costs incurred in respect of the building of the property.

In the past regulations governing the sale of council houses have generally included the requirement that if the house is resold within five years then it should first be offered to the local authority at the original price. The 1980 Act marked a considerable change in this respect. If the house is sold within five years then part or all of the discount is repayable. The amount of the discount repayable reduces by 20 per cent each year. For example, if a house is sold between two and three years after the date of purchase then 60 per cent of the discount is refunded and after five years none of the discount need be refunded. The discount is covered by way of second mortgage so any increase in the value of the property now accrues to the purchaser. For building societies this has the great advantage of giving them greater security when they lend.

In addition to giving a tenant the right to improve his house, the Act also gives him the right to a mortgage which, subject to income limits, can be equal to the aggregate of the purchase price and certain other costs.

Building Societies and the Sale of Council Houses

When the Conservative government came to power in 1979 it made it clear that it hoped that building societies would be able to finance a considerable proportion of council house purchases. The advantage to the government of this course of action was that there would be a receipt of capital funds by the public sector, hence a reduction in the public sector borrowing requirement. However, building societies pointed out that in general they could not be expected to give priority to those purchasing their council houses at a time when they were not able to meet the demand from their own investing and borrowing members. Building societies spelt out their policy in detail in evidence to the Environment Committee of the House of Commons which, as one of its first tasks, examined the financial and social implications of the sale of council houses.

Already, in its evidence to the Labour government's Housing Policy Review and in its comments on that Review, the Association had expressed itself in favour of the principle of selling council houses and had indicated a willingness to help finance such sales, funds permitting. In a memorandum of evidence submitted to the Environment Committee on 20 March 1980, the Association said that societies were unlikely to accord special allocations of finance to tenants seeking to purchase council houses. However, it said that those local authority tenants who were building society investors could expect to receive the same preference for loans as building society investors generally and it pointed out that a market research exercise (*Building Societies and the Savings Market*, The Building Societies Association, 1979) showed that 24 per cent of all council tenants were building society investors.

Chapter 7

The Determination and Control of House Prices

The determination and control of house prices would not normally be a subject sufficiently important to merit a chapter of its own in a book on building societies. However, this issue has been a very important one for building societies during the past decade and has been particularly significant in terms of the relationship between building societies and government and in respect of government policy towards the housing market.

The rate of increase in house prices was not an issue until the early 1970s. House prices did rise steadily throughout the 1950s and 1960s but in general the rate of increase was in line with the rate of increase in average earnings, albeit slightly above the rate of increase in the retail prices index. In the 1970s house prices demonstrated a marked volatility with periods of very rapid increase followed by periods of near stability. Trends in house prices, average earnings and retail prices are shown in Table 7.1.

Table 7.1 shows two very rapid periods of house price increase – 1971–3 and 1978–9 – but it also shows that both these periods were followed by a sharp deceleration in price inflation and that over the long term prices have maintained a more or less constant relationship with earnings.

Perhaps the main concern of policy-makers has been periods of rapid increase in house prices which have led to suggestions that houses are beyond the reach of potential house-buyers and that radical changes in methods of financing house-purchase are required. Policy has been formulated partly in response to such rapid increases. However, as Table 7.1 shows, over a long period house prices have not risen disproportionately with earnings or indeed with retail prices and if there is a source of concern then perhaps it should be in respect of the variability of the rate of increase of prices.

The preoccupation with house prices in the 1970s has led to a marked increase in the understanding of the house price mechanism and this chapter makes use of this increase in knowledge to analyse how house prices are determined. The chapter then goes on to examine public policy towards house prices in the 1970s.

The Theory of House Price Determination

House prices, like other prices, are determined by the interaction of supply and demand and the process of house price determination must therefore be examined by reference to the factors affecting the supply and demand

Table 7.1 House Prices, Retail Prices and Average Earnings, 1956–81

Period	Average price new houses £	Increase %	Average price all houses £	Increase %	Average earnings £	Increase %	House price/ earnings ratio	Retail prices index increase %	Real increase in house prices %
1956	2,280		2,230		697		3.21	4.9	
1957	2,330	2.2	2,280		731	4.9	3.12	3.7	– 1.4
1958	2,390	2.6	2,340		756	3.4	3.10	3.1	– 0.5
1959	2,410	0.8	2,360		793	4.9	2.98	0.5	0.3
1960	2,530	5.0	2,480		849	7.1	2.92	1.1	3.9
1961	2,770	9.5	2,710		896	5.5	3.03	3.4	5.9
1962	2,950	6.5	2,890		922	2.9	3.14	4.3	2.1
1963	3,160	7.1	3,100		966	4.8	3.21	1.9	5.1
1964	3,460	9.5	3,390		1,040	7.7	3.26	3.2	6.1
1965	3,820	10.4	3,740		1,114	7.1	3.36	4.8	5.3
1966	4,100	7.3	4,040	8.0	1,187	6.6	3.40	3.9	3.9
1967	4,340	5.9	4,270	5.7	1,230	3.6	3.47	2.5	3.1
1968	4,640	6.9	4,650	8.9	1,326	7.8	3.51	4.7	4.0
1969	4,880	5.2	4,850	4.3	1,430	7.8	3.39	5.4	– 1.0
1970	5,180	6.1	5,190	7.0	1,595	11.5	3.25	6.4	0.6
1971	5,970	15.3	6,130	18.1	1,752	9.8	3.50	9.4	8.0
1972	7,850	31.5	8,420	37.4	1,964	12.1	4.29	7.1	28.3
1973	10,690	36.2	11,120	32.1	2,249	14.5	4.95	9.2	21.0
1974	11,340	6.1	11,300	1.6	2,659	18.2	4.25	16.1	–12.5
1975	12,406	9.4	12,119	7.2	3,320	24.9	3.65	24.2	–13.7
1976	13,442	8.4	12,999	7.3	3,823	15.2	3.40	16.5	– 7.9
1977	14,768	9.9	13,922	7.1	4,170	9.1	3.34	15.8	– 7.5
1978	17,685	19.8	16,297	17.1	4,749	13.9	3.43	8.2	8.2
1979	22,728	28.5	21,047	29.1	5,503	15.9	3.82	13.4	13.8
1980	27,224	19.9	24,307	15.5	6,725	22.2	3.61	18.0	– 2.1

1980	Q.1	26,191	27.1	23,385	24.4	6,230	19.7	3.75	19.1	4.5
	Q.2	27,208	23.0	24,429	19.5	6,581	21.4	3.71	21.5	1.6
	Q.3	27,715	17.2	24,633	11.6	6,950	22.2	3.54	16.4	– 4.1
	Q.4	27,952	11.5	24,664	6.9	7,135	19.5	3.46	15.3	– 7.3
1981	Q.1	28,347	8.2	24,458	4.6	7,264	16.6	3.37	12.7	– 7.2

Notes:

1 From 1975 the average house price figures are taken from a BSA return at the approval stage. Between 1966 and 1974 the figures are equal to new house prices at the approval stage multiplied by the ratio (in the following quarter) of completion stage figures for all house prices to new house price figures from the sample survey results. Prior to 1966 the figures are equal to 0.98 of the actual figures for new house prices at the mortgage approval stage. The series for all prices is therefore far from perfect but it is the best available and is adequate for developing a relationship with average earnings.

2 As there are no officially published figures for average annual earnings, it is necessary to construct a series. The method of construction is as follows:

(a) From 1976 onwards the New Earnings Survey figures referring to weekly earnings in April of each year for those employees whose pay was not affected by absence are used. (The annual rate of pay in April is calculated by multiplying by 52.) Quarterly and annual figures are then calculated by application of the index of average earnings (new series, whole economy seasonally adjusted) to the April base.

(b) From 1970 to 1975 the New Earnings Survey figures are linked to the 'old' index of average earnings (production industries and some services).

(c) From 1963 to 1970 a backwards projection is made by application of the index of average earnings to the first New Earnings Survey, which refers to April 1970.

(d) Prior to 1963 the series is constructed by reference to the percentage increase in the twice-yearly (April and October) survey of average weekly earnings of manual workers in manufacturing industry, with the figures derived from (b) above for April 1963 used as a base.

3 The source for the retail prices index figures is *Economic Trends*.

4 Increases are over previous year or same period of previous year.

Source: BSA Bulletin, No. 27, July 1981.

sides of the market. The housing market is in many respects like any other market but it does have a number of distinguishing features. For the most part, these characteristics stem from the nature of housing. Most commodities are purchased and consumed almost immediately. This is true especially of services such as banking or hairdressing, and perishable commodities, for example, fresh food. Some commodities are consumed over a reasonably short period of time, say, up to ten years – clothes, motor cars and furniture being obvious examples. In contrast, housing is a very durable good, the average life of a dwelling being in excess of sixty years. To this factor must be added another special factor in that virtually everybody is housed in one way or another at any one time. The combination of these two factors leads to three distinguishing characteristics of the owner-occupied housing market:

(a) Most transactions are in respect of secondhand houses. Currently, some 85 per cent of building society loans are to finance the sale of existing houses rather than the purchase of new dwellings. In most markets the price of a secondhand good is well below that of an equivalent new commodity and some secondhand goods have virtually no resale value at all. However, in the case of owner-occupied housing an existing house is a very close substitute for a new house and there is little price difference between the two commodities.

(b) Currently, the housing stock is increasing by under 1 per cent a year and the maximum rate of increase is little more than 2 per cent a year. It follows that there is little scope for the supply of housing to respond to changes in demand and even a massive increase in the rate of new housebuilding would have only a modest effect on the size of the overall housing stock. This can be illustrated by contrasting the market for houses with the market for, say, beer. If the demand for beer doubles from one year to another then it would be necessary for output to double if the demand is to be met. If the demand for housing doubles then the output of new housing would have to increase fifty-fold in order to meet the additional demand within a year.

(c) Because everybody is housed in one way or another at any one time, it follows that for many people the decision to move house or to purchase a house for the first time is a discretionary one which can be brought forward or delayed, perhaps for a considerable time. Also, house-purchase is a major transaction – for most households the biggest financial transaction of their lifetimes – and psychological factors might play an important part in determining when people decide to enter the housing market.

The owner-occupied housing market has been comparatively free of government controls. It is, for example, not possible for the government to attempt to impose price controls on individual houses. However, government tax and housing policy can have an important influence on the supply of and demand for owner-occupied houses. On the supply side, the production of a new house requires land with planning permission and if this is not forthcoming then no new houses can be built. On the demand side, the favourable tax treatment of owner-occupied housing and changes in that treatment can have a material effect on demand. Also, one third of houses in Britain are owned by local authorities and government and local authority policy towards the sale of those houses and the rents which are charged can materially influence the number of council tenants seeking to become owner-occupiers and also the number of private tenants and new households who seek to become council tenants rather than owner-occupiers.

There is sometimes a tendency to equate the supply of owner-occupied houses with the number of new houses built but this is too simplistic. However, new housing is very significant in determining the increase in the number of houses on the market. In the long term, the supply of new houses can be infinite, assuming that land is available, but in the short term the number of houses which can be completed is constrained by the number under construction at the beginning of the period. Given the present circumstances, builders could not step up production to an annual rate of above 150,000 at short notice. However, the supply of new housing is not quite as inflexible as these figures might suggest. In the very short term, the number of sales of new houses can differ quite markedly from the number of new houses completed. In an active market builders might sell at an early stage in the construction process and it is not unknown for speculatively built houses to be sold even before the foundations have been put in. Conversely, in a stagnant market houses may be completed or virtually completed and then left unsold for a considerable time. Also, the construction process may slow down and the building of some houses may stop completely. What this means is that builders can respond to changes in demand by much more than might seem to be the case at first sight by examining the figures for new house-building.

The second important component of the supply of houses for sale are those transferred from the rented sector. Table 3.5 illustrated the importance of this factor in relation to the net increase in the owner-occupied housing. Between 1971 and 1980 sales of privately rented houses for owner-occupation varied between 55,000 and 81,000 a year and these have made a significant contribution to the net increase in the owner-occupied stock. As with new houses, there is probably a little scope for the supply of such houses to respond to demand. In a very active housing market, a higher number of such houses might be put on the market whereas in a weak market the opposite might occur.

In the long term, sales of local authority houses add to the owner-occupied stock in exactly the same way as sales of privately rented houses. However, in the short term sales of local authority houses have far less significance for the behaviour of the owner-occupied housing market. This is because most sales are to sitting tenants who would not otherwise have sought to become owner-occupiers whereas many sales of formerly private rented houses are to people who are not sitting tenants. Thus, the transfer of a local authority house from the rented sector to the owner-occupied sector adds to both supply and demand in the private sector and reduces supply and demand in the public sector.

In summary, the net increase in the stock of owner-occupied houses is made up of new houses and houses transferred from the rented sector. From this total must be deducted losses from the stock through slum clearance and so on. However, such losses have been very small in recent years.

Although the net addition to the owner-occupied stock is vitally important in terms of the determination of house prices, it is also necessary to take account of houses put on the market by existing owner-occupiers as these account for most houses sold each year. Some owner-occupiers move for job reasons while others trade up-market and a few people trade down-market so as to release equity. In terms of numbers, an owner-occupier buying and selling a house has no effect on the overall supply/demand balance. However, there might be some effect in the short term if, for example, people start to buy new houses without making arrangements to sell their existing houses. If a significant number of people act in this way then there might be a sharp increase in demand in relation to supply although inevitably this must be reversed within a very short time.

The final source of houses for sale is those becoming available as a result of household dissolution, emigration and moves by households to other tenures. The *Housing Policy Technical Volume* estimated that in 1981, 135,000 houses would be made available as a result of the dissolution of households and that this figure would increase to 145,000 by 1986. There are also some 70,000 households a year who move from owner-occupation to other tenures and about 30,000 houses a year are made available as a result of emigration. These figures are of significance because they represent a net increase in the supply of owner-occupied housing in relation to demand, other things being equal.

In summary, the supply of owner-occupied houses onto the market can be categorised as follows:

(a) Sales of new houses.
(b) Sales resulting from household dissolution, emigration and moves to other tenures.
(c) Sales of formerly rented houses, not to sitting tenants.
(d) Sales of formerly rented houses to sitting tenants.
(e) Sales of houses by owner-occupiers moving.

In very round terms, the first three sources represent the number of houses available for those entering the market for the first time whereas the final two sources represent an addition to the supply of owner-occupied housing and a corresponding increase in the demand for such housing.

Turning to the demand side of the market, the first point to note is that about half of all houses purchased are bought by owner-occupiers moving. The point has already been made that owner-occupiers moving add to the supply and demand and thus cannot have a significant effect on the supply/demand balance except in the very short term. It is therefore proper to concentrate analysis of the demand for owner-occupied housing on first-time buyers because in anything other than the very short term it is these who are responsible for the net addition to demand in relation to supply.

In the medium term, demand from first-time buyers can be predicted with a reasonable degree of accuracy. Opinion surveys have consistently shown that some 80 per cent of young couples intend to buy houses and already over 60 per cent succeed in so doing. The number of young couples can be forecast by reference to the age structure of the population although there are problems in this respect, notably as a result of the tendency of young single people to own their own houses and also because many couples now prefer to live together rather than to get married.

There are a number of factors which might be expected to lead to changes in the demand from first-time buyers in the short term. These include demographic trends, changes in local authority rents and policy towards the sale of local authority houses. However, for the most part, these have a relatively minor effect and it is evident from an examination of the market that in fact the demand from potential first-time buyers has an instability far greater than that which can be explained by such identifiable factors. It seems that for many potential first-time buyers, the decision as to when to seek to purchase is a voluntary one. This is particularly true for young single people who now account for over 10 per cent of first-time buyers. Many will be living in rented accommodation or perhaps with their parents and at a time of their choosing they will seek to become owner-occupiers. Even for married couples, the decision as to when to purchase a house can often be brought forward or put back by a year or two, depending on prevailing circumstances. Thus, it is not a case of there being an exact number of people seeking to buy their first homes each year but rather a trend level about which there can be substantial variations.

Clearly, the prevailing level of house prices is one factor which might affect variations around this trend. The higher house prices are in relation to earnings, the lower demand is likely to be and vice versa. However, a far more important factor seems to be the rate of increase of real incomes. When people's standards of living are rising rapidly they have an increasing amount of discretionary income to spend and also economic confidence generally is likely to be higher, thus encouraging major decisions like house-purchase. Thus there might be a trend number of first-time buyers of, say, 400,000 a year but favourable circumstances might cause the number of potential buyers in any one year to rise to, say, 700,000 before falling back to, say, 250,000 in each of the two subsequent years. Figure 7.1 helps to explain this position.

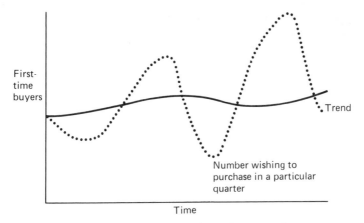

Figure 7.1 **Demand from first-time purchasers**

It is now necessary to bring together the components of supply and demand for owner-occupied housing to examine the determination of house prices. In the long term it is reasonable to expect that there will be a fairly stable relationship between the costs of producing a commodity and its price. This is because if prices run ahead of costs then profits will increase bringing forth an increase in output so as to bring prices back into an equilibrium level with costs. Conversely, if costs run ahead of prices then output will fall and the reduced supply in relation to demand will lead to an increase in prices back to an equilibrium level. However, there is no close relationship between house-building costs and the price of new houses. Probably the main reason for this is the land factor. In examining house prices, land and profit can be added together as a residual. In simple terms, a builder, in examining a potential development project, will ascertain the likely selling price and the cost of production of a dwelling. If, for example, a house could be sold for £30,000 which could be built for £20,000 and the builder requires £4,000 profit then he would be willing to pay £6,000 for the plot of land. If the likely price of the house increases to £40,000 the builder would simply be prepared to pay £16,000 for the plot of land in order to make the same profit. In the normal course of events, an increase in land prices could be expected to lead to an increase in the supply of land but the parts of the country in which there is a plentiful supply of land available for housing and in which such a market mechanism can operate are few and far between. Thus, a shortage of land can mean that a rise in the demand for houses could lead to a rise in land prices rather than an increase in supply.

The point has been made that there is an unsatisfied demand for owner-occupation and given this situation and the fact that there is no close relationship between house-building costs and house prices, it is reasonable to expect that in the long term there will be a relationship between house prices and ability to pay for housing, which in broad terms can be equated with incomes. Table 7.1 shows that there has been a fairly stable relationship between house prices and earnings over the period 1956 to 1980 although the long-term trend has concealed substantial variations. The normal pattern is for the price of commodities to rise less rapidly than earnings but there are good reasons for suggesting that this should not be the case in respect of owner-occupied housing:

(a) The land factor already mentioned.
(b) The quality of the housing stock has been increasing steadily over time, for example, through the installation of central heating, and thus changes in the average price of dwellings overstate changes in the price of dwellings of comparable quality.
(c) Productivity in the house-building industry has been increasing less rapidly than in the economy generally. This is not necessarily because of inefficiency within the house-building industry but rather because the industry itself, being labour-intensive, does not lend itself to mechanisation in the same way as other industries. Therefore it is reasonable to expect that the cost of producing a house should move more in line with earnings rather than manufacturing costs generally.

It is now necessary to explain the causes of the substantial fluctuations in the relationship between house prices and earnings using the theory set out earlier in this section. It is perhaps easiest to explain the mechanism by taking as a starting point a very quiet housing market where house prices are low in relation to incomes and where there has been a substantial build-up in the stock of unsold houses, both new and secondhand, over the previous few years. Assume that there is a rapid increase in real incomes together with a reduction in the mortgage rate such that more people are both willing and able to afford house-purchase. The surge in demand would be translated into transactions on the assumption that people willing and able to buy houses are not prevented from so doing by shortage of mortgage funds. Initially, there would be an increase in the number of transactions and although the net increase in the demand for houses exceeds the net increase in the supply, this can safely be absorbed by the stock of houses available for sale and also by builders bringing forward the stage in the construction process at which they sell. However, each first-time buyer must reduce the stock in relation to demand and after a time the point is reached in which the supply of housing is unable to meet demand running above trend level. Builders will have sold all the houses they are constructing and estate agents will have depleted stocks. When this situation is reached, each additional first-time buyer must exert an upward pressure on prices.

Where excess demand does appear then the inevitable rapid rise in prices can feed on itself for a comparatively short period. People may be encouraged to buy simply because prices are rising and owner-occupiers might be tempted to seek to purchase one house while withholding their existing home from the market for some time.

This analysis has suggested that by far the most important factor affecting variations in the rate of increase in house prices is movements in real incomes. Table 7.2 shows that there is indeed a close relationship between the rate of increase in real incomes, represented by real personal disposable income per capita, and the rate of increase in house prices.

Table 7.2   House Prices and R P D I, 1968–80

Year	Average price all houses, increase %	Real house prices increase %	RPDI per capita increase %
1968	8.9	4.0	1.7
1969	4.3	− 1.0	0.6
1970	7.0	0.6	3.7
1971	18.1	8.0	1.1
1972	37.4	28.3	8.1
1973	32.1	21.0	6.9
1974	1.6	−12.5	−0.1
1975	7.2	−13.7	−1.6
1976	7.3	− 7.9	−0.6
1977	7.1	− 7.5	−1.7
1978	17.1	8.2	8.4
1979	29.1	13.8	6.2
1980	15.5	− 2.1	1.8

Sources: Table 7.1; *Economic Trends*, Table 14.

It will be seen that the house price boom of 1971–3 was accompanied by a very rapid rate of increase of real incomes and similarly the boom which occurred in 1978 and 1979 was accompanied by a similar increase.

Recent statistical work has demonstrated the strength of the relationship between changes in house prices in the short term and changes in RPDI. The following equation is taken from the report *The Guideline System* (BSA and DoE, 1980).

Percentage change in 'real' house prices, quarter on quarter =
    0.564 × RPDI (percentage change over corresponding
    (5.2)   quarter of previous year)
    + 0.145 × Advances (000's) to FTBs
    (5.8)
    − 3.07 D4
    (−3.51)
    −11.97
    (−5.8)
    $R^2 = 0.73$ SEE = 2.43   DW = 1.9   t-statistics in brackets

In simple terms, this equation suggests that over half of the variation in real house prices is associated with changes in RPDI; advances to first-time buyers are responsible for much of the remaining variation. The D4 variable in the equation is a seasonal dummy.

Evidence from other countries confirms the strength of the causal relationship between real incomes and house prices. David T. Scheffman and Margaret E. Slade ('An intercountry comparison of housing market trends in the 1970s', in *The Determination and Control of House Prices*, The Building Societies Association, 1981) examined movements in house prices in the 1970s in Great Britain, the United States and Canada. Scheffman's and Slade's main conclusions were:

The fundamental importance of personal disposable income (per capita) in explaining the movements of house prices is revealed both by a simple examination of the data for the three countries and by the results of our regression analyses.

The differential behaviour of the US and Canadian housing markets is a very strong piece of evidence in support of the importance of income as a primary causal factor. In the early 1970s, both the US and Canadian real house prices began to 'take off' (slightly later than in Britain). However, the US recession experienced in 1973–5 cut short the US house price boom while Canadian real house prices continued to rise rapidly. Later, as the US came out of the recession and real income began to rise significantly, house prices in the US 'took off', and a house price boom resulted which has only recently begun to slow down (on a national basis). The recent expansion in British real house prices has also been accompanied by a significant increase in real income.

Before concluding this section on the theory of house price determination, it needs to be stressed that the theory set out in this chapter, while now being generally accepted, is of fairly recent origin and is based partly on the experience of the 1970s when government attempted to control the rate of increases of house prices through manipulating building society lending. Earlier in the 1970s there was a strong school of thought which argued that it was fluctuations in building society lending which were of prime importance in determining movements in house prices.

The 1971/3 Boom and the Memorandum of Agreement

It has been established that the first major house price boom in Britain occurred between 1971 and 1973 and it was this that led to the Memorandum of Agreement and subsequently to the attempt to control house prices later in the decade. The peculiar nature of the 1971/3 boom therefore needs to be described in some detail. The starting point for the boom was the situation in 1970 when house prices were at their lowest relationship with earnings (as is illustrated in Table 7.1) since 1963 and had declined substantially in relation to earnings in the two previous years. Some correction of house prices to earnings therefore seemed inevitable. In 1970, RPDI, which had increased by an average of 1.5 per cent in the preceding three years, rose by 3.7 per cent and this served to increase the demand for house-purchase although, given a plentiful supply of houses, house prices rose by only 7 per cent. Lending continued to increase in 1971 and although the rate of increase of RPDI fell back to 1.1 per cent there was a general air of confidence in the economy. Some additional stimulus to house-purchase was probably given by the announcement that council rents were likely to increase substantially, thus causing some local authority tenants to seek to become owner-occupiers. By the end of 1971, the stock of houses available for sale had probably been run down significantly yet the market received a further stimulus early in 1972 when the mortgage rate was reduced to 8 per cent. The very strong demand continued and began to have a major effect on prices during that year. Probably a contributing factor to the rise in demand at this time was the increase in the number of households as a consequence of the post-war baby boom. However, what was almost certainly the key point in 1972 was the very rapid rate of increase in real incomes, 8.1 per cent during the year, an unprecedented level at the time. As Table 7.1 shows, house prices rose by no less than 37.4 per cent in 1972. The rapid increase in real incomes continued into 1973 and house prices in that year rose by 32.1 per cent.

The house price/earnings ratio climbed to an unprecedented level in 1972 and 1973 and the market was characterised by hysteria with the belief established that prices could continue rising at a rate out of all proportion to the rate of increase of prices generally or earnings. Building society lending peaked in the second quarter of 1972 and then fell, albeit erratically, throughout the second half of 1972 and 1973. However, demand continued at a strong level and as the stock of houses available for sale had already been run down substantially, the reduced number of transactions was not sufficient to prevent house prices continuing to rise at a rapid rate.

The inevitable downturn occurred towards the end of 1973. The rise in interest rates in the economy led to the BSA recommended mortgage rate being increased from 8.5 per cent at the beginning of the year to 11.0 per cent in August. The combination of this sharp increase in mortgage rates together with the rise in house prices brought owner-occupation onto the political stage in a big way and building societies were subject to some criticism both for the increase in interest rates and, more significantly, for having fuelled the house price boom. There was a possibility that direct controls might be imposed on building societies. However, following lengthy discussions between government officials and The Building Societies Association, in October 1973 the Memorandum of Agreement on Building Society Mortgage Finance was drawn up. The objectives of the Memorandum were set out in Chapter 6 but the significant one in respect of house prices was objective (c) which was to 'contribute towards the stabilisation of house prices'. The Memorandum went on to spell out how the objectives could be best achieved. It included a section by which the Council of the Association agreed to be ready 'to advise member-societies to adjust their lending policies, especially as regards second-time purchasers, if it appears at any time that excessive mortgage funds might otherwise be released in relation to the number of purchasers and the supply of dwellings with a consequent undesirable rate of increase in house prices'.

Thus the Memorandum implicitly assumed that house prices could be influenced by manipulation of lending policies and it should be noted that it was lending policies with regard to second-time buyers which were felt to be particularly significant. This is in contrast to the analysis earlier in this chapter which suggests that it is the number of first-time buyers which is of significance. The difference is partially explained by the fact that the Memorandum of Agreement was a political document in which it would be unacceptable to suggest that the housing market could be controlled by preventing people from becoming owner-occupiers.

The Memorandum of Agreement coincided with the slump in the housing market which began to make itself felt in 1973 and reached a low point in 1974. RPDI declined and fell more significantly in the following three years. House prices were virtually stagnant during 1974 and increased only modestly in 1975, notwithstanding a very rapid rate of increase of prices generally.

The Establishment of the Guideline System

The Memorandum of Agreement led to the establishment of the Joint Advisory Committee which subsequently met approximately monthly. The JAC quickly spawned a Technical Sub-Committee comprising economists and statisticians from various government departments and The Building Societies Association. The JAC and the Technical Sub-Committee were initially concerned with implementing the policy objectives set out in the Memorandum of Agreement but significantly attention appeared to be focused almost entirely on the house price objective. In April 1975, a working arrangement designed to contribute towards the achievement of the objectives set out in the Memorandum was announced by the JAC. This comprised:

(a) An assessment of the level of building society lending that the market was thought able to absorb without undue risk of an excessive increase in house prices.

(b) Monthly monitoring of house prices and of the housing market generally.
(c) An understanding that the BSA would ask member-societies to adjust the volume of their gross mortgage approvals if the JAC's assessment indicated that a lower level of lending would be desirable.

These arrangements came to be known as 'the guideline system' and the calculated desirable level of building society lending came to be known as 'the guideline'. The agreement again assumed that building society lending could be manipulated to control house prices. It included the sentence 'The agreed arrangements, by providing for adjustment of lending, should help avert a house price explosion.'

Subsequently, the Technical Sub-Committee of the JAC calculated, on a six-monthly basis, the guideline level of lending. The theoretical basis of the guideline system depended crucially on three propositions:

(a) That in the short run the supply of new and secondhand houses for sale was largely unresponsive to house price changes and the state of the housing market.
(b) That the underlying demand for house-purchase from creditworthy borrowers could only become effective if credit for house-purchase became available.
(c) That the effective demand for owner-occupation depended, within a fairly wide range, on the supply of mortgage funds from building societies.

The guideline calculation itself was a supply-based calculation covering a period of six months only. Basically it comprised five important features:

(a) An estimate of the net addition to the supply of houses for owner-occupation over the following six months on the assumption that supply would not be constrained by lack of effective demand.
(b) A calculation of house price levels required to enable builders to earn a normal profit margin so that supply would not be constrained by builders' inability to realise an adequate return.
(c) A resultant estimate of the total house-purchase funds required, given the estimated net addition to supply and the calculated house price.
(d) An estimate of the number of transactions likely to be wholly financed from sources other than building societies.
(e) An assumption about the size of percentage advance required from building societies by first-time purchasers and existing owner-occupiers moving, thus yielding an estimate of the total desirable building society lending for house -purchase.

This is a very mechanistic approach and in practice there were frequent disagreements between the government and the BSA as to the size of the various variables and at the end of the day the calculated guideline resulted as much from political bargaining as from economic analysis. However, from 1975 to 1977 this was of academic importance because for the most part building society lending was constrained by lack of funds and was well below the calculated guideline level. Moreover, the housing market was still in a depressed state following the inevitable collapse after the 1971/3 boom. House prices rose only modestly between 1973 and 1977 and the house price/earnings ratio was back to a low level by the end of 1977.

The Attempt to Control House Prices in 1978

By the end of 1977 the house price/earnings ratio had fallen to 3.34, almost as low as the 3.25 recorded in 1970 prior to the boom in the early part of the 1970s. Building society lending had been running at record levels in 1976 and 1977 and the stock of houses had been gradually run down such that by the end of 1977 there were signs of pressure in the market. The market received a major stimulus in 1978 when real incomes rose by no less than 8.4 per cent compared with a decline of 1.7 per cent in the previous year. Early in 1978 the rapid rise in house prices was beginning to show through in the figures and was causing political concern.

In fact, calculation of the guideline for the first half of 1978 had proved difficult because the conventional calculations produced a house price figure below that actually obtaining at the end of 1977. This in turn led to a calculated level of commitments below current lending. The Technical Sub-Committee put forward a lending figure of £670 million a month for the first half of 1978 but this was increased by the JAC to £700 million for January and £680 million for February and March. The government requested a 10 per cent cutback in building society lending with effect from March and this was implemented by the BSA on a quota system based on the existing assets of societies.

As Table 7.1 showed and as the analysis in this chapter has suggested, the curb was not successful. Fuelled by the rise in real incomes, house prices continued to rise rapidly. The reduction in building society lending, which at best was modest, was compensated for by a decline in the average percentage advance as purchasers sought additional funds from other sources. There was a sharp increase in borrowing from banks, insurance companies and other mortgage lenders.

By the end of 1978, the increase in the general level of interest rates had reduced building societies' competitiveness to such an extent that the guideline curb was no longer necessary and it was allowed to lapse from the end of the year.

The Guideline System Report 1980

The apparent failure of the guideline called into question the theory on which it was based. Moreover, The Building Societies Association, while it had acquiesced in government policy, had never been entirely happy with the guideline as a concept. At its meeting in November 1978, the Technical Sub-Committee of the JAC suggested that a review of the guideline method-ology was necessary. The JAC endorsed this proposal later that month and the Technical Sub-Committee began its work early in 1979. Discussions took over a year to complete but in the spring in 1980 a document was submitted to the JAC. The government and the Council of the Association decided that the report should be made more widely available as a contribution to discussion on the working of the owner-occupied housing market and the report was published in July 1980 (*The Guideline System*, a Report by the Technical Sub-Committee of the Joint Advisory Committee on Building Society Mortgage Finance (Department of the Environment and The Building Societies Association, 1980)).

Much of the analysis in the report is in line with the theory set out in this chapter. The report examined in detail the three basic propositions that underlaid the guideline system. It pointed out that it was too great a simplification to assume that changes in underlying demand could affect house prices only if they were made effective by building society credit. It was felt that they could also influence the strength of bidding in the market and thus influence house prices. The report also pointed to the immense practical difficulties in working out the appropriate guideline figure.

The report recognised that the owner-occupied housing market was much more complex than was allowed for in the guideline. It accepted that demand factors were the major short-term influence on house prices and noted that there were many factors influencing demand and that it was generally agreed that important factors were actual and expected personal incomes and the availability of building society mortgage commitments. However, it was noted that there was no straightforward relationship between the availability of building society loans and the movement in house prices, partly because there were alternative sources of funds. The report concluded that 'control of building society lending cannot sensibly be used for fine-tuning the housing market, even though such lending is clearly an important influence on the housing market, because house prices are influenced by many important factors other than the availability of building society mortgage commitments'.

The report effectively marked the end of the guideline system and there has been no attempt to resurrect it. Moreover, the analysis in the report is increasingly accepted and provides a much sounder basis for an understanding of housing market conditions. The report rather leaves the JAC without the role which occupied it for many years but it has remained in being as a forum for discussion between representatives of the government and The Building Societies Association.

Chapter 8

Co-Operation between Building Societies and Local Authorities

The Importance of Local Authorities in the Owner-Occupied Housing Market

At the end of 1980, 31.6 per cent of houses in Great Britain were rented from local authorities or other public bodies. This proportion has grown from virtually nil at the end of the Second World War. Local authorities therefore play a vital role in the housing market in that they own nearly one third of the housing stock.

The main thrust of local authority housing activity has been in respect of the provision of rented housing but many local authorities have also been concerned directly with the owner-occupied housing market by lending to home-buyers. Money lent by local authorities comes from their general borrowing and interest charged to borrowers had, until recently, to cover the full cost of all the local authority's debt. The Housing Act 1980 provides that the rate of interest charged on local authority loans should be the higher of this 'pooled' rate or a national rate to be established by the Secretary of State, which in practice is the BSA recommended rate.

Local authorities have statutory housing duties and they can make mortgage loans in pursuance of those duties. In the past, some local authorities have confined their lending to cases which come within their overall housing strategy while others have attempted to develop an extensive home loans programme as an objective in its own right. The *Housing Policy Technical Volume* (chapter 7, paragraph 56) merits quoting in this respect:

In the past, local authorities have developed to a certain extent their own interpretation of the categories (of home-buyers) which were applicable. This means there has been a diversity of practice in local authority lending with some authorities taking a wider view than others of their role. Knowledge of this is limited, but it is thought that the result has been that in some areas borrowers were able to turn to the local authority only in special circumstances (eg if they were seeking an older property needing improvement), while in other areas local authority lending was widely available and not necessarily only to those who could not obtain a building society loan.

In general, local authority lending has been at a fairly modest level and well below building society lending. This is illustrated in Table 8.1

which compares lending by the two sets of institutions for the period of 1970–80.

Table 8.1 Local Authority and Building Society Gross Advances, 1970–80

Year	Building society lending	Local authority lending	Local authority/ building society lending
	£m.	£m.	%
1970	2,021	118	5.8
1971	2,758	127	4.6
1972	3,649	133	3.6
1973	3,540	293	8.3
1974	2,950	455	15.4
1975	4,965	636	12.8
1976	6,117	152	2.5
1977	6,889	135	2.0
1978	8,734	155	1.8
1979	9,103	244	2.7
1980	9,614	134	1.4

Note: The table does not strictly compare like with like. The building society figures are for the UK and include some lending other than for house-purchase. The figures for local authorities are for England and Wales and are in respect of loans to private persons for house-purchase. The financing of council house sales is excluded.
Source: Housing and Construction Statistics.

Table 8.2 Numbers of Building Society and Local Authority Loans, England and Wales, 1970–80

Year	Building society loans	Local Authority loans	Local authority/ building society loans
	000's	000's	%
1970	509	44	8.6
1971	613	47	7.7
1972	638	45	7.1
1973	504	59	11.7
1974	397	75	18.9
1975	601	102	17.0
1976	653	28	4.3
1977	681	23	3.4
1978	742	27	3.6
1979	611	35	5.7
1980	628	16	2.5

Sources: A compendium of Building Society Statistics, 3rd edition (The Building Societies Association, 1980); Housing and Construction Statistics; BSA Bulletin.

It will be seen that in 1971 and 1972 local authority lending was running at less than 5 per cent of building society lending but the proportion climbed rapidly to reach 15.4 per cent in 1974. The volume of local authority lending further increased in 1975 but then fell back sharply and has been at little more than minimal levels in the last few years.

Table 8.1 is inadequate in many respects because accurate data is not available to compare building society and local authority lending for house-purchase. Slightly more reliable figures are shown in Table 8.2 which compares the numbers of loans made by building societies and local authorities in England and Wales only.

The proportions are higher than in Table 8.1, partly reflecting the fact that the building society and local authority figures are both for England and Wales but also as a result of the fact that local authority loans have been smaller than building society loans. In 1974 and 1975 the number of local authority loans was between 17 and 19 per cent of the number of building society loans, a very high proportion.

Initially, the increase in local authority lending could be attributed to the sharp cutback of building society lending in 1973 and 1974. Also, because of the way that local authorities charged interest on their mortgage loans, that rate tended to lag behind building society rates and in 1974 many local authorities were able to offer loans at cheaper rates than building societies. The government, anxious to avoid an increase in building society mortgage rates, was happy to acquiesce in an increase in local authority lending. Tables 8.1 and 8.2 show the very sharp increase in lending in 1974. However, local authority lending gained a momentum of its own and when building society lending picked up again in 1975 local authority lending, far from reducing, increased further with a record 102,000 loans being made in England and Wales, twice the level of a few years earlier.

Local authority loans have been more concentrated on poorer properties and poorer borrowers than have building society loans. However, the sheer volume of building society lending, together with the relatively liberal lending policies employed by societies, has meant that even when local authority lending was at its peak, building societies tended to make more downmarket loans than local authorities. Certainly, some local authorities were willing to make loans on properties on which some building societies were not willing to make loans, but in general the increase in local authority lending was in respect of properties which building societies would readily have mortgaged had they had the money available. At the time there were suggestions that building societies were unwilling to lend, for example, on pre-1919 properties yet at that time published figures showed that some 17 per cent of building society loans were on properties in this age category.

The Cutback of Local Authority Lending and the £100 Million Scheme

By early 1975, the government was under considerable pressure to bring public expenditure under control and thought was given to reducing local authority lending as a means of achieving this. In April 1975, the government informed the Association that it intended to cut back local authority lending. The government asked whether societies would be prepared to fill the gap, and government identified a figure of £100 million as the required size of 'replacement lending' in the financial year 1975–6 although this was subsequently increased to £105 million. Building societies readily agreed to take on this additional lending.

To some extent this agreement and the government's request were political as it has already been seen that there was a considerable overlap between building society and local authority lending. However, the government could not be seen to be cutting back on local authority lending without some visible alternative being put in its place.

In June 1975 the Secretary of State for the Environment announced that building societies were willing to co-operate and he said that discussions would be held at regional level to identify the local authority lending schemes which were directly linked to housing objectives and where building society participation would be appropriate. The original intention was therefore that local authorities should use building society lending not in respect of individual cases but rather in respect of projects which they felt were relevant to their housing objectives, for example, rehabilitation work in housing action areas and general improvement areas. The discussions continued on this basis for some months and the intention was that the DoE regional controllers should identify such projects. In fact, the scheme has never operated in this way. Rather, societies have been dealing with individual cases sent to them by local authorities.

In July 1975 the Department of the Environment split the £100 million between regions and its regional controllers allocated the total between local authorities. The Building Societies Association approached the ten largest societies and they agreed to participate in this scheme. The Association appointed regional co-ordinators to act in each region. Similar arrangements were put in hand for Scotland and Wales.

A first meeting between representatives of The Building Societies Association, the local authority associations and the Department of the Environment was held in September 1975. This was in many ways an historic meeting in that building societies and local authorities had never before met formally to discuss housing matters, a somewhat surprising situation bearing in mind the importance of the two sets of institutions in the housing market and their obvious areas of mutual interest. The meeting was somewhat acrimonious, largely because of misunderstandings on both sides. The local authority representatives were critical of building society lending criteria and one frequently suggested solution was that local authorities should guarantee building society loans. The building society representatives replied that their lending criteria were much less rigid than was frequently supposed and that the existence of a guarantee would be unlikely to make much difference to a society's willingness to lend.

The scheme was very slow to get off the ground and it was the final quarter of 1975 before any loans were made. In December 1975 the Association issued a statement committing itself to co-operation with local authorities and indicating that local authority representatives had been invited to attend a meeting to discuss difficulties which had arisen over the original scheme.

In January 1976, the Secretary of State for the Environment announced a further reduction in local authority lending and he indicated that he had been encouraged by the recent commitment of building societies to the principle of helping local authorities through the support scheme. A circular was issued to local authorities asking them to restrict their lending to the following categories:

(a) Existing local authority tenants; people high on an authority's waiting list for housing; people displaced by slum clearance and people whom an authority would otherwise have been obliged to rehouse.
(b) Applicants who are homeless or who are threatened with homelessness or living in conditions that are overcrowded or otherwise detrimental to health.
(c) Applicants who wish to buy larger houses for only partial occupation by themselves in areas where conditions of overcrowding seem liable to develop.
(d) Applicants who wish to buy an older property suitable for single family occupation and especially people who wish to buy a house with a view to improving it subsequently.

A further meeting between the local authority associations, The Building Societies Association and the DoE was held in January 1976. The main problem with the £100 million scheme had been the time taken to build up local liaison. A working party was set up to look at the problem and this duly reported in April 1976. A succession of meetings served to increase considerably the level of understanding between societies and local authorities and the results were reported back to individual societies and authorities and no doubt led to some re-examination of policies in a number of societies. Activity under the scheme picked up during the second quarter of 1976 and averaged over £10 million per month. Technically, the £100 million scheme was for the financial year 1975–6 but total approvals under the scheme exceeded £160 million.

The 1977–8 Scheme

In July 1976 the government indicated to the building societies that it was envisaging a further substantial cutback of local authority lending during the financial year and also during 1977–8. Again, the building societies agreed to help fill the gap thus created even if this gap was of more politcal than real significance. A figure of £276 million was identified by the government as legitimate local authority lending during 1977–8 and the government wanted building societies to take on £176 million. The scheme operated in much the same way as the original £100 million scheme, that is, individual local authorities were given a quota by the Department of the Environment and the Association matched individual societies with local authorities. Applicants were referred by local authorities to societies who would then grant loans in the normal way.

The introduction of the scheme was somewhat rushed and it also coincided with a sharp increase in normal building society lending. Perhaps as a result of this, lending under the support scheme fell well short of the target and only £105 million was committed.

The scheme has continued to operate, at least formally, in much the same way since that time. In 1978–9, £300 million was agreed as the appropriate support scheme lending figure and the reduction in building society lending during this time, partly as a result of the guideline cutback, meant that almost the entire allocation was taken up. For 1979–80 and 1980–1, The Building Societies Association agreed to a £400 million support scheme figure in each year but the high level of building society lending meant that the money was not wholly taken up. It was becoming increasingly clear that the level of support scheme lending was inversely proportional to the overall availability of building society funds, thereby confirming the already well-established overlap between the categories of applicant catered for by societies and local authorities. Partly in recognition of this, the support scheme figure for 1981–2 was agreed at £350 million.

The Effects of the Support Scheme

The building societies have always maintained that the benefits from the support scheme have not, for the most part, been reflected in figures for lending under the scheme but rather have been the increased understanding between societies and local authorities which in turn has enabled societies to plan their lending policies with a sounder knowledge of housing market conditions. The support scheme has acted as an important catalyst in bringing together societies and local authorities at both national and local level. At national level, in addition to the meetings which have already been mentioned, building society speakers are frequently invited to address local authority audiences and vice versa. At local authority level, many authorities have invited building society managers to meetings to explain their housing strategies and other informal contacts have been developed.

It is not easy to assess the exact extent of this increased understanding and co-operation but one variable which is relevant in this respect is the number and proportion of loans on pre-1919 houses. These houses include the most marginal properties which building societies are frequently accused of not being willing to finance. Certainly, local authorities did concentrate their lending on this type of property when they had sufficient funds.

Table 8.3 shows trends in lending on pre-1919 houses in England and Wales.

The table shows that in 1975 when local authority lending was at its peak, 19.2 per cent of building society loans went on pre-1919 houses. The cutback of local authority lending in 1976 was accompanied by an increase in the proportion of loans on pre-1919 houses to 22.9 per cent. The number also increased sharply with the result that the total number of loans made on pre-1919 houses in England and Wales in 1976 was almost exactly the same as in 1975. If the entire 3.7 per cent increase in building society loans is attributed to the cutback of local authority lending then this represents some 24,000 loans. It will be noted that the proportion of building society lending going on pre-1919 houses has continued to rise significantly and the number of loans on such properties in England and Wales has not fallen below the 1975 level when local authority lending was at its peak.

These figures are sufficient to show that building societies have taken over a substantial proportion of the lending previously done by local authorities.

Table 8.3   Building Society and Local Authority Loans on Pre-1919 Houses in England and Wales, 1970–80

Year	Building society loans 000's	Local authority loans 000's	Total loans 000's	BS pre-1919 loans/ total BS loans %
1970	85	27	112	16.7
1971	112	29	141	18.2
1972	123	28	151	19.2
1973	91	37	128	18.1
1974	74	47	121	18.7
1975	115	63	178	19.2
1976	152	20	172	22.9
1977	160	17	177	23.5
1978	177	23	210	24.0
1979	148	33	182	24.3
1980	187	15	202	27.7

Notes:
1   For most of the period, figures on the percentage of loans on pre-1919 houses by region are not available from the sample survey of mortgages. It is assumed that the percentage for England and Wales is the same as that for the UK.
2   For 1970–5 it is assumed that 62 per cent of all local authority loans went to purchasers of pre-1919 houses – the actual 1975 proportion. For subsequent years the proportion has been taken to be 94 per cent – the actual 1976 proportion.
Sources: 5 per cent sample survey of building society mortgage completions; DoE.

The figures are also very much greater than those for the support scheme and they indicate therefore that the bulk of this increase in lending has not been through the support scheme but rather has been through the normal course of societies' business.

Direct Lending by Building Societies to Local Authorities

When local authority lending was cut back initially, fears were expressed that building societies either could not, or did not wish to, take over the lending previously done by the authorities and the suggestion was put forward that societies should lend money directly to local authorities for on-lending to home-buyers. In fact arrangements were already in hand for such a scheme with the Northern Ireland Housing Executive. Societies resisted such a policy, arguing that their lending policies were sound and they did not wish to see a proportion of their funds being taken away from them and allocated, perhaps not as efficiently, by local authorities. Societies also made the point that they had some £2,000 million invested with local authorities in the normal course of their business and it was up to the authorities how they wished to use these funds.

This issue was pursued at a political level for some time with the suggestion being made by some sections of the Labour Party that building societies should hand over 10 per cent of their funds each year for on-lending by local authorities. Perhaps because of the success of the support scheme and the clear indication that building societies had been taking over lending previously done by the local authorities, such suggestions received little support and died a natural death.

Local Authority Guarantees for Building Society Mortgages

In the early discussions which took place between building society representatives and the local authority associations, the suggestion was made that local authorities should guarantee building society mortgages and that this would enable societies to lend on all the properties on which local authorities had previously lent. Certainly the concept was a superficially attractive one, removing as it would all risk from building societies while allowing those people who would have bought homes financed by local authority loans to continue to be able to obtain loans. In reality the position was far more complicated in that building society representatives argued strongly that the existence of a local authority guarantee would in practice make little difference to societies' willingness to lend. A building society is able to lend only on the security of freehold or leasehold estate and it cannot lend on the security of a guarantee. If a society did not feel that a loan was justified then it would not make the loan regardless of whether the guarantee was available.

Moreover, one problem which had existed with local authority guarantees in the past was the accompanying bureaucracy. Local authorities had been able to guarantee loans under the Housing (Financial Provisions) Act 1958. However, the scheme was very bureaucratic with local authorities vetting each case individually and requiring written notice of any arrears.

Building societies have for many years operated the standard indemnity scheme by which high percentage loans can be granted. Partly as a result of the discussions with the local authority associations, arrangements were made to increase the limit for 100 per cent loans under the indemnity scheme to £14,000 with effect from 1976. Subsequently the limit has been further increased to £20,000.

It became generally accepted that in practice a local authority guarantee could offer only limited benefits to societies and would not lead to a radical change in lending policy. Nevertheless, the Labour government announced its intention to strengthen the powers of local authorities to guarantee building society mortgages and provisions to this effect were included in the Housing Bill published in 1979. The relevant sections of the Bill were reintroduced by the Conservative government and subsequently enacted in the Housing Act 1980.

Basically, the Housing Act 1980 enables local authorities to guarantee building society loans and the guarantee is, as far as the society is concerned, every bit as good as an insurance company guarantee. Moreover, the local authority is empowered, if it so wishes, to take over the mortgage. It is envisaged that these guarantee powers will be used in marginal areas where a society might not normally be willing to lend. In effect, the local authority would be backing its own redevelopment policy by offering to buy out any building society loans which go wrong. The effect of these provisions remains to be seen. One problem with any guarantee is that it cannot protect the borrower should he lose through no fault of his own. For example, if a purchaser buys a house for, say, £10,000 in a poor area and has every expectation that the area will improve but subsequently finds after five years that his property is worth only £8,000, then he has no protection. As long as he continues to pay the mortgage then the guarantee powers will not be called upon. The guarantee can only operate when the building society has suffered a loss and there is still no adequate protection for a borrower in such circumstances.

Improvement Grants

Local authorities in their direct lending have been particularly concerned with lending on properties to be improved. Building societies have also been willing to lend on such properties and indeed to finance improvements but they operate under different legal rules from the local authorities. Societies' normal policy is to lend only on houses which either have the basic amenities already installed or which will have them installed immediately after purchase. A major purpose of the improvement grant system is to allow the basic amenities to be installed so obviously there is an important link between the willingness of building societies to lend and the availability of improvement grants.

The statutory conditions relating to improvement grants caused problems for building societies after the enactment of the Housing Act 1974. This provided that when an improvement grant was made, the statutory conditions would attach to the property, generally for five years from the date on which the property was fit for occupation following completion of the works. For the first of these five years the property had generally to be occupied exclusively by the owner and during the next four years it had, if he did not occupy it, to be let or kept available for letting. If the property was sold the conditions would still apply. If the new purchaser wished to occupy the property himself then the local authority was entitled to seek repayment of the grant together with compound interest. Inevitably a building society would have to take this into account when deciding whether to lend on a property to be improved and, moreover, these conditions probably prevented some improvements from taking place.

The Association put forward the suggestion that the Housing Act 1974 should be amended but failing this it proposed an administrative solution. The local authority would be asked to give the society a written undertaking that if the society had to exercise its power of sale during the five year period, any repayment of an improvement grant would be limited to the proceeds of the sale remaining after satisfaction of the mortgage debt and the costs of realisation. Many local authorities were prepared to give such an undertaking and undoubtedly this did make it easier for societies to lend on properties to be improved.

The Housing Act 1980 effectively remedied the problem by removing the statutory conditions referred to above. There was virtually unanimity between the organisations concerned with housing that such a change in the law was necessary and this is perhaps one manifestation of the benefits of increased understanding and co-operation between societies and local authorities.

In the mid-1970s, there was considerable public debate about the alleged refusal of building societies to lend on certain types of property or in certain areas. The expression 'red lining' was borrowed from the United States and the suggestion was made that building societies drew rings around inner-city areas and refused to lend in those areas for no good reason. Building societies contested such claims and were frequently able to point to loans which they had in fact made inside such 'red lining' areas. The building societies pointed out that they had a responsibility towards potential owner-occupiers not to encourage them to buy a property which would not represent value for money. Many properties in run-down inner-city areas came into this category and in some cases a valuer would not recommend the property as being a suitable mortgage security. However, in many cases there is no doubt that building society managers were not as aware as they might be of local housing conditions and that loans were sometimes refused which could perhaps have been made. The support scheme had the significant effect of bringing together societies and local authorities and so removing such doubts and misunderstandings. Building societies could publicly voice their concern about lending in particular areas and the local authority, if it was so able, might reassure societies. In other areas, it was generally accepted that the provision of finance for owner-occupation would not be appropriate.

There were suggestions that building societies should be forced to disclose the pattern of their mortgage lending as has happened in the United States. But building societies themselves pointed out that this would be very costly and would lead to doubtful benefits. However, the government wanted evidence that something was being done about this matter and the Association agreed, somewhat reluctantly, at the end of 1977, to set up an appeal procedure to operate as from 1 April 1978. Under this procedure, applicants nominated by local authorities to building societies and who were subsequently refused a loan because of an unfavourable valuation report, could appeal first to a higher level within the society and if still dissatisfied to a review board comprising selected vice-presidents of the Association. In the event, not a single case has yet been put to the review board.

Chapter 9

Sources of Funds and
The Stow Report

In the second half of the 1970s, one important area for debate within the building society industry, and also in a wider field, was whether building societies had the capacity to fund the likely increase in demand for owner-occupation in the 1980s. The suggestion was made that building societies were rapidly approaching saturation point in respect of their share of the savings market and that they were 'running out of investors'. This chapter sets out the nature of these fears and then examines in detail the response of the building society industry in the form of the Stow Report.

The Argument that Building Societies can run out of Investors

At first sight, it is a plausible argument that building societies must, in the not-too-distant future, run out of investors and hence not be able to grow and to meet the additional demand for owner-occupation which is likely to occur in the 1980s. The argument has frequently been put in the form that it requires a certain number of investors to provide sufficient funds to enable one loan to be made. Certainly, an examination of the statistics shows an apparently alarming rise in the ratio of shareholders to borrowers. This is illustrated in Table 9.1.

It will be seen that the number of shareholders per borrower has risen from 1.50 in 1950 to 2.81 in 1970 and 5.69 in 1980. Moreover, the relationship between the increase in the number of shareholders and the increase in the number of borrowers shows an even more marked trend. The ratio has been very variable for reasons which are not entirely clear but between 1970 and 1980, on average, the number of shareholders increased eleven times as fast as the number of borrowers.

It is accepted that the figures in Table 9.1 are misleading in that many shareholders have accounts with more than one building society. Nevertheless, there is still no doubt that the number of individual shareholders has risen sharply in relation to the number of borrowers. The proportion of the adult population with building society accounts increased from an estimated 11 per cent in 1965 to 48 per cent in 1980 whereas the proportion of households with building society mortgages increased from about 16 per cent to about 25 per cent over the same period.

Building societies have also enjoyed a significant increase in their market share. Table 2.5 showed that societies' share of short-term household financial

Table 9.1 Shareholders and Borrowers, 1930–80

Year	Shareholders	Borrowers	Shareholders/ borrowers	Increase in shareholders over previous year	Increase in borrowers	Increase in shareholders/ increase in borrowers
	000's	000's		000's	000's	
1930	1,449	720	2.01	184	91	2.02
1940	2,088	1,503	1.39	(−64)	(−23)	2.78
1950	2,256	1,508	1.50	78	65	1.20
1960	3,910	2,349	1.66	93	103	0.90
1970	10,265	3,655	2.81	1,180	185	6.38
1971	11,568	3,896	2.97	1,303	241	5.41
1972	12,874	4,126	3.12	1,306	230	5.68
1973	14,385	4,204	3.42	1,511	78	19.37
1974	15,856	4,250	3.73	1,471	46	31.98
1975	17,916	4,397	4.07	2,060	147	14.01
1976	19,991	4,609	4.34	2,075	212	9.79
1977	22,536	4,836	4.66	2,545	227	11.21
1978	24,999	5,108	4.89	2,463	272	9.06
1979	27,878	5,251	5.31	2,879	143	20.13
1980	30,640	5,383	5.69	2,763	132	20.93

Sources: Annual Reports of the Chief Registrar of Friendly Societies as reproduced in *A Compendium of Building Society Statistics*, 3rd edition (The Building Societies Association, 1980); *Building Societies in 1980* (The Building Societies Association, 1981).

assets increased from 24 per cent in 1966 to 35 per cent in 1972 and 43 per cent in 1980. Given that there is a finite number of investors and also that the market for personal savings is not unlimited, there is indeed a very plausible argument to suggest that these trends cannot continue forever.

However, such an argument is far from valid, the reasons for this being set out in the first part of Chapter 2. The number of investors is not of great significance to building societies. Rather, what matters is the volume of personal sector financial intermediation. It may be that societies have 20 million investors out of an adult population of 44 million but the fact is that over 5 million of these investors have, between them, less than £300 million in their accounts. Clearly if they all closed their accounts there would be a dramatic reduction in the investor/borrower ratio but in practice nothing of significance would change.

Moreover, Chapter 2 showed that building society lending itself contributes to the funds of the personal sector and therefore increases the size of the market within which building societies compete. However, it is easy to put forward such an analysis in retrospect but the fact is that in the late 1970s there were many who did not accept these arguments but rather considered that building societies were shortly going to approach a crisis point in terms of their ability to attract the funds needed to meet the demand for owner-occupation.

The cyclical nature of the building society industry, with there being significant swings in the volume of net receipts which societies are able to attract, has meant that there have been recurring suggestions for a reform of the housing finance system. Each time societies are at the bottom of their cyclical trough, the suggestion is made that they need to diversify their sources of funds because they are not able to attract as much as they require. Such arguments tend to disappear as societies' fortunes improve. The first official sign of concern as to the ability of societies to attract the necessary volume of funds came with the publication of the Consultative Document *Housing Policy* (Cmnd 6851, HMSO, 1977). Chapter 7 included a section entitled 'An Adequate Supply of Mortgage Funds', which in fact accepted that societies may be able to fund mortgage demand from their traditional sources. It went on to comment:

> But there can be no certainty about financial flows some years ahead. It is, therefore, possible that the building societies will only be able to meet demands placed upon them for advances if they supplement their traditional sources of finance by raising funds from other financial institutions – in particular life and pension funds. The form of security would have to suit the investing institutions, and might be medium term or long term for the most part.

The Green Paper added that if fresh sources of funds had to be tapped then building societies might well be able and prefer to deal directly with financial institutions but it also raised the possibility of a special financial intermediary.

No direct action was taken as a result of the Consultative Document in respect of this matter (or indeed in respect of most other matters) and as building societies were on the cyclical up-swing throughout 1977 the issue did not merit much attention. However, in May 1978 the Governor of the Bank of

England, Mr Gordon Richardson, in an address to the annual conference of The Building Societies Association, returned to the same theme. Mr Richardson said he believed that 'there may be a case for looking at the introduction into your balance sheets of some small portion of longer-term money at some future date'.

The Establishment of the Stow Committee and the Heseltine Group

Interest rates moved against building societies in 1978 and 1979 and in the latter year in particular the supply of mortgages fell well short of the demand. House-builders were particularly concerned that this might represent a long-term tendency and asked building societies to examine alternative sources of funds. In May 1979 the new Conservative government came to power, committed to a huge expansion in the level of owner-occupation. It was understood that the Secretary of State for the Environment, Mr Michael Heseltine, was considering establishing a committee to look at this question.

Partly in response to the concerns which were being felt, the Association established, in August 1979, a working party to consider the case for societies' seeking to attract funds from sources other than the personal sector. The terms of reference of the working party were as follows:

(a) To estimate the medium-term demand for building society mortgage finance and to consider the extent to which this demand can be financed by traditional means.

(b) To examine and comment on the sources of investment funds received by societies.

(c) To consider the methods by which and the terms on which alternative sources of funds might be raised.

(d) To consider the implications of raising funds from alternative sources for the operation of societies and the rest of the financial system.

(e) To consider the merits of raising short-term funds from the money markets as a means of maintaining lending at a high level at times when building society rates are uncompetitive.

The working party was chaired by Mr Ralph Stow, the then immediate past-Chairman of the Council of the Association, and, significantly and unusually for the building society industry, it included two prominent outsiders – Mr John Wilmot, a partner in the stockbroking firm of Laurie Milbank & Co., and Mr Richard Harrington, a lecturer in economics at the University of Manchester. The working party was completed by two building society executives – Joe Bradley from the Nationwide and George McKenzie from the Abbey National – and by Mark Boléat from the Association.

Meanwhile, the government was making slow progress in establishing its own working group and not until November 1979 did the Secretary of State for the Environment, Mr Heseltine, make the following announcement:

It is the Government's policy to encourage a substantial growth in home-ownership. I am therefore establishing a group including people of experience from the main financial institutions to consider and review possible options on ways and means of securing an adequate and stable flow of funds in order to achieve this objective.

Mr Heseltine indicated that the group would be led by his department but it had on it a number of distinguished non-civil service members including Mr Alan Cumming, then Deputy Chairman of the BSA Council, Mr F. W. Crawley, a deputy general manager of Lloyds Bank, Mr Philip Chappel, director of Morgan Grenfell & Co. and also representatives of insurance companies and pension funds. This group came to be known as the House-Purchase Finance Review Group. However, its report has never been made public.

The Stow Report

The Association's working group rapidly came to be known as the Stow Committee and its subsequent report (*Mortgage Finance in the 1980s*, The Building Societies Association, 1980) as the Stow Report. The Committee completed its deliberations in the short period of four months, no doubt partly wishing to publish its results prior to those of the government's House-Purchase Finance Review Group. The report was completed late in 1979 and was published by the Association early in January 1980. In many respects, the report represented the first attempt by the Association to do a detailed statistical analysis into building society operations and indeed much of the analysis has been drawn on in preparing this book. The report also had important policy implications and for both of these reasons it is examined in detail in this chapter.

The report began by examining briefly the demand for building society loans. In this examination the point was made immediately that the demand for building society mortgage finance, like the demand for other goods and services, must to some extent depend on the price of that finance, that is, the mortgage rate in relation to the price of other forms of finance. The report set out tentative figures for the underlying demand that societies might expect to face during the 1980s and these are reproduced in Table 9.2.

The section on demand went on to say that if societies were asked to finance 85,000 council house sales a year then this would require an additional £60 million a month net receipts at 1979 prices.

In analytical terms, probably the most important part of the report is the second chapter which explains the sources of building society funds. This noted that in recent years, net receipts accounted for 45 per cent of building society funds, interest credited 17 per cent and repayment of mortgage principal 38 per cent. The report added that about 75 per cent of mortgage repayments are redemptions, most of which are linked to new loans being taken out. It was therefore pointed out that there are two mechanisms by which building societies are in effect self-financing:

(a) Interest credited to investors' accounts.
(b) The regular mortgage repayments, part-redemptions and complete mortgage redemptions where borrowers do not seek a new loan.

Table 9.2 The Demand for Building Society Loans, 1975–85

Year	Number of loans	Amount advanced	Net receipts required	
			Per year	Per month
	000s	£m.	£m.	£m.
1975	651	4,970	3,190	270
1976	715	6,120	2,280	190
1977	737	6,720	4,720	390
1978	802	8,730	3,370	280
1979	710	8,900	3,400	280
1980	810	11,350	6,100	510
1981	840	12,950	6,600	550
1982	865	14,450	7,000	580
1983	890	16,100	7,500	630
1984	915	17,700	7,800	650
1985	940	19,400	8,150	680

Note: Figures for 1975–8 are actual; 1979 figures are estimates and figures for 1980–5 projections.
Source: Mortgage Finance in the 1980s (The Building Societies Association, 1980).

The report then went on to develop the concept of the last-time seller. It was noted that about 85 per cent of building society loans are on the security of existing houses and that the money lent by building societies to purchasers of existing houses must eventually be received by people who are selling houses but not buying others with loans. In some cases these would be elderly people moving out of their large owner-occupied houses and perhaps into sheltered accommodation or they might be people inheriting the houses of their parents when they die. The report estimated that some £4,500 million was realised by these 'last-time sellers' in 1979 and that such money is available for investment in building societies if societies' rates are sufficiently attractive. The report included the following table analysing the sources of building society funds.

Table 9.3 An Analysis of the Sources of Building Society Funds

Source	Percentage of total
Mortgage redemptions replaced by a new loan	26
Mortgage redemptions not replaced by a new loan	4
Regular mortgage repayments	8
Net receipts from 'last-time sellers'	17
Interest credited to investment accounts	15
Net new receipts	30
Total	100

Source: Mortgage Finance in the 1980s (The Building Societies Association, 1980).

Having made this theoretical point, the Stow Committee naturally went on to conclude that building societies should experience no difficulty in raising an adequate supply of funds and that the problems which they had experienced in the past had been cyclical, caused by their interest rates being below a competitive level, especially at times of rising interest rates. To help prove its point, the Committee examined interest rates in a number of other countries and showed that in Britain the rate of interest on mortgage loans had traditionally been below other rates of interest whereas in other countries the opposite position had obtained.

The report went on to examine in more detail the nature of the savings market in which building societies operate and the analysis in the report forms the basis of the first part of Chapter 2 of this book. The report stressed that expenditure on existing houses need not have any relation to aggregate net saving. The following example was given. Assume in a simple economy that the net saving of the personal sector equals £100 and is all lent to firms for productive investment. Now assume that person A saves an additional £50 which he pays to person B for the purchase of a house and person B promptly spends the whole amount on consumption. Aggregate net saving is unchanged. It would be the same if, instead of A saving £50, it was C who saved £50, depositing it with a building society which lent the money to A. As long as the ultimate recipient of the money spends it on consumption then net saving is not increased. The report went on to conclude that it would be theoretically possible, although admittedly unlikely, for new deposits and lending of building societies to exceed the total net saving of the personal sector. The point was made that deposits with building societies come from gross saving and this is made up of three components:

(a) Net saving out of income plus net capital transfers.
(b) Loans.
(c) Sales of company securities.

It was noted therefore that building societies make capital funds available to the personal sector through their lending. It was also argued that a rise in house prices did not have the effect on the ability of societies to fund mortgage demand that is sometimes claimed. That is, while a rise in prices increases the demand for mortgage funds, that very same rise in prices results in a greater amount of capital being received by last-time sellers and therefore a higher volume of funds which building societies are able to attract if their rates are right.

Having established that building societies are able to meet mortgage demand from their traditional sources, the report nevertheless examined in detail alternative sources of funds. It was noted that in fact it is only the personal sector which directly or indirectly can provide the funds for building societies. The question was whether societies should attempt to raise their funds retail, that is, directly from the personal investor, or rather wholesale, that is, through the intermediary of pension funds and life insurance companies. That these are the only two significant alternative sources of funds is illustrated in Table 9.4 which shows personal sector acquisition of financial assets.

It will be seen that between 40 and 50 per cent of the personal sector's

Table 9.4 Personal Sector Acquisition of Financial Assets, 1974–78

Asset	1974 £m.	%	1975 £m.	%	1976 £m.	%	1977 £m.	%	1978 £m.	%
Life assurance and pension funds	3,493	40	4,426	44	5,398	45	6,121	43	7,976	47
Public sector assets	1,333	15	1,206	12	2,571	22	2,080	15	1,601	9
Bank deposits, notes and coins	3,326	38	1,397	14	1,626	14	1,046	8	3,840	22
Company and overseas securities and unit trusts	−1,242	(14)	−1,283	(13)	−1,174	(10)	−1,855	(13)	−1,785	(10)
Building society deposits	1,969	23	4,161	41	3,301	28	5,932	42	4,906	29
Other	− 162	(2)	234	2	222	2	752	5	601	4
Total	8,717	100	10,141	100	11,944	100	14,076	100	17,139	100

Source: Bank of England Quarterly Bulletin, June 1979.

acquisition of financial assets has been in the form of contributions to life assurance and pension funds. The report noted that there were three ways in which societies could raise funds from the personal sector via these inter-mediaries:

(a) Direct loans.
(b) The issuing by societies of a marketable security.
(c) The establishment of secondary mortgage markets.

The report considered the first two options together and noted that pension funds and life assurance companies were commercial organisations with a fiduciary duty towards policy holders and beneficiaries. To ascertain what type of investments might be attractive to these companies, the report set out the composition of the assets which they acquired in 1978. Table 9.5 reproduces this information.

Table 9.5   Pension Funds and Assurance Companies:
Increase in Financial Assets, 1978

Financial asset	Assurance cos.		Pension funds	
	£m.	%	£m.	%
Bank deposits, notes and coins	224	5	229	7
Government stocks	2,644	61	1,310	39
Ordinary shares	644	15	1,155	34
Fixed interest securities	66	2	− 63	(2)
Loans	428	10	207	6
Other assets	318	7	560	16
Total	4,324	100	3,398	100

Source: Bank of England Quarterly Bulletin, June 1979.

Table 9.5 shows that 61 per cent of the financial assets acquired by assurance companies were government securities (almost entirely long-dated) and a further 15 per cent were ordinary shares. Loans accounted for a modest 10 per cent of the total. Government stocks accounted for 39 per cent of the increase in the financial assets of pension funds and equities accounted for a further 34 per cent.

The Stow Committee argued that these figures showed that if building societies had to raise substantial funds from assurance companies or pension funds then they would need to compete with government stocks, given that any investment similar in concept to equities would not be possible. The Committee considered that because of the advantages which government stocks have over other securities (in particular the exemption from capital gains tax) then societies would have to offer any security at a premium over gilts. Enquiries amongst financial institutions indicated that any security would have to be at fixed rates of interest and that this would be sufficiently unattractive to societies to be no real option at all.

The report considered the argument which is frequently made that if societies could raise a modest proportion of their funds at a premium rate of interest then it would not be necessary to increase the rate of interest on the bulk of their funds. The Committee did not accept this argument. It pointed out that any such policy would lead to a rise in the general level of interest rates and also traditional investors would find a mechanism by which they could invest in any new high interest rate security.

The Stow Committee examined the viability of a secondary mortgage market in Britain, drawing heavily on the experiences of the United States and Canada. The Committee concluded that it would be impossible to establish a secondary mortgage market in Britain. It was noted that the market existed in America primarily because of the inadequacy of the primary market and in particular the prohibition on financial institutions of trading across state borders. It also commented that in order to be marketable, a mortgage had to have a fixed rate of interest.

Having made the case for building societies being able to attract an adequate volume of funds from the personal sector, the Stow Report went on to look at the implications of building societies operating with competitive interest rates so as to meet mortgage demand. Such a policy was felt to be particularly beneficial for the housing market and especially house-builders in that mortgages would be available on demand and therefore transactions would be less likely to be held up, either because of a direct shortage of mortgage funds or because of chains breaking down which in turn might be caused by shortage of mortgage funds.

The report considered briefly the effect on societies themselves of the building society industry operating with competitive interest rates and set out five possible implications:

(a) Competitive interest rates imply interest rates set by the market and not by administrative decision.
(b) Because the mortgage rate has persistently been below a competitive level, it has been possible for even the few less efficient societies to prosper. If societies operated with competitive interest rates, this would no longer be the case.
(c) If there was competition for mortgage business then it might be necessary to implement tighter prudential controls for granting mortgages, otherwise there would be the danger of risky lending.
(d) If societies could meet normal mortgage demand then they would be in a better position to finance loans for home improvements and other purposes for which there is at present a substantial unsatisfied demand.
(e) Competitive interest rates would make it practical for mortgage loans to be assumed – that is, taken over by the purchaser of a house by way of transfer of equity.

The Stow Report concluded with an examination of policies to stabilise building society lending. It was pointed out that if societies operated with competitive interest rates then this in itself would make a major contribution to stabilising lending. However, it was recognised that building society rates could never fluctuate as much as those of other institutions.

The using of liquidity ratios as the stabilisation mechanism was still deemed to be the most effective means by which fluctuations in net inflow could be prevented from leading to fluctuations of equal magnitude in advances. However, the Committee considered alternative methods by which lending could be stabilised. It was noted that in the United States the Federal Home Loan Bank Board (FHLBB) raised funds from the market and on-lent them to savings and loan associations at a rate of interest which was above the cost of those funds to the FHLBB but slightly below the mortgage rate charged by the savings and loan associations. This enabled the associations to operate on very low liquidity ratios. However, the Committee thought that this would not be practicable in Britain because the mortgage rate tended to be substantially below market interest rates for much of the time and such bank borrowing could prove very expensive for societies.

The Committee suggested that the most effective means of borrowing short-term funds to enable a society to stabilise lending would be a building society certificate of deposit. It was suggested that a market in building society CDs could be established if certain conditions of issue could be met:

(a) A life of three to six months.
(b) Large denominations, not less than £50,000.
(c) A fixed rate of interest.
(d) The payment of interest gross.

However, in general, the Committee was not keen on borrowing from the money market as a means of stabilising lending, largely because of the high costs that would be entailed.

By far the most important conclusion of the Stow Committee's deliberations was that building societies could fund mortgage demand from their traditional sources and the Committee also went on to say that societies should move with all reasonable speed to operating with competitive interest rates. The concluding paragraph of the Stow Report is set out below.

> The major conclusion of the Committee's work is that building societies should experience no difficulty in meeting mortgage demand from their traditional sources of funds and that there are no alternative sources of funds that would provide more mortgage money at a lower rate of interest. Some of the various alternative sources considered in this Report have their attractions but none could be used effectively unless societies' interest rate structures were at a competitive level. The Committee recommends that societies should move with all reasonable speed to a situation in which their interest rates are competitive as this should enable mortgage loans to be more readily available on demand, as is the case in most other advanced industrial countries.

Reaction to the Stow Report

In general, the Stow Report was very well received, which at first sight might seem surprising, given that it was in effect calling for higher mortgage rates. The quality of the analysis in support of the report's conclusions no doubt played an important part in gaining its acceptability. However, the publication of the report also coincided with a general change in sentiment towards housing with the belief being expressed more frequently that both owner-occupiers and tenants should pay a more realistic price for their housing and that the policy which had generally been adopted of holding down the price of housing artificially had had adverse consequences.

The Phillips Report

Arising from the Stow Report, the Council of the Association established, in March 1980, a working group to consider the feasibility of societies issuing marketable term securities and certificates of deposit (CDs). The group, which consisted entirely of building society executives, was chaired by Mr Brian Phillips of the Nationwide and it completed its report in August 1980. The working group examined in detail the various technical aspects and concluded that it would be worthwhile for building societies to raise money from the wholesale market. The Committee's conclusions are summarised below:

(a) Building society certificates of deposit could help to stabilise lending. However, societies would have to maintain a permanent presence in the CD market.
(b) Ready access to the wholesale money markets would permit building societies to operate with lower liquidity ratios.
(c) Building society CDs should have a 3–6 month duration, a minimum denomination of £100,000 and interest should be paid gross.
(d) All building societies could raise time deposits on the wholesale market.
(e) Building societies could offer a marketable, longer term, variable interest security.

To date, no building society has issued CDs or longer term marketable securities. However, two societies have issued marketable bonds, similar to local authority yearling bonds.

Chapter 10

Competition for Funds and the Wilson Report

The Growth of Competition Between Banks and Building Societies

The British financial system is unusual in that there are a variety of financial institutions, each operating in a specialist part of the market. Thus traditionally the merchant banks have been concerned with helping companies raise money, the clearing banks have provided a money transmission service and have provided funds for industry and the building societies have acted as savings banks and have provided mortgage loans. This sharp division of functions is unusual in other countries. In Western Europe, the general pattern is for there to be a closely integrated financial system with a number of types of institution competing with each other in the various markets. The savings banks are particularly strong, not only as providing homes for savings but also as mortgage lenders and, indeed, lenders to industry. In the other advanced industrial countries, building society-type organisations exist but there has tended to be a much closer overlap between their functions and those of the commercial banks and the savings banks. In Britain, however, building societies and banks, the two largest retail financial institutions, have tended to operate in separate segments of the market. The banks have been primarily concerned with the corporate customer and with providing a money transmission service for the personal individual. The banks have not sought to make mortgage loans nor have they been particularly vigorous in attracting savings deposits. By contrast, the building societies have confined their activities almost entirely to providing a savings bank service and to giving mortgage loans.

A common trend in recent years in those countries where there are specialised financial institutions such as building societies has been for there to be greater competition between these institutions and the more general banks. This is true of Britain, the United States, Canada, South Africa and Australia. A number of reasons can be deduced for this trend:

(a) Technological advances have made it considerably easier for the non-bank financial institutions to offer sophisticated services to personal customers and thus for these institutions to compete more directly with the banks. This is less true in Britain than in South Africa, Australia and the United States where the specialised housing finance organisations offer a money transmission service.

(b) The banks have increasingly realised that the mortgage market is a growing market and one in which there is a place for them to operate at a substantial profit. They have also seen mortgage lending as a means of introducing other business.

(c) The public have become more sophisticated financially and look for a higher standard of service from their financial institutions. One way of achieving this is for one institution to provide all the financial services that an individual needs and partly for this reason the various institutions have found it necessary to increase the range of services which they offer.

Chapter 2 traced the growth in building societies' share of the short-term personal deposit market. To a considerable extent, this growth went unnoticed until the mid-1970s. However, at about that time, the banks became increasingly concerned at the erosion of their share of the deposit market and it was natural to point to the growth in building societies' share of that market as being the cause. Table 10.1, taken from the evidence which the clearing banks submitted to the Wilson Committee, shows percentage shares of deposit holdings of UK residents with the principal institutions.

It will be noted that the London clearing banks suffered a very sharp decline in their market share between 1962 and 1976. To a significant extent, this was explained by an increased market share of the 'other banks', for the most part American banks. The market share for all banks declined only modestly over the period. The significant increase in building society market share appears to have been largely at the expense of the National Savings Bank and, to a lesser extent, the trustee savings banks.

The American banks have enjoyed considerable success in attracting deposits by concentrating on the most profitable part of the market. They have not offered a money transmission service but rather have attracted large deposits and made large loans, thereby enabling them to work on a very small operating margin. However, by the mid-1970s, the clearing banks in their public statements became increasingly critical of the special advantages which building societies were alleged to enjoy and no doubt they were influenced by the very visible growth in building society activity, not least through the ever-increasing number of branch offices. The totally different frameworks within which banks and building societies operate no doubt played a part in framing the banks' criticisms. The American banks, since 1971, have operated under much the same regulations as British banks and therefore logically the British banks could not argue that they enjoyed any unfair advantages.

The Establishment of the Wilson Committee

At the same time as the banks began to express publicly their concern about building societies, there was also a growing debate on the adequacy of the whole financial structure, in particular, whether the financial institutions were partly responsible for Britain's poor economic performance by being unwilling to provide sufficient funds to enable industry to invest. The opinion was also expressed in certain sections of the Labour Party that, on principle, the clearing banks should be nationalised.

Table 10.1 Deposit Holdings of UK Residents with Principal Institutions in UK: Percentage Shares, 1962–76

End-year	London clearing banks	Scottish and N. Ireland banks	Other banks	Total banks	Building societies	National Savings Bank	Trustee savings banks	Other	Total
1962	43.4	5.4	2.6	51.4	21.2	10.7	9.2	7.5	100.0
1963	42.2	5.1	3.6	51.0	22.2	9.9	9.5	7.4	100.0
1964	41.2	4.8	4.2	50.1	23.0	9.3	9.7	7.9	100.0
1965	39.9	4.7	4.9	49.5	24.3	8.6	9.6	8.0	100.0
1966	38.5	4.6	5.2	48.4	26.5	8.1	9.7	7.3	100.0
1967	37.5	4.6	6.4	48.5	28.3	7.2	9.2	6.7	100.0
1968	36.9	4.6	7.3	48.8	29.3	6.7	9.0	6.2	100.0
1969	35.2	4.4	7.6	47.3	31.4	6.3	8.7	6.3	100.0
1970	34.1	4.3	7.9	46.2	33.5	5.8	8.4	6.0	100.0
1971	31.8	4.0	7.5	44.5	36.0	5.4	8.3	5.8	100.0
1972	30.7	3.9	8.7	46.7	35.6	4.9	7.8	5.1	100.0
1973	31.5	4.1	12.1	50.3	33.3	4.2	6.8	5.4	100.0
1974	34.0	4.5	14.7	49.9	33.6	3.8	6.4	6.3	100.0
1975	32.4	4.3	11.4	48.1	36.4	3.4	6.2	5.8	100.0
1976	31.2	4.2	12.1	47.5	37.7	3.2	6.1	5.6	100.0

Note: There is a significant discontinuity in the series in 1971.
Sources: Financial Statistics; The London Clearing Banks (CLCB, 1978).

Perhaps to quieten down the general debate, the government announced the establishment of a Committee to Review the Functioning of Financial Institutions. The terms of reference, as set out in a Treasury minute of 5 January 1977, were:

> ... to enquire into the role and functioning, at home and abroad, of financial institutions in the United Kingdom and their value to the economy; to review in particular the provision of funds for industry and trade; to consider what changes are required in the existing arrangements for the supervision of these institutions, including the possible extension of the public sector, and to make recommendations.

It will be noted that the emphasis was very much on the provision of funds for industry and trade and moreover that the committee was asked specifically to examine the possible extension of the public sector.

The chairman of the committee was the former Prime Minister, Sir Harold Wilson, and the committee quickly came to be known as the Wilson Committee, an expression used in this book. The committee had eighteen members and, like similar committees, comprised the usual mixture of trade unionists, academics, journalists and representatives of the City. Significantly, the building society industry was not represented.

The deliberations of the Wilson Committee came to be the forum in which competition between building societies and banks was discussed and it also enabled the two sets of institutions to air their differences. The report of the committee contributed further to the discussion.

The terms of reference of the Wilson Committee were such as to lead The Building Societies Association to feel initially that the main thrust of the committee's work did not concern building societies and for this reason there was no necessity to produce a detailed volume of evidence. It was only when the banks' evidence, including as it did several criticisms of building societies, was published that The Building Societies Association decided to submit a major volume of evidence.

The Evidence Submitted by the London Clearing Bankers to the Wilson Committee

The banks were obviously the central target for the Wilson Committee's deliberations and for this reason the main representative organisation of the banks, the Committee of London Clearing Bankers, devoted considerable resources to preparing evidence for the committee. The CLCB made a preliminary submission to the committee on 'channelling funds to industry and trade' in April 1977 and a supplementary paper on this subject was issued in June 1977. The main volume of evidence was submitted in November 1977 and was subsequently published under the title of *The London Clearing Banks*, Evidence by the Committee of London Clearing Bankers to the Committee to Review the Functioning of Financial Institutions (Committee of London Clearing Bankers, 1978). This evidence in itself provides very valuable information on the banking system, in particular, the terms on which banks lend money. Among the major general points made in this evidence were:

(a) The main changes in the clearing banks' role in recent years have been their development into international institutions, their diversification and the increasingly competitive nature of their operations.

(b) In general, the UK financial system is well-equipped to meet the economy's needs.

(c) There were significant structural changes in the banking industry in the late 1960s as a result of mergers. All of the banks have extended their representation overseas and at home have developed merchant banking services and medium-term lending. The banks also now have wholly-owned finance house subsidiaries and are involved in credit cards.

(d) Virtually the entire cash distribution system in Britain depends on the clearing banks which also handle most non-cash payments. Cash and cheques remain dominant and talk of a 'cashless society' is premature.

(e) Balances in current accounts have grown more slowly than other deposits and they have become more expensive to operate. Since 1971 the banks have made greater use of large-scale deposits raised on the wholesale markets. The banks' deposit structure is predominantly short-term. The personal sector is the main provider of the banks' sterling deposits and they are in competition with a wide range of institutions and have lost market share to building societies in particular.

(f) Clearing banks maintain a substantial margin of liquid assets and they must also demonstrate their solvency by showing an appropriate margin of assets over liabilities. The banks welcome the fact that the Bank of England's responsibilities for the banking system are being extended and formalised but are concerned about the proposed deposit protection scheme.

(g) The need for monetary and credit controls is accepted but they should not be allowed to impede competition or supress innovation. Two regrettable developments were the corset controls and the restriction on bank deposit interest rates.

(h) The banks' lending role is conditioned by their deposit-taking activities but generally is responsive to demand. There is no evidence that investment has been held back because of lack of bank finance. Banks lend money on a variety of terms and conditions.

(i) Partly as a result of inflation, capital deposit ratios have deteriorated despite the raising of fresh capital. The banks' rates of return have been lower than those for industry in general and have been low in relation to those of major banks abroad.

(j) Increasingly the banks have dealt directly with government departments rather than through the Bank of England.

(k) There has been an erosion of the traditional demarcation lines between financial institutions. The banks welcome increased competition but savings banks and building societies enjoy various fiscal advantages and are exempt from monetary controls.

(l) There are no grounds for nationalising the banks.

The section of the evidence which achieved most publicity was that relating to the banks and other financial institutions. The relevant chapter (18) began by noting that there had been an erosion of the lines of demarcation separating the activities of the various sectors of the financial system. The banks themselves were held to have played a major role in this process by diversifying their own activities. It was noted that the banks had acquired finance house subsidiaries, developed personal loan schemes, offered credit cards and extended their 'merchant banking' activities. The evidence noted the growth of foreign banks in the City of London and commented that these provided very strong competition, especially in the field of the provision of finance for U K business of overseas companies and for multi-national and other large U K companies.

These developments were described as involving the commercial part of the financial system but the evidence went on to comment on the increase in competition between the clearing banks and the mutual and public sector institutions. The evidence argued that the overlap in lending services between these institutions and the banks was not unimportant; thus, although the clearing banks did little mortgage lending, it could well be the case that a person who takes out a large building society mortgage may have less need to borrow from a bank.

The evidence argued that the mutual and public sector institutions 'are endowed with artificial competitive advantages'. Examples given included the fiscal advantages enjoyed by the building societies, the advantages of savings banks and national savings in respect of payment of interest on savings, the inadequate capital base on which the Giro is allowed to expand its range of banking services and the unequal application of monetary and credit controls.

The detailed comments concerning building societies merit quoting in full as they set out virtually all of the alleged unfair advantages which building societies are held to enjoy:

18.13 The building societies have a less direct but important fiscal advantage in the arrangements whereby the societies are allowed to pay income tax on behalf of their depositors at the agreed 'composite rate'. This acts as an inducement to those paying income tax to place their funds with building societies rather than with banks; the societies benefit from the fact that tax-paying investors are evidently more sensitive to interest differentials than non-taxpayers. Building societies also have the advantage of a special low rate of corporation tax (40 per cent); moreover neither building societies nor savings banks are liable to corporation tax on gains arising on the sale of government securities, provided they have held them for more than twelve months.

18.14 The building societies, savings banks and Giro are all exempt from the monetary controls imposed on banks, though it is intended in due course to bring the T S Bs and Giro within the system. Building societies do have portfolio constraints of their own; but these are in force for prudential purposes rather than to limit the growth of the societies' liquid liabilities. Thus the building societies are not obliged to hold $12\frac{1}{2}$ per cent of their liabilities in the form of reserve assets. Much more important, however, has been the building societies' exemption from credit ceilings in the period up to 1971, and more recently from the 'corset' controls on interest-bearing deposits described in chapter 6. In addition the clearing banks were subjected between September 1973 and February 1975 to a restriction on their deposit rates in order to limit their ability to compete with building societies.

18.15　The prudential constraints which these institutions are expected to observe in order to ensure their capital adequacy are also less onerous than those observed by commercial banks. Again, it is intended eventually to bring the TSBs within the same framework as the banks, although it is not yet clear how they will be furnished with the necessary capital resources. The inadequate capitalisation of the Giro has been defended by a government spokesman with the observation that the resources of the Post Office stand behind it. Clearly this involves subsidisation of the Giro by other parts of the Post Office. The clearing banks believe that a formal separation of the Giro from the rest of the Post Office would make it much easier for the Giro to be treated in the same way as other institutions.

18.16　The nature of the competition between the banks and the building societies and TSBs is also affected by these institutions' mutual form of organisation. Not only does this mean that they are able to add to their capital resources sums which a commercial bank would have distributed in dividends, but it may also affect their attitude to new investment in their businesses and to the rates of interest they charge and pay. Provided that they are earning a sufficient surplus to maintain suitable prudential ratios, they have no clear incentive to ensure that new ventures are profitable. In this respect the position of the building societies and TSBs is quite different from that of mutual insurance companies, where the benefits of profitable management are enjoyed by the policyholders in the form of bonuses. Where institutions are not effectively owned by anyone, there can sometimes arise in an especially acute form the problems of the separation of ownership from control. In the case of the TSBs no such problems appear to have arisen hitherto; but this has been largely because their discretion has been severely limited by government controls and they have been unable either to earn worthwhile surpluses or to expand and diversify their business. Now that these controls are to be relaxed it remains to be seen how far the TSBs will feel constrained by commercial disciplines.

18.17　In the case of the building societies the clearing banks recognise that the advantages bestowed on them reflect an official commitment to support the ideal of home ownership. The banks do not disagree with the importance of this ideal but they consider that there is a need for some rationalisation of the authorities' sometimes inconsistent attempts to encourage the flow of resources to a multitude of sectors (such as industry, housing, exports and the government itself). The building societies are now of such size and importance that fuller consideration than hitherto should be given to the effects of their activities on other financial institutions and markets so as to avoid undesired distortions in the allocation of savings and credit. In particular, the banks consider that there is a strong case for providing any subsidy to home ownership which the authorities deem appropriate directly to home buyers and letting the building societies compete with other institutions on equal terms.

18.18　In the first place this would reduce the present distortion in the distribution of intermediation between the building societies and other institutions and might encourage other institutions to compete with the building societies in the home mortgage market. How far they would wish to do so is hard to say, but the extra flexibility so created could only be beneficial. Secondly, the present privileged financial circuit would cease to exist and the way would be open for the building societies to become more integrated with the rest of the financial system. On this subject the clearing banks note with interest two suggestions in the government's recent consultative document on housing policy. These were that building societies should be prepared to raise short-term loans on the money market and that consideration should be given to the possibility of channelling funds from the investing institutions into housing finance. Thirdly, the cost of the subsidy would be known and subject to public scrutiny and it would be met by the exchequer rather than distributed arbitrarily among a range of participants in the financial markets. (*The London Clearing Banks*, Evidence by the Committee of London Clearing Bankers to the Committee to Review the Functioning of Financial Institutions, Chapter 18, CLCB, 1978)

The Evidence Submitted by The Building Societies Association to the Wilson Committee

The point has already been made that initially The Building Societies Association considered that the Wilson Committee would not be greatly concerned with the activities of societies. The Association responded to an invitation from the Committee to submit evidence on the supply of funds to industry and trade. A short paper on the provision of building finance was duly submitted in June 1977. The Association was then invited to submit evidence on the structure and functioning of financial institutions. This was done in September 1977. It was only after the submission of this evidence that it became clear that the clearing banks intended to comment critically about building societies in their evidence. Following publication of the clearing banks' evidence early in 1978, the Association decided to submit a more detailed volume of evidence and this was done in September 1978.

The first two sections of the evidence described the development and structure of the building society movement and the role of The Building Societies Association. The third section explained the prudential and credit controls to which building societies are subject, pointing out inter alia:

(a) Societies are able to lend only against the security of a mortgage held on freehold or leasehold estate.
(b) The special advance limit means that the bulk of such loans must be of modest size.
(c) Societies must maintain a proportion of their funds in liquid form and the manner in which they can invest those funds is closely circumscribed.
(d) In practice, societies must meet the requirements for designation for trustee status.

The Association commented that the adequacy of the prudential controls is evidenced by the fact that societies have an exceptionally good reputation for safety. Concluding this point, the Association stated:

Taking all factors into account, the Association believes that the controls to which building societies are subject are, for the most part, those appropriate to their operation. The controls are different from those applying to other institutions because the nature of the societies' business is specialised and strictly circumscribed. The requirement that societies should lend only against the security of freehold or leasehold estate, together with the controls on the manner in which liquid funds can be invested are, combined with a cautious lending policy, such as to ensure that the risk of loss is very small indeed. This means that societies need a smaller margin of assets over liabilities than do other institutions whose activities are not controlled so tightly.

Turning to credit controls, the Association commented that it was correct to say that building societies have not been subject to the controls imposed on the banking system but argued that the reason for this is that societies' lending is confined to mortgage loans and other loans relevant to housing so that general credit controls would not be appropriate. The Association added that the government had sought to influence building society lending in the context of the housing market through the medium of the Joint Advisory Committee.

Section IV of the Association's evidence set out the role of societies in the savings market. This section begins with an historical analysis of the role of societies in the savings market and a description of the capital structure of building societies and the characteristics of their investors. The Association offered the following comments on the reasons why building societies have grown so rapidly as savings institutions:

(a) They have expanded their branches in order to attract additional savings and branches are open for nearly as many hours a week as retail shops.
(b) Savings have been attracted because of the role of societies as providers of mortgage finance. Many investors originally open an account so as to assist them in obtaining a loan.
(c) Societies have kept their service simple and by efficient administration they have been able to keep their costs to a minimum.

The Association commented briefly on the composite rate of income tax, arguing that it was not introduced to give societies a competitive advantage but that it was of great administrative convenience to societies and to the Inland Revenue. However, the Association admitted that without the composite rate, the cost of the interest paid to investors and therefore the amount charged to home-buyers would rise to some extent although it went on to argue that this would not significantly affect the overall demand for mortgages because the mortgage rate is always held below a market clearing level.

The Association commented on competition which societies faced from government and argued that this competition had become distorted in that the government has given fiscal advantages to holders of its own securities. For example, national savings certificates are particularly attractive to higher rate taxpayers as are low coupon gilts with a guaranteed tax-free capital gain.

The most significant part of the Association's evidence was Section V which dealt with the economic and financial effects of building society lending. To a large extent this section replied to the accusation that building societies had been too successful and by attracting an ever-increasing volume of funds and using these funds to finance house-purchase, they had been depriving industry of the funds needed to finance investment. The Association emphatically rejected such arguments. It was noted that only one fifth of bank lending was to manufacturing industry as such and, more significantly, it added that the evidence showed quite clearly that industry had not been suffering from lack of capital funds but rather there had been a lack of demand for capital by the corporate sector. In this respect, the Association was echoing the evidence submitted by the Committee of London Clearing Bankers.

The evidence analysed in detail the influence of building society lending on the use of real resources in the economy. The difference between financial and real resources was emphasised. It was noted, for example, that if bank notes totalling £10 million were destroyed in a fire then there would, in real terms, be no loss at all and bank notes of a further £10 million could be printed at no material cost to the economy. However, if a factory worth £10 million was destroyed then it would be necessary to rebuild it and this would require the use of real resources that might otherwise have been put to some alternative use. It was noted that it had been fashionable some time earlier to argue that Britain devoted an exceptionally small proportion of resources to housing but that recently it had become more common to argue that too many of the country's resources were going into housing at the expense of industrial investment. The Association pointed out that investment in dwellings had in fact been accounting for a declining proportion of total gross fixed capital formation, from about 20 per cent of the total in 1967 to 17 per cent in 1977. Moreover, it was noted that total investment in dwellings as a percentage of GDP had declined from 4.4 per cent in 1967 to 3.1 per cent in 1977. The Association reproduced a table from the Consultative Document *Housing Policy* showing that the proportion of GDP accounted for by investment in housing was lower in Britain than the average for other advanced industrial countries.

The Association argued that not all investment in housing was financed by borrowing, particularly in the private sector where many purchasers put in a fairly substantial deposit. It was noted that only one half of total expenditure on new private housing was financed by building society loans and that of all capital expenditure on housing, only a quarter was financed by societies.

The evidence pointed out that the bulk of building society lending was on the security of existing dwellings and that such lending had no direct influence on the allocation of real resources in the economy. The relevant section of the Association's evidence is reproduced below.

It is important to establish that building society lending on existing dwellings does not influence the real economy directly. Taking the most simple example, if two existing owner-occupiers wish to exchange their houses and both redeem building society loans on the houses which they are selling, and take out loans for an equal size on the houses which they are purchasing, then all that has happened is that the two people have moved house, yet building societies will have advanced money to both, even though, in net terms, the advances will have been zero and there would be no effects on the economy as a whole.

Whenever a building society lends money to enable someone to purchase an existing house, the vendor will receive a cheque from the purchaser. Thus, a financial liability is incurred on behalf of the purchaser while a financial asset is created on behalf of the vendor. (Conversely, the purchaser acquires a real asset at the expense of the vendor.) The money which the vendor receives does not 'disappear' so the building society lending is not, in any way, 'used up' in the purchase of existing housing. The crucial point is that, for every purchaser of an *existing* asset, there must also be a seller and funds cannot, in any way, be 'used up' in the purchase of an asset. It is only expenditure on new dwellings and the improvement of existing dwellings which utilises real resources; expenditure on secondhand houses merely involves a redistribution of financial and real liabilities and assets.

The real debate therefore should be about the distribution of the economy's real resources, the balance between the community's income and consumption, and the proportion of real investment absorbed by housing and other forms of real investment. In the final analysis, the real resources available for all types of investment (including housing) are determined by the balance between the country's real income and real consumption. The personal sector, the corporate sector and the Government sector both save and invest and any imbalance between total domestic savings and investment must be reflected in a balance of payments surplus or deficit.

For a given level of real income (either at full employment or at a policy-determined level) if the community's investment plans exceed total real savings then the claims on the country's real resources will exceed the available supply. This will be reflected in a combination of rising prices and a balance of payments deficit. However, in the final analysis, only at full employment (that is where the country's real resources are fully utilised) can it be argued that the housing sector may be absorbing real resources that might otherwise have been available for industrial investment. For many years Britain has not been in this situation because the economy has been operating at less-than-full capacity and the industrial sector's investment demand has been weak. Building societies have done no more than respond to the clear preferences of individuals by channelling savings to where the demand is greatest; that is, to finance house-purchase loans. The fact that societies are seldom able to meet the demand for mortgage funds indicates that the community's preference for private housing is not being met in full, notwithstanding the weak industrial demand for credit.

Section V of the Association's evidence concluded with a brief discussion of the effect of building society intermediation on the volume of credit. It was noted that societies could make loans only after they had received investments and the effect of their activity on the total volume of credit depended on what would otherwise have been the alternative use of the investments received. Four major alternatives were identified:

(a) Deposits with a clearing bank.
(b) Spending on goods and services.

(c) Loans to the public sector.
(d) Loans elsewhere in the private sector.

In the case of (a), the transfer to building societies would increase the potential aggregate volume of credit and the level of aggregate demand because the lending ability of building societies would be raised while the credit potential of the banking sector would not be affected. In the case of (b), the aggregate volume of credit would be increased and when the funds were on-lent to home-buyers, the overall effect would be an unchanged level of aggregate demand because the decrease in aggregate demand as a consequence of investors refraining from the purchase of goods and services would be counterbalanced by the increase in demand via loans for house-purchasers. In the case of (c), there would be an increase in the total credit potential of the financial sector and possibly also an increase in the volume of bank deposits. In the case of (d), then only the structure of a given volume of credit and aggregate demand would be altered.

On this point, the Association concluded that the overall effects of building society intermediation upon the volume of credit and the money supply were complex and it was noted also that if building societies did not lend for house-purchase then their acquisition of government debt could affect the money supply by enabling the government to finance its deficit in a non-inflationary way.

Section VI of the Association's evidence concerned rates of interest. This section began with the Association arguing that societies were convinced 'that stability is desired by the majority of their investing and borrowing members'. It was pointed out that since the beginning of 1975 the mortgage rate had changed seven times whereas M L R had been changed fifty-four times. It was noted that because societies steer a steady course without following every change in the general level of interest rates, it follows that they experience substantial variations in their competitive position vis-à-vis other institutions and hence in the volume of net inflow which they are able to attract. To prevent these fluctuations leading to fluctuations of equal magnitude in the level of new lending, the Association pointed out that societies have operated a stabilisation policy whereby liquid assets are built up when savings inflow is at a high level and these assets are run down when net inflow falls off.

In this section of its evidence, the Association pointed to the importance of the variable rate mortgage. It was noted that such was the volume of funds which societies are required to raise that a substantial proportion of their capital will always need to be raised on a short-term basis. However, mortgage loans had to be made for long terms. The device which made it possible for societies to borrow short and lend long was held to be the variable interest rate mortgage which means that in the event of a rise in the general level of interest rates, societies are able to increase the rates charged on practically all existing mortgages and thereby raise sufficient income to enable higher interest rates to be paid to their investors.

The Association considered the argument that building societies might change their investment rate more often while making less frequent adjustments to the mortgage rate. The Association was sceptical about this proposal, pointing out that it would be very difficult to reduce the investment rate without there being a reduction in the mortgage rate because of public and political pressure. There was also the prudential danger that what appeared to be a short-term increase in interest rates might turn into a long-term increase and societies might therefore run into margin problems.

In a letter to the Bank of England dated 27 January 1978 and widely leaked to the press, the Committee of London Clearing Bankers had noted that building society interest rates were relatively inflexible and argued that this had a disruptive effect on other financial institutions. The Association replied to this point by saying that less frequent interest rate adjustments did not confer any advantage on societies but rather reflected the demands of their consumers.

Finally in Section VI the Association commented very briefly on the recommended rate system by which societies pay and charge on the bulk of their business the rates recommended by The Building Societies Association. The Association recognised that some disadvantages could be claimed for the relative lack of competition between societies on interest rates but argued that societies were convinced that any major discrepancy in the rates offered to investors by the larger societies would quickly be eliminated and also that in any foreseeable circumstances free competition would result in a generally higher level of mortgage interest rates. On this subject, the Association concluded that it considered: 'that, on balance, stability and order are preferable to the uncertainties in the minds of millions of investors and borrowers which unbridled competition would bring'.

Shortly after submitting their volume of written evidence, representatives of the Association were invited to give oral evidence to the Wilson Committee and this was duly done on 28 November 1978. Little that was new came out of this session of oral evidence and for the most part the questioning related to matters which were internal to the building society industry.

The Committee showed a particular interest in the growth of the management expense ratio of societies and on 25 January 1979, the Association submitted a further memorandum to the committee (reprinted in *Studies in Building Society Activity 1974–79*, The Building Societies Association, 1980). This memorandum pointed out that an increase in the rate of inflation has a direct effect on the total of management expenses but an effect only on the increment to savings balances. Therefore, an increase in the rate of inflation will increase management expenses in relation to savings balances and so the management expense ratio. The Association commented that this theoretical approach was confirmed by empirical evidence and also by the experience of other financial institutions. The memorandum pointed out that the average cost of operating each building society account had declined in real terms since 1969, notwithstanding an increase in the number of transactions per account.

The Wilson Committee Report

The Report of the Wilson Committee was published in June 1980 (*Committee to Review the Functioning of Financial Institutions, Report*, Cmnd 9357, HMSO 1980). The Report runs to nearly 400 pages and is accompanied by a volume of appendices comprising a further 200 pages. The evidence submitted to the Committee had been published previously in a series of volumes.

The Report itself provides a valuable description of the functioning of financial institutions and the operation of the money markets and, as with the Green Paper *Housing Policy*, the usefulness of the analytical work will continue long after the major conclusions of the Report have been forgotten.

Before dealing in detail with the sections of the Report concerned directly with building societies, it is helpful to set out the major conclusions of the committee's deliberations.

(a) The financial institutions, and especially the pension funds and insurance companies, have been assuming growing importance in the capital market. This has far-reaching implications for the rest of the financial system.

(b) The contention has been made that real investment in the UK has been unnecessarily constrained by shortages in the supply of external finance but given the highly developed state of the British financial system and the relative freedom accorded to the institutions operating in it, it was no great surprise to find that this was not generally the case. It is the price of finance in relation to expected profitability which is the major financial constraint on real investment.

(c) High and fluctuating rates of inflation have had pervasive effects on the financial system and on real investment. One important manifestation of this has been the drying-up of new issues of long-term industrial bonds. A medium term re-discount facility might help ameliorate the immediate effects and in the longer term, experimentation with index-linked industrial bonds should be considered.

(d) So as to assist the provision of finance to small firms, the establishment of a loan guarantee scheme is recommended together with the creation of an English development agency to supplement the existing Welsh and Scottish development agencies.

(e) The operation of financial institutions and competition between them is influenced by biases in the taxation system and by controls imposed for prudential or monetary reasons. Building societies in particular have benefited from the favourable tax treatment accorded to them and also by the reliefs given for owner-occupation. Complete neutrality of treatment for different types of financial institutions is neither necessary nor desirable but unintended and unnecessary divergencies from neutrality should be avoided.

(f) Building societies have grown very fast but the competition between them is severely constrained by the recommended rates system which should be abolished.

(g) The contrast between statutory and non-statutory forms of regulation is less sharp than is often made out and no recommendation is made in favour of greater statutory controls. However, the present system is felt to be not wholly satisfactory, partly because of the extent to which non-statutory regulation takes the form of self-regulation.

(h) There is a need for an open and publicly accountable body with responsibility for reviewing the overall arrangements for the regulation of the financial system.

(i) The role of the Bank of England has been broadened in recent years and the Bank's accountability itself has been widened through it being subject to the Parliamentary Select Committee on the Treasury and Civil Service Department. Non-executive directors of the Bank should be drawn from a wider range of backgrounds.

(j) No extension of the public sector by the nationalisation of existing institutions is called for.

The Report noted the substantial rise in the volume of personal sector intermediation and the resultant role of the financial institutions in the economic life of the nation. Two chapters of the Report are specifically concerned with building societies:

(a) Chapter 8 – 'Building societies and the recommended rates system'.
(b) Chapter 24 – 'The prudential regulation of building societies'.

Following is a summary of the major points made in these two chapters and also one or two points from other chapters which touch on the operation of building societies:

(a) Building societies have grown rapidly, partly because they offer a simple, efficient, easily understood service to depositors for which no explicit charges are levied. Probably the main reason for their growth has been the attractiveness of home-ownership, which stems partly from the tax advantages available to owner-occupiers. Another factor has been the composite tax.
(b) The interest rate 'cartel' produces doubtful benefits and, by encouraging non-price competition, is wasteful of resources. The only way to provide a competitive spur to building societies is to end the recommended rate system and the Committee recommends its abolition. Pressure to set competitive rates should encourage administrative efficiency and cutting of costs. The Committee recognised that the mortgage rate would probably rise. However, the housing market and the construction industry would benefit.
(c) More competitive behaviour by societies should go hand-in-hand with a more even treatment of them, relative to other institutions, by the authorities.
(d) On balance, building societies should not be brought within the scope of monetary control at present. The case for doing so would become stronger if they were to extend their range of lending in competition with banks and finance houses.
(e) Owner-occupation enjoys considerable tax privileges which in total constitute a substantial inducement to borrow for personal housing purposes and to maximise the proportion of total borrowing by way of mortgage. One way of avoiding future unintended changes in the value of relief would be to replace it with a direct interest rate subsidy, similar to the arrangements for life assurance premiums.
(f) The composite rate system gives building societies a competitive advantage; moreover, the Committee believes it is wrong to allow non-taxpaying building society depositors (many of whom are not aware of the true situation) to subsidise taxpaying depositors or the house-purchaser. The Committee recommends that the composite rate arrange-

ment should be terminated and that some means should be found to allow non-taxpaying depositors to receive interest at the gross rate. It also recommends that consideration should be given to putting the tax treatment of interest payments by all deposit-taking institutions on a common basis.

(g) The Committee recommends that building societies should pay corporation tax at 52 per cent rather than the reduced rate of 40 per cent.

(h) Investment in housing in the UK has not been excessive by international standards in recent years and some stimulus to house-building might be given by extending the option mortgage arrangements to index-linked loans thereby encouraging societies to tap the pension funds.

(i) The building society movement has a good record over the last twenty years in terms of avoiding losses to depositors but it would be wrong to continue relying on this, particularly if competition between societies increases. The opportunity offered by the need to legislate to implement the European Community directive should be taken to strengthen the prudential arrangements in five areas:

  (i) The conditions for registration should be tightened up; for example, a minimum level of reserves should be set statutorily for all societies and the chief registrar should have the power to prescribe minimum liquidity ratios.

  (ii) The chief registrar should be given powers to promote mergers or to enforce the winding-up of a society for prudential reasons.

  (iii) A more formal and comprehensive monitoring system is required and the Registry can no longer continue to place the same degree of reliance on the validity of accounts submitted. The Committee recommends that the scope and frequency of Registry contacts with individual societies should be reconsidered and that the present voluntary cash flow statements should become a statutory requirement.

  (iv) The building society aspects of the Registry's work should be separated from its other functions and steps should be taken to equip the new organisation with additional suitably qualified staff.

  (v) A deposit protection scheme should be set up on a statutory basis and there is a strong case for giving the same 100 per cent protection that is now implicitly provided to members of the Association.

Reaction to the Wilson Committee Report

It needs to be remembered that the Wilson Committee was established by a Labour government and one of the objectives of the government was to remove from public debate, and more particularly debate within the Labour Party, the question of nationalising the various financial institutions. The Report was published after the Conservative government had gained power and therefore, inevitably, it had less impact on the government than might have been the case had the Labour Party still been in power. If only by inaction, the government made it clear that it did not intend to take any action as a result of the recommendations of the Wilson Committee although it was of course open to any financial institution to seek changes based on the recommendations of the committee.

The committee's most critical comments were reserved for building societies and these received a considerable amount of publicity. The Association felt it necessary to issue a press statement about the report. The following points were made in this statement:

(a) It was noted that the report recommended the abolition of the recommended rate system. The Association argued that the prime effect of the system was to bring order and stability into the financial markets which directly affect millions of people. The abolition of recommended interest rates would mean higher mortgage interest rates which would have profound consequences for existing borrowers. The Association pointed out that the recommended rate system was not rigid and societies were free to pay and charge whatever rates they wished. The Association rejected the suggestion that the recommended rate system was wasteful of resources but rather argued that branch offices and advertising were essential to attract deposits and that societies' management expenses were low compared with those of other institutions.

(b) With regard to the composite rate arrangements, the Association pointed out that there was no subsidy from the Exchequer but that abolition of the arrangements would cause an increase in the mortgage rate. It was noted that the system was of great administrative convenience to the Inland Revenue, societies and their investors.

(c) The extension of the option mortgage scheme to replace the present tax relief system on mortgage interest would, the Association noted, increase the cost of home loans for higher rate taxpayers and would have wider implications which would need to be carefully studied.

(d) The Association accepted that any deposit protection scheme needed to be on a statutory basis but did not see why building society depositors should have 100 per cent protection whereas the protection scheme for the banks provides for only 75 per cent protection.

There has been little further discussion of the Wilson Report's recommendations and indeed it was not until January 1981 that the matter was debated in the House of Commons and then it was on a Private Member's motion. The government made no commitment towards implementing any of the recommendations. However, the importance of the Wilson Report should not be underestimated in that it provided a very valuable analysis of the financial system in Britain and this alone has helped to provide for more educated debate.

Publication of the Report probably helped to change attitudes in favour of a more competitive environment for financial institutions. Direct controls on the banking system were eased in favour of a market approach to controlling the rate of growth of the money supply. At the same time the banks saw the need to expand their services to the personal sector and the combination of these two factors led to aggressive bank marketing of both savings and mortgage schemes. The implications of this competition are considered in detail in Chapter 16.

Chapter 11

Building Societies and Monetary Policy

One issue which the Wilson Committee touched on but did not examine in depth was the importance of building society activity for monetary policy. Inevitably, as building societies increased in size in relation to the banks, the opinion began to be expressed that building society deposits were similar in nature to bank deposits and should therefore be included within any definition of the money supply which the authorities sought to control. The reason for building societies being outside of the traditional framework of monetary policy was set out by the Governor of the Bank of England in his speech to the annual conference of The Building Societies Association in May 1978:

> The building societies lend predominantly to a specialised market in which the banks are hardly engaged, save as providers of bridging finance. This traditional demarcation has justified a difference of treatment by the authorities in respect of guidance or other official influence on lending. However, the greater the breaking down of this demarcation as a result of ventures into house lending by the banks or increased use of loans from building societies to finance purchases other than of houses, the stronger the case would be for treating building societies and banks similarly for monetary policy purposes.

The Association had largely relied on this reasoning in giving its evidence to the Wilson Committee although this did briefly examine the effect of building society activity on the volume of credit and, as has already been noted, it was pointed out that the overall effect of building society intermediation was complex and depended to a large extent on the alternative use to which funds invested in building societies might otherwise have been put and on the ultimate destination of building society loans.

The Wilson Committee itself devoted just one paragraph to this issue. It noted that a change in relative interest rates could cause a sizeable shift of deposits from the building societies to the banks or vice versa and therefore recognised that there was a case for including societies within any monetary control scheme. However, the report went on to note that societies do not compete in the short-term credit markets and also that the supply of mortgage finance was of special political importance. On balance, the committee did not think that building societies should be brought into the scope of monetary control although, echoing the views of the Governor of the Bank of England in 1978, it concluded by saying: 'The case for doing so would, however, become stronger if they were able to extend their range of lending in competition with banks and finance houses.'

The Rationale for Monetary Policy

In order to examine this issue, it is first necessary to analyse why government seeks to control the money supply. This is of course an economic issue and discussion of this point will be found in any standard economic textbook. What follows is a very brief summary.

Monetarist theory, as it has come to be known, rests on the principle that the rate of increase in prices can be related directly to the rate of growth of the money supply. Monetarists argue that an increase in the supply of any commodity, including money, relative to the supply of all other commodities, will cause the commodity in question, including money, to fall in value as against all other commodities. This theory rests on three basic assumptions:

(a) That the demand for money is stable and changes to a known and relatively fixed extent in response to changes in other variables in the economy, such as incomes and rates of interest.
(b) That the magnitude of the stock of money is not determined by the level of activity taking place in the economy but rather can be determined by government.
(c) Money does not enter the economy in order to accommodate changes in incomes or prices but rather causes those variables to change.

Monetarist theory has been increasingly accepted in recent years and has formed the basis of British economic policy, albeit with varying degrees of enthusiasm, since the visit of an IMF team to London in 1976.

The Definition of Money

In order to control the money supply, it is first necessary to decide what constitutes money and this is not as simple as might appear to be the case at first sight. Money is usually defined as anything which is generally acceptable by the public in payment for goods, services or other assets. Legally, only notes and cash are acceptable for these purposes but transfers from current bank accounts are of course generally acceptable as a means of payment. Current accounts with banks together with notes and coins form the narrowest definition of the money supply, known officially as M1.

A considerable volume of funds is held on seven-day deposit with banks and as these are easily withdrawable on demand they exhibit many of the characteristics of bank current accounts. A wider official definition of money (M3) includes deposit accounts in banks in addition to the components of M1. Sterling M3 (£M3) excludes UK residents' deposits held in foreign currencies. These components of the money supply are shown in Table 11.1.

Table 11.1   Main Components of the Money Supply, 15 July 1981

	£m.	£m.
Notes and coins in circulation with the public	10,472	
+ U K private sector sterling sight deposits	21,833	
= Money stock M1		32,305
+ Private sector time deposits	39,033	
+ Public sector time and sight deposits	1,336	
= Sterling money stock £M3		72,674
+ U K residents' deposits in other currencies	10,101	
= Money stock M3		82,775

Source: *Financial Statistics*, August 1981, Table 7.1.

At first sight, there are grounds for saying that shares and deposits in building societies are as liquid as bank deposits. Most money deposited with building societies can be withdrawn on demand and indeed the fact that building society branches, unlike bank branches, are open on Saturday mornings makes societies an even more liquid source of funds than bank accounts for some people. It is also a fact that building societies do have the capacity to create credit in that their lending can come back to them in the form of deposits. However, building society deposits, unlike bank deposits, cannot be transferred by cheque and therefore cannot normally be used as a medium of exchange.

However, it can be argued that building society deposits, like the deposits of other non-bank financial intermediaries, are different in nature from bank deposits. A simple example can illustrate this. Assume an individual wishes to reduce his bank deposit balance and to increase his building society balance. He therefore pays to the society a cheque for, say, £100. Obviously the individual's bank account falls by £100 and his building society deposit increases by £100, but equally obviously the total amount of bank balances is not affected because the society has a bank balance £100 higher and the individual a bank balance £100 lower. Similarly, when the building society lends the £100, the recipient of the funds will initially have a bank account £100 higher, the building society an account £100 lower. Thus, the nominal amount of bank deposits is not for the most part affected by changes in building society deposits and sterling M3 is therefore largely unaffected by building society activity.

However, it has to be accepted that this argument is valid only if the source and destination of building society deposits are bank accounts. The crucial question is the extent to which building society activity induces a transfer of funds to or from the public sector. This point was touched on in the Association's evidence to the Wilson Committee and indeed has already been described briefly in the previous chapter. The point needs to be developed in more detail. If societies attract deposits away from national savings or induce net private sector sales of gilt-edged stock, the government may be forced to issue Treasury Bills to cover its short-term needs. This results in an increase in reserve assets for the banking system and creates the possibility of a multiple creation of credit by the banks. David Llewellyn ('Do building societies take deposits away from banks?' *Lloyds Bank Review*, January 1979) summarised the position as follows: 'The initial monetary effect of a switch of funds to the building societies is either a rise in the money supply (and possibly an increased supply of reserve assests to the banking system) to the extent that the inflow is from the public sector debt, or simply a change in ownership of bank deposits.'

Having attracted deposits, building societies have three options open to them:

(a) To lend to the public sector through increasing their liquidity.
(b) To lend on mortgage.
(c) To acquire bank deposits.

Lending to the public sector will reduce the need for the government to fund its borrowing requirement from the banking sector and hence will tend to reduce £M3. As has already been pointed out, the acquisition of bank deposits will leave the money supply unchanged. An increase in mortgage lending will not affect the money supply but will lead to an increase in the amount of credit in the economy. Thus in summary societies have the power to inflate the money supply if they are able to acquire funds from the public sector.

This influence on the level of activity in the economy is far less direct than is the influence of a growth in bank deposits and therefore there are grounds for treating deposits with building societies and bank deposits separately for purposes of monetary control although the point has already been made that the more similar banks and building societies become, the greater is the case for shares and deposits in building societies being within the target money supply variable.

Although official policy has been to exclude building society shares and deposits from the main monetary aggregates at which control is directed, there has been an increasing interest in wider measures of liquidity. Some City analysts have developed their own concepts of 'M4' and 'M5' which include other liquid deposits such as Treasury Bills, local authority deposits and shares and deposits with building societies. In 1979, the Bank of England decided that it would be appropriate to introduce an official wider definition of liquid assets held by the private sector. An article in the *Bank of England Quarterly Bulletin* ('Components of private sector liquidity', *Bank of England Quarterly Bulletin,* September 1979) set out a selection of short-term financial assets which, for the most part, were limited to sterling assets within one year of maturity or realisable within a year without significant loss of interest or capital. Obviously, shares and deposits with building societies were included in this definition. However, because not all building society shares and deposits are liquid, some adjustment to the overall totals had to be made. The figures excluded term shares with an original maturity of over one year, SAYE deposits and shares and deposits held by overseas residents. In order to avoid double counting, building society holdings of money, money market and other savings instruments had to be excluded from the total.

Following the publication of the article, the government has regularly published tables for two measures of private sector liquidity which have come to be known as PSL 1 and PSL 2. PSL 1 includes money, other money market instruments and certificates of tax deposit. The second wider measure, PSL 2, includes retail liquidity of the personal sector in the form of building society shares and deposits and other similar forms of liquid savings instruments. Table 11.2 shows the components of private sector liquidity as at 15 July 1981 and the figures can usefully be compared with figures for the money supply as at the same date shown in Table 11.1.

Table 11.2   Components of Private Sector Liquidity, 15 July 1981

Component	£m.	£m.	£m.
Money (seasonally adjusted)		69,922	
+ Other money market instruments		4,434	
+ Certificates of tax deposit (gross)		1,311	
= PSL 1 (seasonally adjusted)			75,667
Shares and deposits with building societies	45,762		
+ Deposits with trustee savings banks	5,940		
+ Deposits with the National Savings Bank	4,404		
+ National savings securities	1,890		
− Savings institutions holdings of money, money market instruments and deposits in other institutions	3,567		
= Savings deposits and securities		54,429	
Savings deposits and securities (seasonally adjusted)			54,129
+ PSL1 (seasonally adjusted)			75,667
− Savings institutions holdings of certificates of tax deposit			237
= PSL2 (seasonally adjusted)			129,559

Source: Financial Statistics, August 1981, Table 7.6.

It will be seen that shares and deposits with building societies accounted for 84.1 per cent of savings deposits and securities and 35.3 per cent of the total PSL 2. It is significant to note that included with building society shares and deposits in the definition of 'savings deposits and securities' are deposits with the National Savings Bank, deposits with trustee savings banks and national savings securities. Such instruments are comparable to building society shares and deposits and therefore need to be treated in a similar manner in measuring definitions of money or liquidity. It is also relevant to note that from November 1981 deposits in the trustee savings banks are included in sterling M3.

Figures for PSL 1 and PSL 2 are published regularly and are monitored by the government and financial analysts along with figures for the more readily accepted definitions of the money supply, M1 and £M3. Should the government decide to concentrate on a wider monetary aggregate as its target for monetary policy then PSL 1 and PSL 2 provide the means by which this can be achieved.

Recent Developments in Monetary Policy

Recent discussion as to whether building society shares and deposits should be included within the definition of the money supply which the government seeks to control has been accompanied by a change in the techniques of monetary control. To a considerable extent these changes remove the complaints which banks justifiably had in that they were subject to a competitive disadvantage by being singled out as the means by which monetary policy was implemented. Also they partially remove from discussion the need to 'bring building societies within monetary controls'.

In order to develop this point it is necessary first to explain how monetary policy has been implemented in the past. The government's main target has been sterling M3 and the ways in which this can be influenced can best be explained by showing an identity:

Change in £M3 = public sector borrowing requirement
    − sales of public sector debt to non-bank private sector
    + sterling lending to UK private sector
    − external financial outflows.

Broadly speaking, the government can control the money supply in two ways. Either it can cut the public sector borrowing requirement by increasing taxation or reducing expenditure or it can seek to influence the level of interest rates. A high level of interest rates will help to finance sales of public sector debt and will also reduce private sector demand for bank finance, albeit after a considerable time lag. High interest rates may also induce financial inflows from abroad however and can thus serve to frustrate a restrictive monetary policy unless the exchange rate is allowed to appreciate.

The Bank of England used to be able to influence interest rates directly by manipulating minimum lending rate or more recently by its own operations in the open market. Also, the banks were subject to a reserve asset ratio by which they were obliged to hold 12.5 per cent of their eligible liabilities (basically sterling deposit liabilities) in specified reserve assets. Included in these assets were balances with the Bank of England, Treasury Bills, money at call with the London money markets, gilt edged stock with less than a year to maturity, certain local authority bills and certain commercial bills of exchange. The requirement to hold reserve assets could have been used to control the rate at which the banks were capable of creating credit. In simple terms, a bank could not create credit unless it could increase its supply of reserve assets. However, in practice, the authorities were not able to control the supply of reserve assets for a number of reasons. One of these was that institutions other than banks also held reserve assets. For example, building societies hold Treasury Bills and gilt edged stock with less than a year to maturity and if a bank found that its reserve asset ratio was in danger of falling below 12.5 per cent then it could attract such securities away from building societies, therefore enabling it to create credit.

The monetary authorities have also used another instrument – special deposits. The Bank of England has power to take liquidity directly from the banks by requiring them to deposit a specified percentage of their eligible liabilities with the Bank of England. To make such deposits, the banks may be forced to sell investments and this will increase the rate of interest generally and therefore have the effects described earlier.

These two instruments, together with government open market operations, did not prove successful in controlling the money supply and instead the monetary authorities sought to act directly on the level of bank deposits because it is these which must ultimately determine the banks' ability to lend. The supplementary special deposit scheme (better known as the corset) was first introduced in 1973 and was in effect for much of the remainder of the 1970s. Under the scheme, the Bank of England sought to restrain any growth of interest-bearing eligible liabilities (that is interest-bearing deposits). The Bank of England set a maximum growth level for such deposits and any growth above this resulted in the offending bank being required to deposit a proportion of the excess with the Bank of England in a non-interest-bearing account. The effect of the corset was to limit the ability of banks to attract deposits and therefore to make loans. In practice, the corset did not work this way. Rather, it led to various means by which the banks circumvented the control. One such method was the 'bill leak'. Instead of banks performing their traditional function of attracting deposits from one group of people and lending these deposits to another group in the form of loans, the banks acted as brokers between those wishing to invest and those wishing to borrow. A company seeking to borrow would issue a bill which would be guaranteed by the bank and this bill would be purchased directly by, perhaps, a company with funds to invest. Thus, in effect credit had been created but without any movement of funds into or out of a bank.

The corset in particular, and to a lesser extent the other direct monetary policy measures, were among the competitive disadvantages which banks claimed to be under compared with building societies; it was suggested from time to time that the building societies should be subject to similar controls.

In reply, building societies pointed out that those who seek to apply monetary controls to them frequently seemed to be more concerned with ensuring equality of treatment between building societies and banks than with ensuring that monetary policy achieved its macro-economic objectives. Societies pointed out that applying the reserve asset ratio to building societies would not significantly affect their behaviour as they would be readily able to acquire reserve assets and that in fact this would not limit their lending. Also, it was pointed out that applying the corset to building societies would hardly be appropriate as almost all of societies' liabilities are interest-bearing. In general, the banks' complaints were directed not so much at building societies being exempt from monetary controls but rather that monetary controls were being applied to banks alone than to the entire financial system.

The Conservative government elected in May 1979 was more 'monetarist' than its predecessor and immediately embarked on a review of the means by which monetary policy is implemented. There was considerable discussion about the possibility of 'monetary base control' which would concentrate control on the deposits held by the banks with the central bank. In the event, the government's review turned out to be less far-reaching than had been anticipated but significantly the conclusions served to remove many of the complaints which the banks previously had.

A Green Paper *Monetary Control*, Cmnd 7858 (HMSO, March 1980) acknowledged the defects of the methods of monetary control previously employed and proposed a number of changes:

(a) The phasing out of the supplementary special deposit scheme (the corset). This was implemented in June 1980 and thereby served to remove one

of the major complaints which the banks had had against the techniques by which monetary policy has been implemented.
(b) The abolition of the reserve asset requirement for monetary control purposes. This was implemented in August 1981.
(c) The liquid asset requirement for prudential purposes is to be retained.
(d) The requirement that the clearing banks keep 1.5 per cent of their liabilities in the form of balances at the Bank of England is to be retained and extended to all banks. Special deposits will also be retained. These two instruments will enable the Bank of England to continue to influence short-term interest rates.

The Green Paper was accompanied by a brief government statement on monetary policy; the main features of this are set out below:

(a) The government's policy was stated as being 'to sustain downward pressure on prices by a progressive reduction in the rate of growth of the money supply over a period of years'.
(b) The main instruments by which the government will limit monetary growth must continue to be fiscal policy and interest rates. In particular, the government announced its intention of bringing down, over time, the public sector borrowing requirement.
(c) It was stated that no single statistical measure of the money supply could fully 'encapsulate monetary conditions'. The government said that in assessing monetary conditions the authorities would have regard to a range of monetary aggregates, including not only M1 and M3 but also wider measures of private sector liquidity including, for example, non-bank holdings of Treasury Bills and short-term investments in building societies and local authorities.
(d) Sterling M3 would continue to be the main aggregate at which monetary policy would be directed but the government would take account of the growth in the other aggregates.

The Green Paper is significant in marking a further step towards implementing monetary policy through the market mechanism rather than through direct controls on bank lending which had existed in the 1960s and on the growth of bank deposits such as the corset scheme which applied throughout much of the 1970s. Building societies are directly affected by variations in interest rates and thus the Green Paper can be said to be bringing societies more within the scope of monetary control. However, by removing direct controls, the government virtually ended the argument as to whether societies should be brought within such controls. Significantly, the government is also retaining sterling M3 as the main target although the Green Paper and subsequent government statements have indicated that the monetary authorities would also have regard to a wider range of monetary aggregates.

From November 1980 the monetary authorities placed greater emphasis on open market operations and the significance of M LR declined. On 20 August 1981 the Bank of England formally discontinued its practice of posting a continuous M LR although it reserved the right to reintroduce the rate 'in some circumstances'.

Prudential Supervision

A Brief History of Prudential Supervision

The development of laws and regulations relating to the supervision of building societies is set out in Chapter 1 of this book and Chapter 4 explains the reserve and liquidity requirements that societies have to meet in order to achieve and maintain trustee status. The first section of Chapter 12 chronicles the most important developments in this area in the post-war period:

1947   BSA recommended a 5 per cent reserve ratio.

1951   BSA recommended a 7.5 per cent minimum liquidity ratio.

1952   BSA regulations on liquidity introduced.

1957   BSA repeated its recommendation for a 5 per cent reserve ratio but added that 2.5 per cent should be seen as a minimum ratio.

1959   The House Purchase and Housing Act introduced trustee status for deposits in building societies. The minimum reserve requirement was 2.5 per cent (2 per cent for assets over £100 million), minimum liquidity ratio 7.5 per cent and size £0.5 million. The BSA made it a requirement of membership that societies eligible for trustee status by virtue of their size should have such status but did not reduce its own reserve ratio minimum below 2.5 per cent for assets in excess of £100 million.

1960   The Building Societies Act gave the Registry greater powers to prescribe the way in which societies' liquid funds could be invested. More generally, the powers of the Registry were increased; for example, the Chief Registrar was empowered to stop a society raising money and to control its advertisements. The special advance concept was also introduced.

1962   The Building Societies Act consolidated existing legislation.

1966   The Prices and Incomes Board report commented on building society reserves and liquidity and recommended the Association to establish an independent committee to look at these matters.

1967   The Hardie Committee duly reported and in 1968 the present sliding scale for reserves was adopted.

1981   The concept of authorisation was introduced.

Perhaps it is significant that there have been few major developments with respect to prudential supervision since 1967. The 1970s saw turmoil in financial markets generally and regulations governing other institutions have been tightened. That the prudential requirements relating to building societies have not been significantly strengthened indicated that those requirements, perhaps, have been adequate.

However, it is interesting to note in this respect the effect of inflation in effectively reducing the 'real' reserve requirements of societies. To maintain the 1968 real value, the minimum size for trustee status would need to be £4 million rather than £1 million and the 2.5 per cent requirement would apply up to £400 million rather than £100 million. (The minimum size for trustee status is to be increased to £10 million, but this does not affect societies below that size which already have trustee status.) The sliding scale has also meant that all societies have effectively experienced a reduction in their minimum reserve requirement. For example, in 1968 a society with assets of £1,000 million would have been required to maintain a reserve ratio of 1.8 per cent. In 1980 a society with assets of £1,000 million in 1968 prices, that is with assets of £4,000 million, would need to maintain a reserve ratio of 1.39 per cent. Notwithstanding the erosion of the reserve ratio requirement in real terms, there has been no move to increase the various thresholds.

More generally, little attention has been given by the government to major changes in building society legislation, partly, no doubt, because the industry was thought to be running fairly smoothly. However, it is becoming increasingly apparent that the legislation under which building societies operate is not wholly appropriate to their present day status. As Chapter 1 has indicated, the law rather treats building societies as being mutual organisations and is concerned with the protection of members from the possible misdeeds of directors and managers. The law envisages a building society being run in much the same way as small friendly societies where people know each other and can actively participate in elections for directors and in the management of the society. Building societies ceased to operate like that a long time ago but the law has not been changed to meet their changed status. Societies and the regulatory authorities, in the form of the Chief Registrar, have adapted well to the changed conditions but inevitably some thought has had to be given to bringing building society law more up to date.

Chapter 1 of this book has indicated that major changes in legislation have generally followed problems of one form or another. In the 1950s, the difficulties experienced by the Exeter Benefit, State and Scottish Amicable Societies led to the 1960 Act and to controls on the manner in which liquid funds could be invested. The 1960s were fairly quiet in this respect but in the 1970s two scandals, relating to the Wakefield Building Society and the Grays Building Society, came to light and drew attention to the possible need for a tightening of prudential requirements. At the same time, thought had to be given to amending the law to take account of developments in the European Community. The remainder of this chapter is concerned with the problems of the late 1970s while the implications of the European Community for building society law are examined in detail in Chapter 15.

The Wakefield Building Society

There is a general presumption that building societies are efficient, well-managed organisations in which the savings of individuals are perfectly safe. People who run building societies are assumed to be honest and working for the benefit of the community. Moreover, because building societies deal with money as their stock-in-trade, so elaborate procedures have been developed both internally and by external auditors to ensure that money cannot be misappropriated. For the most part these presumptions are soundly based and the general belief was that a big fraud was not capable of happening in the building society industry.

This belief was changed by the Wakefield Building Society affair. In 1976, during the course of the audit of the accounts of the society, major defalcations came to light. These had been perpetrated by the general manager of the Wakefield Building Society, William Robinson, and inadequate auditing allowed them to remain undetected for a long time. The extent of the defalcations amounted to £633,000, a very substantial amount, but one which was safely covered by the society's reserves and still allowed the society to maintain a reserve ratio sufficiently high to qualify for trustee status. Nevertheless, it was thought that press publicity about the affair could have an adverse effect on the society and consequently the Halifax Building Society agreed to take a transfer of engagements from the Wakefield.

Following these events, the Chief Registrar of Friendly Societies, on 16 September 1976, wrote to the Chairman of each society, drawing attention to the duties imposed upon the society and its directors by section 76 of the Building Societies Act 1962. This lays down that it is the duty of a society to establish and maintain:

(a) a system of control and inspection of its books and accounts, and
(b) a system for supervising its cash holdings and all remittances and receipts.

The letter pointed out that section 76 (5) of the Act required directors to take all reasonable steps to ensure that a society has established and maintained these systems. The Chief Registrar emphasised that societies should not assume that the section of the Act had been complied with merely because auditors had not reported to the contrary.

Police charges were preferred against Mr Robinson and he was committed for trial on 28 August 1977. The case was heard on 16 January 1978 and Mr Robinson pleaded guilty to nineteen specimen offences. He was convicted of all offences and sentenced to terms of imprisonment ranging from two to six years, the sentences to run concurrently. Some of the money stolen from the society was recovered and, somewhat paradoxically, investors in the former Wakefield Building Society received several bonuses after the society's engagements had been taken over by the Halifax. This was because, notwithstanding the defalcations, the Wakefield Society had a substantially higher reserve ratio than the Halifax, although at the time of a takeover of any society in such circumstances there must be uncertainty as to whether any further losses will come to light.

The Grays Building Society

The Wakefield affair led to a tightening of procedures in many societies, particularly the smaller ones. However, in 1978 a much greater fraud came to light. The society concerned was the Grays Building Society, a very small building society with total assets on paper of some £11 million and operating predominantly in the Grays area of Essex. Previously, the affairs of the Grays Building Society had caused some concern to the Chief Registrar of Friendly Societies, primarily because of the rather antiquated methods of accounting adopted by the society and also because of the age of the directors. Moreover, the chief executive of the society, Mr Harold Percy Jaggard, was 79 years old and occupied the positions of both Chairman and Secretary.

The first indication that something was seriously wrong came on 17 March 1978. One of the auditors' staff, whilst auditing the books, said to Mr Jaggard that something was wrong. Mr Jaggard replied that he would attend to it later and promptly went home and committed suicide. When his suicide was discovered, a hastily summoned meeting of the board of directors of the Grays Building Society was held and this was attended by an assistant registrar from the Registry of Friendly Societies. The Building Societies Association was informed of the position and arrangements were made with the Woolwich Equitable Building Society to take over the engagements of the Grays Society. It was anticipated at the time that the defalcation was probably fairly minor and no greater than that which had been found at the Wakefield Building Society.

By 22 March, it was evident that the deficiencies could amount to at least £2 million. The Woolwich Building Society put a team into the Grays to investigate the position for itself and by 26 March it had become clear that the deficiencies totalled £7 million out of published total assets of £11 million. The Woolwich Equitable Building Society could not possibly be expected to take over such a large liability and arrangements were put in hand by The Building Societies Association to obtain financial support from other members of the Association.

Fortunately, these developments occurred over the Easter weekend but it was evident that the society could not open its doors on 28 March and an announcement was made to this effect together with a statement that the Association was considering ways of safeguarding the interests of members of the society. As a first step, the Association secured agreement from the five largest societies to make good any deficiency pending an approach to all societies. This enabled a full statement to be made on 2 April.

The rescue operation consisted of setting up a fund under section 43 of the Building Societies Act 1962. This allowed for societies to contribute to a guarantee fund but some legal doubt was expressed as to whether such a fund could be set up after the need for it had become established and whether a society which was, in essence, bankrupt could become a member of such a fund. In order that there should be no doubt about the matter, application was made in May 1978 for a declaration of the High Court which duly declared in favour of the arrangements, the implementation of which was put in hand. After three months, the investors in the Grays Society were able to have access to their money, the deficiency being made good by every single member of The Building Societies Association in Great Britain with the Woolwich Building Society taking over the management and engagements of the Grays.

On 30 March 1978, the Chief Registrar of Friendly Societies appointed Mr Ian Davison of the firm of chartered accountants, Messrs. Arthur Anderson & Co., under section 110 of the Building Societies Act 1962, as an inspector to enquire into and report on the affairs of the Grays Building Society. In May of that year, Mr Murray Stuart-Smith, QC was also appointed as an inspector. The Report of the inspectors was published in May 1979 (Registry of Friendly Societies, *Grays Building Society*, Investigation under section 110 of the Building Societies Act 1962, Cmnd 7557, HMSO, 1979). The Report makes fascinating reading and no more than a brief summary of it is attempted in this book.

The principal finding of the inspectors was that a long-running fraud had been perpetrated on the Grays by Mr Jaggard. Evidence of defalcations was found as far back as 1938 and it was possible that they were occurring before that time. Moreover, money was stolen as recently as 1978. The fraud was facilitated by the lack of an adequate system of internal control for which the directors were held responsible and remained undiscovered 'because of the persistent gross failure of the auditors to discharge their professional duties properly'. Mr Jaggard was held to have acted alone and managed to dominate the scene at the Grays.

The inspectors attempted to trace the growth of the deficit in the accounts. In 1951, the deficit was estimated at £680,000 out of total assets of £2 million. By 1966 the deficit was put at £2.7 million out of £5 million. The final deficit was put at £7.1 million out of £11 million. The total amount of money actually stolen was estimated at about £2 million with the remaining £5 million representing interest which would have been earned had the £2 million not been stolen. The bulk of the money stolen went to meet Mr Jaggard's gambling debts and he was also generous to his family.

Mr Jaggard stole money by a process known in accounting circles as 'teeming and lading'. His theft involved a three-stage operation:

(a) The misappropriation of cash from the society's takings.
(b) A cover-up by accelerating the banking of cheques received in a subsequent accounting period.
(c) The abstraction of cheques to fill the gap which would appear when misappropriations had reached a certain level.

In order to do all of this, Mr Jaggard had to have complete control of money coming into and out of the society and this he achieved partly by dealing with the post personally. In particular, several redemption and investors' cheques were expropriated.

Obviously such theft would normally be uncovered in the course of an internal audit but the Grays Building Society, like other societies of its size, did not have an internal auditor. However, again in the normal course of events it would be reasonable to expect that the external audit which each society has, by law, to have by a qualified auditor, would uncover such defalcations. Mr Jaggard was faced with a very difficult problem with respect to the annual accounts. The accounts of individual investors and borrowers were perfectly maintained and the Woolwich Building Society, when it took over the accounts, could find little at fault with them. However, there was a glaring difference between the addition of the individual accounts and the sums which could be shown in the annual accounts. To cover this up, Mr Jaggard falsified the accounts which were then audited. This was facilitated by negligent auditors.

The report was a thorough one and showed very much that the problem was not one of an inadequate supervisory framework but rather that the requirements of the law had not been carried out. It follows that the recommendations emanating from the report did not call for major changes in legislation. The inspectors held that Mr Jaggard's fraud had remained undetected for so long because of a combination of factors, the most important of which were:

(a) Bad auditing.
(b) Lack of appreciation by the directors of their duties and their poor management and control generally of the society's affairs.
(c) Abuse by Mr Jaggard of his dominant position.
(d) Lack of trained or qualified staff.

The inspectors said that the possibility of one or more of the factors occurring in small to medium-sized building societies remained a real one for the following reasons:

(a) Auditing of building societies is regarded as being relatively undemanding work.
(b) There is difficulty in obtaining directors of the right calibre and experience in small to medium sized societies.
(c) Because small societies tend not to have many, if any, executive directors, the chief executive is inevitably a key figure.
(d) Routine office work in a building society is not demanding and this can mean that new blood is not brought into small societies with knowledge or experience to question the procedures in use.

For the most part the inspectors were not critical of the Registry's handling of the Grays affair but they did suggest that changes had to be made in the Registry's monitoring procedures.

With regard to auditors, the inspectors said that the Grays experience showed it may no longer be prudent for the Chief Registrar to rely upon the fact that the auditor is qualified as a guarantee that the audit has been properly performed. After considering various possibilities, the inspectors merely recommended that section 129 of the Building Societies Act should be amended so as to render an auditor an officer of a building society, so that he would therefore be required to furnish information to the Registry if called upon to do so. The inspectors made a number of recommendations with respect to the auditors' statement.

With respect to directors, the inspectors suggested that the Registry should provide guidance for new directors and that it would be desirable if new directors could attend a short course and if existing directors could attend a refresher course occasionally. It was recommended that directors should be required to resign and seek annual re-election upon reaching the age of 70 as is the case for companies.

It was recommended that the chairman of a building society should not also be the chief executive and also that two executive directors should be required for societies with trustee status.

Following the Grays affair, the Chief Registrar of Friendly Societies wrote, on 9 June 1978, to the Chairmen of all building societies suggesting three points:

(a) That if a board had not recently carried out a reappraisal of systems of control, inspection and supervision then it should do so.
(b) That directors should not consider that section 76 of the Building Societies Act had been complied with merely because the society's auditors had not reported to the contrary.
(c) That audits should be fully effective for all purposes.

Two weeks later, the President of the Institute of Chartered Accountants in England and Wales wrote to auditors of building societies reminding them of their responsibilities under the Building Societies Act and under the accountants' Ethical Guide.

Since the Grays affair, the Registry has devoted much of its limited resources towards enquiries into building societies' affairs. Visits to societies by officers of the Registry have been intensified by the establishment of a programme of in-depth inquiries which are subsequently followed by meetings with boards of directors and also with the society's auditors. Also, the Chief Registrar and his assistant registrars have been engaged on a separate programme of meetings with societies' boards.

The Chief Registrar's Evidence to the Wilson Committee

Chapter 10 commented briefly on the Wilson Committee's comments about the prudential supervision of building societies. The Wilson Committee's deliberations came soon after the Grays affair and obviously the Committee wanted to examine this issue. The Chief Registrar of Friendly Societies gave written evidence to the Wilson Committee on the supervision of building societies in November 1978 and his statement provides probably the best description of how societies are currently supervised.

The main points made in this evidence were as follows:

(a) The Registry has a total staff of 120 of whom about 15 are engaged almost wholly upon matters relating to the registration and supervision of building societies. In terms of man hours, approximately a quarter of the time of the Registry is spent on building society work.
(b) The Registry has been closely associated with the formation, en-

couragement and development of mutual and co-operative societies and partly because of this the Chief Registrar is able to exercise an influence in matters other than those specifically governed by the statutes which he administers.

(c)   The statutory safeguards and powers in some respects still fail to provide a completely coherent scheme of control in the interests of building society members but they confer on the Chief Registrar a measure of discretion in relation to certain of his functions.

(d)   Supervision of building societies is exercised in the following main areas:

  (i)   the establishment of societies or the absorption of a smaller society by a larger unit;
  (ii) the operation of societies;
  (iii) the financial position of societies.

(e)   The Chief Registrar aims to ensure that the constitution of societies is consistent with their mutual nature; that their business is carried on within the limitations of the Act, and that they are prudently managed and financially sound.

(f)   The Registry maintains close liaison and continuous dialogue with The Building Societies Association.

(g)   Before allowing a new society to become established, the Registrar will discuss the proposal with its founders to ensure that its business will be conducted on secure and conventional lines and that it will be able to comply with prudential requirements.

(h)   The Registry is invariably informed of merger discussions at an early stage and can use its influence where necessary.

(i)   The financial performance of societies is monitored by a critical appraisal of information sent periodically to the Registry. Societies must file copies of their annual accounts and directors' report and also their annual return. The Chief Registrar prescribes the form and content of the annual return and societies' accounts.

(j)   Societies provide a monthly financial statement to the Registry on a voluntary basis and this provides up-to-date information about cash flow.

(k)   If the examination of the various returns shows possible weaknesses, this is pursued with the society by correspondence, by on-the-spot enquiries or by a combination of methods as appropriate.

(l)   The Registry has a statutory power to prohibit the taking of investments by a society and this of course can have a dramatic effect. However, this power is unsatisfactory in some respects in that it might be counter-productive through increasing the likelihood of failure of a society. Once prohibition has been imposed the society concerned is almost certain to experience a run on its liquid funds which it will be unable to satisfy. Existing investors will therefore be 'locked in'.

(m) The Registry has power to prohibit advertising and this may be imposed where it is desirable to slow down the rate of expansion of a society.

The final paragraph of the Registrar's evidence is worth quoting in full as it indicates the possible areas of weakness in the existing statutory framework:

In connexion with the Registrar's powers considered in the preceding paragraphs, it is worth drawing attention to the fact that they leave some gaps which cannot always be made good in practice. Whilst the powers may protect the investing public from further investment in an unsound society, once used they do little or nothing to enable protection to be given to existing investors. One obvious solution is the provision of more positive powers for the Registrar, in particular the power to require a transfer of a society in difficulties to another willing and financially able to accept it, and the power to petition for compulsory winding-up of such a society. Again, unless persuasion is effective, which may not always be the case, powers such as those relating to advertising have to be used to achieve indirectly any desirable limitation of a society's expansion or of its use of high interest rates. Whilst to a great extent the Registrar's accepted position and influence enables him to overcome the deficiencies in his statutory powers, there is a need to review these powers in the light of the protection required both by actual investors and the investing public generally.

It will be noted that the Chief Registrar expressed particular concern at his inability to protect existing investors and put forward as a possible solution more positive powers for the Registry to enforce a transfer of engagements.

The Wilson Report and Prudential Supervision

The Wilson Committee report devotes one brief chapter (Chapter 24) to the prudential supervision of building societies. This chapter begins with the observation that there has been no systematic review of the prudential supervision of societies since 1962 and goes on to say: 'The present arrangements in some respects give the appearance of not having fully come to terms with the great growth in building societies' importance over the last two decades.' The committee noted that weaker and more inefficient societies had been cushioned from normal commercial pressures by the recommended rates system and argued that if this was dismantled then societies would be forced to operate in a much more competitive environment which would place them under considerable strain and would require more stringent prudential supervision.

After describing the Registry's functions the Wilson Report examined the adequacy of the supervisory arrangements. It accepted that the Chief Registrar's informal influence over the building society movement had been reasonably effective and it noted that the industry had a good record in terms of avoiding losses to depositors. However, the report went on to say that it would not be right to continue to rely on this particularly if competition between societies is to be promoted and it suggested that legislation was required in five areas:

(a) A minimum level of reserves should be set statutorily for all societies and the Registrar should have authority to prescribe minimum liquidity ratios.

(b) The Chief Registrar should be given greater powers of control, particularly over small societies. The Committee recommended that the Chief Registrar should be given powers to promote mergers or to enforce the winding-up of a society for prudential reasons subject to the appropriate right of appeal.

(c) The Grays and Wakefield affairs show that the Registry can no longer rely on the validity of published accounts. The Committee recommended that the scope and frequency of Registry contacts with individual building societies should be reconsidered and that the present voluntary cash flow statements should become a statutory requirement. (The Registry has increased its contacts with societies significantly although this is largely a consequence of the Grays affair rather than the Wilson Report.)

(d) The building society aspects of the Registry's work should be separated from the other functions of the Registry and the new organisation should be equipped with suitably qualified staff.

(e) The building society industry has had a good record over the years for voluntarily dealing with the consequences to investors of failures but it would be consistent with the treatment of banks and insurance companies if a statutory deposit protection scheme could be established. Moreover, 100 per cent protection should be given as this protection is implicitly given already by arrangements which the Association has implemented where necessary.

A Deposit Protection Scheme

The Wilson Committee published its report at the same time as The Building Societies Association was itself giving consideration to the question of a deposit protection scheme. Societies willingly contributed to the Grays rescue fund and public confidence in the industry had been preserved. However, inevitably a failure of the size of the Grays led to pressure for the establishment of a more formal system of deposit protection as the Association was in no position to guarantee to investors in any society that their savings would be protected.

Moreover, the government became committed to ensuring that building societies had an adequate deposit protection fund. Following the secondary banking crisis in the early 1970s, consideration was given to establishing a deposit protection scheme for bank investors. Provision for a scheme was made by the Banking Act 1979. Building societies were not within this scheme but during the parliamentary debate on the subject the government indicated that it believed that societies were evolving a voluntary scheme and it gave assurances that if necessary it would legislate to ensure that protection to building society depositors would be given.

Policy holders with insurance companies are also protected through the Policy Holders' Protection Act 1975. Not unreasonably, there was therefore justification for giving building society investors similar protection.

The initial reaction of the Association was that the industry itself should formulate a voluntary scheme rather than have a statutory scheme which would probably be bureaucratic and which might bring unwelcome restrictions in its train. A scheme was developed by the Association and this was very much modelled on the scheme for banks set out in the Banking Act 1979. In a speech to the Association's annual conference in 1979 the then Chairman of the Council, Mr Ralph Stow, expressed the majority view of the Council of the Association that a private or voluntary scheme would be preferable to a statutory scheme. A voluntary scheme had been worked out with the following features:

(a) It would be open to any building society not subject to an order by the Chief Registrar but members of the BSA would be obliged to join as a condition of membership of the Association.
(b) It would be managed by trustees appointed by the Council of the Association.
(c) An initial basic fund of £1.5 million would be established. This would be brought into being by every society paying £7,150 or in the case of a very small society, a sum not exceeding 0.3 per cent of assets. (This 0.3 per cent figure was borrowed from the Banking Act.)
(d) If additional funds were required then they would be raised proportionately to total assets up to a maximum of 0.3 per cent.
(e) Cover should be 75 per cent of the investors' loss.

Following the statement there was a lively debate on the merits of deposit protection and this has continued. The arguments are very finely balanced. The main argument in favour of a deposit protection scheme is that building societies stand together in terms of confidence. If one building society fails then other societies might well feel an effect and the industry could suffer withdrawals on a massive scale. Fear of such a development was one of the factors leading societies to contribute to the Grays rescue fund. Moreover, the view was expressed that a deposit protection fund would further enhance the existing good reputation of societies as safe homes for personal savings. It was noted that in the United States in particular savings and loan associations (the equivalents of building societies) advertised insurance of their deposits.

However, the arguments against a voluntary deposit protection scheme, and indeed against any deposit protection scheme, were also strong. The main argument is that 100 per cent deposit protection would benefit those societies indulging in more risky business at the expense of those managed on conservative lines and would remove from the investor any possible risk in investing with a given society. Some societies operate on higher rates of interest than others and it was argued that it was a matter for investors to decide whether the risk of investing in a high rate society was worth taking. A deposit protection fund to some extent would reduce the risk. (The major clearing banks had expressed similar concern with respect to the deposit protection scheme under the Banking Act. In effect they were being asked to guarantee aggressive smaller banks which might not be as prudently managed.)

There was also the point that the size of a deposit protection fund would be limited. The 0.3 per cent of assets maximum contribution would fix a maximum size for the fund at £120 million (in 1979). What this would mean in effect was that any society with assets of under £120 million would be fully protected while larger societies would not be able to advertise that deposits with them would be protected. Thus the reserves of the largest societies would exceed the total deposit protection fund and therefore effectively they could not say that because of the fund their investors were protected whereas very small societies could use such an argument.

A voluntary scheme also raised immense problems in that societies might have to change their rules to enable them to contribute. The question might be asked at annual meetings as to why efficient societies were willing to contribute to a fund to prop up less efficient societies.

Eventually the Council of the Association decided that it would not be practical to establish a voluntary deposit protection scheme and the government was duly informed of this. There was therefore every expectation that a Building Societies Bill, which was expected during the course of 1980, would include provision for a statutory deposit protection scheme and the industry was ready to accept this. However, for reasons which will be discussed later in this chapter, the 1980 Bill did not materialise and there seems no prospect of primary legislation on building societies for several years. The government has not yet indicated whether it intends to legislate for a deposit protection fund in anticipation of more wide ranging legislation. The Association is now reconsidering its position on a voluntary scheme, at least as a temporary measure.

New Legislation: The Building Society View

In anticipation of legislation which was initially expected in 1980, the Council of The Building Societies Association drew up a list of amendments which they would like to be made to existing legislation. Details of the building society proposals were given by Mr Sydney Burton, a former Chairman of the Association's Practice Committee, at the South Eastern Association of Building Societies conference in 1980. Among the points listed by Mr Burton were the following:

(a) Large societies should be allowed to set up their own insurance companies under the Insurance Companies Act. Smaller societies should be empowered to join together to set up an insurance company to serve them all.
(b) Currently a society can be formed by 10 persons, each with a stake of £500. The number should be increased to 25 and the stake £2,500 each. (The Authorisation Regulations effectively increased the £500 figure to £5,000.)
(c) The special advance requirement causes problems, largely because it is based on the current year's lending and it is not always easy for a society to know exactly what proportion of its loans will be special advances. The Association proposed that the special advance limit should be 15 per cent of advances made in the previous year or 10 per cent of advances made in the current year, whichever is the greater.
(d) The requirement for an increase in the special advance limit to be approved by each House of Parliament should be removed and it should be variable simply by an order from the Registry.
(e) The cost of sending out notices of meetings and annual accounts to

investors is prohibitive and consideration should be given to easing the requirements on societies.

(f) A figure of £250 should be the required holding in order for a member to exercise a vote on a special resolution. Mr Burton indicated that current thinking was that instead of a single member being able to propose a special resolution, the requirement should be 100 members where the membership of the society exceeds 1,000 or 10 per cent of the membership for smaller societies.

(g) A resolution should be passed at each annual meeting appointing the auditor or auditors.

It should be noted that all of these points, with the exception of the suggestion that societies should be allowed to set up insurance companies, are points of detail. They are concerned with improving the existing statutory framework rather than with bringing building society law up to date to reflect the rapid growth of societies and the quite different nature that they now have compared with that which existed when the basis of the present law was enacted.

New Legislation Postponed

It has been noted that there was general expectation that there would be a Building Societies Bill in 1980. The prime purpose of the Bill would be to implement the first European directive on credit institutions but it was expected that the Bill would contain much else. The European aspect of the Bill is considered in detail in Chapter 15.

However, somewhat to the surprise of the building society industry, the Financial Secretary to the Treasury, Mr Nigel Lawson, made the following statement in Parliament on 8 August 1980:

The government intend to apply to building societies the first European directive on credit institutions by means of regulations to be made in the next session of Parliament under the European Communities Act 1972. We have no immediate plans for primary legislation: we shall be considering this further when the European directive has been implemented.

The Chief Registrar explained the thinking behind the government's decision in an article in the *Building Societies Gazette* in September 1980. Mr Brading, the Chief Registrar, noted that consideration had been given to a number of technical amendments to the 1962 Act but he pointed out that these could not be regarded as being high on the scale of urgency or essentiality. Mr Brading went on to indicate that the 1962 Act had served the industry remarkably well. He suggested that it would be difficult to argue convincingly that the case existed for legislation and expenditure of Parliamentary time to make such modest amendments to existing legislation.

Mr Brading considered the necessity for legislation following the Grays affair and pointed out that already the Registry, the accountancy bodies and the societies themselves had gone a very long way towards strengthening the prudential supervision of societies. He suggested that even if legislation in response to Grays was to be proposed it would probably now be slimmer than it would have been a few years' earlier and in a few years time the government would be even better placed to judge the situation.

The Chief Registrar did comment on the question of a deposit protection scheme and he said that this would obviously be a matter for further consideration in the period ahead.

Perhaps the most significant part of Mr Brading's article was his observation that in the next few years there would be a continuation and an expansion of discussion within the industry on quite fundamental matters and that any developments which result may have relevance for future legislation. Perhaps Mr Brading was thinking of the increased competition between societies which might require greater prudential supervision and possibly also of the corporate nature of societies with many building society executives questioning the concept of mutuality.

Mr Brading amplified these points when he spoke to the South Eastern Association of Building Societies conference later in 1980. He indicated then that greater competition between societies might affect monetary control policies and could possibly involve legislation. He also raised the question of the rights of building society members and he asked whether it was still practicable and realistic to assume that the ultimate responsibility for the management of societies could lie with the members themselves. If not, he suggested that the time may be approaching when it will be necessary to regard the basis of the constitution of building societies as needing fresh consideration.

Chapter 13

The Income Tax Arrangements

In Chapter 10 it was noted that the banks have objected to the special income tax arrangements which building societies have with the Inland Revenue, claiming that they confer on societies a competitive advantage. Furthermore, the Wilson Committee report recommended that the special arrangements should be abolished. The income tax arrangements have also been a subject for discussion within the building society industry over recent years, although largely on moral rather than on competitive grounds. In discussing the special arrangements, there are therefore two aspects which need consideration:

(a) Whether the special arrangements give building societies a competitive advantage.
(b) Whether the special arrangements are fair.

Basically, the taxation of interest which building societies pay is very simple. In the case of most other institutions, interest is either paid gross and taxed as income in the hands of the recipient, or, alternatively, interest is paid after basic rate tax has been deducted. In the latter case, those investors not liable to tax are able to claim a refund. For building society interest, a special rate is calculated that is sufficient to discharge the basic rate tax liability of all those who receive building society interest. Those liable to the basic rate of tax only have no further tax liability but those not so liable are unable to claim a refund. For those liable to the investment income surcharge or the higher rates of tax, building society interest is assumed to have been received after basic rate tax liability has been discharged and there is therefore a liability to the surcharge or to the higher rates.

In order to understand the nature of these special arrangements, it is first necessary to consider the history of the taxation of interest paid by building societies.

History of the Taxation of Interest Paid by Building Societies

The question of the taxation of interest paid by societies first arose in the second half of the nineteenth century. The question was whether tax should be deducted from interest paid to building society shareholders and the law on the subject was far from clear. There appears to have been individual bargaining between building societies and the tax authorities. In 1869, the newly formed Building Societies Protection Association expressed the view that individual members of societies who may be liable to pay income tax should return income arising from building society shares to the Inland Revenue in common with other items of income. For a time the government sought to obtain from societies the names and addresses of members to whom interest had been paid but it was an open question as to whether the government had power to seek this information and some societies did not provide it. However, for the most part, the question was academic as at the time the tax threshold was £150 per annum and this was well above the income of most building society investors.

In 1887 the Inland Revenue issued a memorandum which provided for a society to furnish to the Revenue a statement of the interest paid or credited to depositors and members whose incomes amounted to £150 a year or more and from whom the society would have the right to deduct the tax, whether or not it exercised that right. However, societies disputed the right of the Inland Revenue to seek information on payments to individual investors and the position remained confused.

The present income tax arrangements had their origin in 1894 when the Inland Revenue issued a Memorandum of Alternative Arrangements, known as 'A' and 'B'. The arrangements began in 1895 and continued almost unchanged until 1932. The motive behind the arrangements was to save the Inland Revenue from routine clerical work in taxing or paying rebates to investors, many of whom did not understand income tax. Arrangement A provided for a society to furnish a statement once a year of the interest paid or credited to depositors and members whose incomes exceeded £160 a year and from whom the society would have the right to deduct tax whether or not it exercised that right. Arrangement B provided for societies to be directly assessed under Schedule D of the Income Tax Acts with half of the total amount of interest being charged for income tax, the remaining half being allowed to cover exemptions. It should be noted at the time that the standard rate of tax was 8d in the £ and the expectation was that income tax would be abolished.

The income tax arrangements ran into difficulty during the First World War as this necessitated a sharp rise in the income tax rate to three shillings (15p) in the £ and the exemption limit was reduced from £160 to £130. Income tax was subsequently raised to five shillings (25p) in the £. This caused problems for those societies which stated in their prospectuses that investors would receive interest free from liability to pay income tax. It was agreed that arrangement B should be modified with the assessment continuing to be made on the basis of half of interest but the assessment was based on the unearned rate of income tax applicable to incomes not exceeding £500; three shillings (15p) rather than five shillings (25p) in the £.

In 1921 the Association agreed with the Inland Revenue that arrangement A would be continued only for societies already registered under it. For arrangement B the assessment would be one half of the standard rate of tax on one half of the interest paid or credited. However, one problem was that some societies were obtaining large deposits from corporate bodies and the interest they were paying on these deposits was liable to tax under arrangement B. In 1924 it was agreed that arrangement B should not apply to any deposit or share in excess of £5,000 or any amount held by a limited company or other incorporated company or society. (It should be noted that this limit, in effect, still applies today and stands at only £20,000, a considerable reduction in real terms compared with 1924.) For money paid to companies or on shares in excess of £5,000, the full standard rate tax had to be paid. The assumption which underlaid arrangement B was that half of the total amount of interest was payable to investors who were exempt from tax and therefore the 50 per cent tax rate paid to the Revenue represented the full amount which would be raised if all societies' investors were individually assessed. In the 1920s investigations were carried out to ascertain whether this was in fact the true position.

As a result of the investigations arrangement B was withdrawn and replaced by Document no. 13A (1932) which came into effect for three years from April 1932. The main features of the new arrangements were that:

(a) Societies would be directly assessed at the standard rate on all dividends and interest on investments exceeding £5,000, all dividends and interest paid to an incorporated company and also the profits of the society.
(b) Societies would be directly assessed at two-fifths of the standard rate in respect of the balance of the dividends or interest paid to investors.
(c) Societies were required, in the case of each new or additional investment of £500 or more, to obtain a declaration sufficient to establish whether the investment should be charged at the standard rate or two-fifths of the standard rate (that is the composite rate).

Investigations carried out in 1933 and 1934 proved that the two-fifths proportion was about right, that is about two-fifths of the interest payable by building societies was received by those liable to tax. In 1935 new arrangements were drawn up which were to operate for at least four years and from year to year thereafter. The war resulted in the arrangements continuing longer than had been anticipated. In 1935 the standard rate of tax stood at 4s 6d (23p) in the £ and the agreed composite rate was 1s 8d (9p). During the war years the drastic increase in direct tax caused sharp rises in the composite rate. The rate rose from 12.96 per cent in 1939/40 to 30 per cent by the end of the war.

Immediately after the war it was thought that the Board of the Inland Revenue proposed to abolish the income tax arrangements but, in 1950, the then Chancellor of the Exchequer announced that he intended to give the arrangements permanent effect and statutory sanction. Parliamentary sanction was originally given in section 23 of the Finance Act 1951. This section was repealed and re-enacted with consequential modification in section 445 of the consolidating Income Tax Act 1952. In turn, this section, together with subsequent provisions, was consolidated in section 343 of the Income and Corporation Taxes Act 1970. This remains the statutory provision for the taxation of interest paid by building societies although there have been subsequent amendments through the Finance Act 1971, the Finance Act 1972, the Finance (No.2) Act 1975, the Finance Act 1978 and the Finance Act 1980.

The Present Arrangements

Section 343 (1) of the Income and Corporation Taxes Act 1970 (as amended), states:

> The Board and any building society may, as respects any year of assessment, enter into arrangements whereby:
>
> (a) on such sums as may be determined in accordance with the arrangements the society is liable to account for and pay an amount representing income tax calculated in part at the basic rate and in part at a reduced rate which takes into account the operation of the subsequent provisions of this section; and
> (b) provision is made for any incidental or consequential matters, and any such arrangements shall have effect notwithstanding anything in this Act:
>
> Provided that in exercising their powers of entering into arrangements under this section, the Board shall at all times aim at securing that (if the amount so payable by the society under the arrangements is regarded as income tax for the year of assessment) the total income tax becoming payable to, and not becoming repayable by, the Crown is, when regard is had to the operation of the subsequent provisions of this section, as nearly as may be the same in the aggregate as it would have been if those powers had never been exercised.

In order to calculate the composite rate, it is necessary for the Inland Revenue to estimate how much income tax would be raised if the arrangements did not exist. Before describing in detail how this is achieved, it is important to note at this stage that the composite rate does not apply to all investments held with building societies but only to investments which are:

(a) beneficially owned by individuals, or
(b) held in trusts (other than discretionary and accumulation trusts) such that no persons other than individuals are beneficially interested, or
(c) held by persons, bodies of persons or trustees of funds (other than by the Crown, by any exempt pension fund or by any company) entitled to exemption from income tax under schedule D.

In addition, the arrangements apply only to investments under certain limits, currently £20,000 for an individual and £40,000 for a joint account. The interest paid on all other investments held with societies is subject to the basic rate of tax and the society must account for this to the Inland Revenue.

The composite rate is calculated by means of periodic statistical investigations undertaken by the Inland Revenue and societies are obliged to co-operate in these as a condition of taking part in the arrangements. The most recent investigation was conducted in 1978/79. The sample comprised

0.14 per cent of investments of under £1,000, 1.33 per cent of investments between £1,000 and £15,000 and 15 per cent of investments in excess of £15,000. Between investigations, the composite rate is calculated by reference to changes in incomes and tax allowances.

Calculating the composite rate is a time-consuming exercise and the results of the investigation are far from conclusive. The final rate is negotiated between the Inland Revenue and The Building Societies Association. The time taken to calculate the composite rate necessarily causes problems for building societies. The rate is applicable for financial years but it is not always possible for societies to work out their tax liability at the beginning of financial years. In some recent years the basic rate of income tax has not been fixed until some time into the financial year and more importantly the composite rate can change for other reasons, in particular, changes in income tax allowances. Thus in the 1977/8 financial year, the composite rate was eventually fixed at 24.25 per cent in December and this yielded to societies a considerable unexpected profit.

This problem became particularly acute for the 1980/1 tax year. In the normal course of events, the statistical investigation carried out in 1978/9 would have been used to calculate the composite rate for the year 1980/1. The composite rate in 1979/80 had been fixed at 21 per cent and as a result of the Budget measures in 1980, in particular the abolition of the 25 per cent tax band, societies anticipated an increase in the composite rate to 22.5 per cent and budgeted accordingly. However, preliminary results from the statistical investigation (which became available in July 1981) showed that the composite rate was more likely to be between 25 and 26 per cent. This was a cause for concern to societies because it meant that they would have no way of knowing for quite some considerable time what the exact composite rate would be and the very high increase would cause budgetary problems. To overcome this problem, the government introduced, in the Finance Bill, an amendment to the income tax arrangements such that any information (other than on tax rates or allowances) becoming available after the beginning of the relevant tax year would not be taken account of in calculating the composite rate. The effect of this was that the 1978/9 investigation would be used for the first time in 1981/2. As a result, the composite rate was fixed in 1980/1 at 22.5 per cent rather than perhaps 25.5 per cent or 26.0 per cent.

The 1978–9 statistical investigation showed that in fact the composite rate in 1980/1 would have been 25.5 per cent had the law not been changed. With the basic rate of tax at 30 per cent, this implies that 85 per cent (25.5 per cent divided by 30 per cent) of interest received by building society investors subject to the income tax arrangements was received by those liable to the basic rate of tax. The rate for 1981/2 was fixed at 25.5 per cent.

Composite Tax Rates and Revenue

Table 13.1 shows the composite rate and the standard or basic rate of tax for each year since 1939/40 together with the composite rate as a percentage of the standard or basic rate.

Table 13.1   Composite and Standard/Basic Rates of Tax, 1939–40 to 1981–2

Financial Year	Composite rate %	Standard/basic rate %	Composite rate as percentage of standard/basic rate
1939–40	12.96	35.00	37.0
1940–1	20.77	42.50	48.9
1941–2	28.75	50.00	57.5
1942–3	28.75	50.00	57.5
1943–4	28.75	50.00	57.5
1944–5	30.00	50.00	60.0
1945–6	30.00	50.00	60.0
1946–7	23.75	45.00	52.8
1947–8	22.50	45.00	50.0
1948–9	21.25	45.00	47.2
1949–50	25.83	45.00	57.4
1950–1	24.58	45.00	54.6
1951–2	26.25	47.50	55.3
1952–3	25.83	47.50	54.4
1953–4	24.17	45.00	53.7
1954–5	25.42	45.00	56.5
1955–6	24.17	42.50	56.9
1956–7	26.67	42.50	62.8
1957–8	27.50	42.50	64.7
1958–9	27.92	42.50	65.7
1959–60	25.62	38.75	66.1
1960–1	26.67	38.75	68.8
1961–2	27.08	38.75	69.9
1962–3	27.50	38.75	71.0
1963–4	27.08	38.75	69.9
1964–5	29.17	38.75	75.3
1965–6	30.83	41.25	74.7
1966–7	31.25	41.25	75.8
1967–8	31.25	41.25	75.8
1968–9	32.08	41.25	77.8
1969–70	32.25	41.25	78.2
1970–1	32.75	41.25	79.4
1971–2	31.00	38.75	80.0
1972–3	30.00	38.75	77.4
1973–4	23.50	30.00	78.3
1974–5	26.25	33.00	79.5
1975–6	27.75	35.00	79.3
1976–7	27.75	35.00	79.3
1977–8	24.25	34.00	71.3
1978–9	22.50	33.00	68.2

Table 13.1 – *cont.*

Financial Year	Composite rate %	Standard/basic rate %	Composite rate as percentage of standard/basic rate
1979–80	21.00	30.00	70.0
1980–1	22.50	30.00	75.0
1981–2	25.50	30.00	85.0

Notes:
1 In 1973–4 the standard rate of tax was replaced by the basic rate. Under the standard rate, income from employment was taxed at 7/9 of the standard rate whereas now it is taxed at the full basic rate. Thus the reduction in the tax rate in 1973–4 was more apparent than real.
2 The rates prior to 1971–2 have been converted from £-s-d. The composite rate is always rounded – currently to the nearest 0.25 per cent.
Sources: *The Building Societies Year Book* (Franey & Co., Annual) and The Building Societies Association.

It will be seen that the composite rate more than doubled during the war years, reflecting the rapid increase in the standard rate of income tax and also the reduction in tax allowances. The composite rate reached its highest ever level in 1944/5 and 1945/6, that is, 30 per cent at a time when the standard rate was 50 per cent. In the immediate post-war years, the composite rate fell significantly as a proportion of the standard rate although there was a sharp increase in 1949/50. The rate then fell again in relation to the standard rate until 1953/4, after which time it increased steadily to average over 75 per cent of the standard rate in the late 1960s and reaching a peak of 80 per cent in 1971/2.

That proportion was maintained until 1977/8 when the very sharp increase in tax thresholds, particularly for elderly people, resulted in an unprecedented reduction in the composite rate in relation to the basic rate. A further reduction occurred in 1978/9 such that the composite rate stood at 68.2 per cent of the basic rate, the lowest proportion since 1959/60. This trend was reversed modestly in 1979/80 and more sharply in 1980/1 as a consequence of the abolition of the 25 per cent tax band. It has been noted that the statistical investigation showed that, had the law not been changed, the composite rate would have been 25.5 per cent in 1980/1 and in fact this rate was eventually settled for 1981/2. This is equal to 85 per cent of the basic rate, the highest ever proportion and a significant change on the position of just three years earlier.

Variations in the ratio of the composite rate to the standard or basic rate of income tax can be explained either by changes in the tax thresholds or by the actions of non-taxpayers. For example, if non-taxpayers suddenly decide that they can invest their money more profitably elsewhere, then the composite rate will rise in relation to the basic rate. However, in practice it seems that variations in the composite rate as a proportion of the basic rate can largely be explained by changes in the tax thresholds rather than by changes in the behaviour of individual investors. The general tendency has been for the real level of tax thresholds to decline over time and therefore for the number of non-taxpayers to fall. It follows that the composite rate has increased in relation to the basic rate. This is illustrated in Table

13.2 which shows the composite rate as a percentage of the standard or basic rate and also the tax thresholds for a married couple with two children as a percentage of average earnings.

Table 13.2   Tax Thresholds and Relationship Between Composite and Standard/Basic Rate of Tax, 1949–50 to 1976–7

Year	Tax threshold for married couple with two children as percentage of average earnings	Composite rate as percentage of standard/basic rate
1949–50	98	57
1955–6	97	57
1966–7	75	76
1968–9	63	78
1972–3	63	77
1973–4	55	78
1974–5	54	80
1975–6	47	79
1976–7	49	79

Sources: The figures in the second column are taken from Table 13.1. The figures in the first column are taken from: A. B. Atkinson and J. S. Fleming, 'Unemployment, social security and incentives', *Midland Bank Review*, Autumn 1978.

The table shows that in 1949–50 the tax threshold for a married couple with two children was 98 per cent of average earnings and the composite rate stood at 57 per cent of the then standard rate. By 1966–7 the threshold had fallen to 75 per cent of average earnings and the composite rate had increased to 76 per cent of the basic rate. However, since that time the tax threshold has continued to rise substantially in relation to average earnings but the increases in the composite rate in relation to the basic rate have been less marked. The main reason for this could well be that a substantial proportion of investments with building societies are held by elderly investors, the earnings of many of whom have remained well below the tax threshold. Also, the allowances available to elderly investors have been increased substantially, particularly for the tax year 1977–8. The statistical investigation carried out in 1978–9 indicates a return to the long-term trend of the composite rate rising in relation to the basic rate.

The amount of composite rate tax actually paid by building societies depends of course not only on the tax rate but also on the total volume of savings invested with societies that are subject to the composite rate. Unfortunately, figures are not available to show composite rate tax liability for each year. However, Table 13.3 does show the income tax provided for in societies' accounts between 1965 and 1980.

It will be seen that the income tax provided for in societies' accounts has increased considerably from £89 million in 1965 to £1,372 million in 1980.

Societies pay their income tax in January and February of each year and the large sums involved necessarily have a substantial effect on societies' cash flow. When interest rates are at a high level, tax liability can be equal to as much as one per cent of the total assets of building societies.

Table 13.3 Building Societies and Income Tax, 1965–80

Year	Composite rate tax provided for in building society accounts £m.	Year	Composite rate tax provided for in building society accounts £m.
1965	89	1973	312
1966	100	1974	449
1967	123	1975	555
1968	151	1976	660
1969	189	1977	694
1970	226	1978	667
1971	248	1979	925
1972	277	1980	1,372

Notes:
1   The amounts paid include provision for tax at the standard or basic rate on the small proportion of investments held by individuals and bodies not liable to the composite rate.
2   The figures are in respect of societies' financial years and thus cover in many cases more than one tax rate. (Until 1975–6 societies were assessed at the composite rate applying at the end of their financial year for the whole of that financial year. In that year the system was changed such that the tax is charged at the rate applicable when interest is actually credited or paid out.)

The Effects of the Composite Rate

It was noted at the beginning of this chapter that there are two aspects of the income tax arrangements which merit special consideration:

(a) Whether the special arrangements give building societies a competitive advantage.
(b) Whether the special arrangements are fair.

The point about equity is a relatively simple one. The income tax arrangements effectively average out the basic rate tax liability of building society investors. The rate paid is a weighted average of a zero tax rate and the basic rate of tax. Both taxpayers and non-taxpayers receive the same net-of-tax return but the gross equivalent returns are very different. For example, when the building society ordinary share rate is 9.75 per cent and the basic rate of income tax is 30 per cent, then to an investor liable to tax the gross equivalent yield is 13.93 per cent while for an investor not liable the gross equivalent yield is the same as the net yield, 9.75 per cent. Non-taxpaying investors are invariably able to obtain a higher return from one of the institutions able to pay interest gross such as a clearing bank or the National Savings Bank.

There is therefore the argument that the income tax arrangements effectively involve the subsidisation of taxpaying investors by non-taxpaying investors. In reply, it can be pointed out that non-taxpayers are well aware of the special arrangements and their effect and could well invest with building societies for reasons other than obtaining the maximum return. On the other hand it would be naive to believe that all investors are aware of this and notwithstanding this point it must be regarded as being arbitrary that some investors are able to obtain a higher gross return than others.

Perhaps the more important aspect of the income tax arrangements is whether they give building societies a competitive advantage. The stated view of The Building Societies Association is that the arrangements do enable the mortgage rate to be kept at a lower level than would otherwise be the case and if this is accepted then by definition the arrangements must be said to give building societies a competitive advantage. The basic argument is very simple. For example, with an ordinary share rate of 9.75 per cent, a basic tax rate of 30 per cent and a composite rate of 25.5 per cent, the gross effective yield to taxpaying investors is 13.93 per cent but the gross cost to societies of their funds is just 13.09 per cent. It could therefore be suggested that the mortgage rate can be 0.84 per cent below the level that would otherwise obtain.

However, this is too simplistic in that it assumes that non-taxpayers are not responsive to interest rate differentials whereas taxpayers are. In fact, whether or not the arrangements give building societies a competitive advantage depends solely on the relative elasticities of demand for building society shares and deposits for those liable to the basic rate of tax and those not liable. This can be illustrated by Table 13.4 which shows for taxpayers and non-taxpayers the net yield from a building society, the gross equivalent yield and the cost to societies of savings when the ordinary share rate is 9.75 per cent, the basic rate of tax 30 per cent and the composite rate 25.5 per cent.

Table 13.4   The Effects of the Income Tax Arrangements

Tax liability of investor	Net rate received	Gross equivalent yield	Gross cost to societies with composite rate at 25.5%
Zero	9.75%	9.75%	13.09%
30% basic rate	9.75%	13.93%	13.09%

Table 13.4 shows that although the gross cost to societies of attracting money from basic rate taxpayers is quite substantially less than the yield to those taxpayers, exactly the opposite position obtains in respect of non-taxpayers. The gross yield to such investors in the example is 9.75 per cent but the money costs societies 13.09 per cent.

Thus the income tax arrangements give societies a competitive advantage in attracting money from taxpayers but a competitive disadvantage in attracting money from non-taxpayers. The arrangements as a whole only give societies a competitive advantage if those liable to the basic rate of tax are more interest-sensitive than those who are not liable to the basic rate of tax. This point was accepted by the Committee of London Clearing Bankers in their evidence to the Wilson Committee. The CLCB went on to argue that in fact taxpaying investors were more interest-sensitive than non-taxpaying investors and that therefore societies did enjoy a competitive advantage. This may well be the case but it is impossible to prove or, indeed, to quantify the effect. What can be said is that if the income tax arrangements were abolished then in order to attract the same volume of funds as is currently achieved societies would need to pay a gross rate of interest somewhere between the cost of their funds with the present composite rate and the gross yield to basic rate taxpayers. Taking the example given in Table 13.4, it might be that a gross yield of 13.5 per cent would be sufficient to attract the same volume of funds as would be attracted by a gross equivalent yield of 13.93 per cent to those investors who are taxpayers and 9.75 per cent to those who are non-taxpayers.

The income tax arrangements are seen by some as deliberately conferring on building societies a competitive advantage. The first section of this chapter has shown that the arrangements exist for historical reasons and it has never been the intention that they should give to societies an advantage over other institutions. However, this does not necessarily mean that they do not have such an advantage. Consideration has been given in the building society industry as to whether the income tax arrangements should be amended and the pros and cons are fairly finely balanced. On the one hand, it is accepted that the arrangements may be unfair to non-taxpayers and that to many investors the prospect of a gross yield would be more appealing than a gross equivalent yield. It would also be easier for societies to market a gross yield rather than the present unsatisfactory arrangement of having to quote a gross equivalent yield and then to qualify it by saying that it refers to basic rate taxpayers only. On the other hand, many investors do like the present arrangement whereby, as far as they are concerned, their building society interest is tax-paid and they need not be concerned with the Inland Revenue.

However, at the end of the day it is almost certainly the administrative reasons which provide the main justification for the income tax arrangements. At present the arrangements work very smoothly and require the minimum amount of work on the part of societies or the Inland Revenue although admittedly the statistical investigation is a tiresome process. Calculating the liability of each society in respect of its investors is a relatively simple matter and societies pay over to the Inland Revenue a sum currently in excess of £1,000 million a year when it is due in January or February. The Revenue obtains every penny it is entitled to, in contrast to many other taxes on interest which can relatively easily be avoided or at least deferred for some considerable time. If the arrangements were abolished and, say, building societies paid out interest gross, then the Revenue would need to collect all of the information from societies about interest payments and would have to assess separately some 20 million individuals, many with accounts with more than one society. If societies paid out interest after deduction of basic rate tax then the Revenue would be faced with having to make some five million refunds, probably of fairly small amounts. The government has indicated that the abolition of the arrangements would necessitate an extra 2,000 civil servants and for this reason alone it is unlikely that the arrangements will be abolished in the years immediately ahead.

Official Attitudes Towards the Income Tax Arrangements

The income tax arrangements became a matter for public debate at the end of the 1970s, primarily in the context of the discussion about the competitive advantages of building societies vis-à-vis the banks. The banks argued that the arrangements did give building societies a significant competitive advantage while societies denied that there was a substantial advantage. Inevitably the matter was discussed in quite some detail in the Wilson Committee report. The report argued that the arrangements do enable building societies to pay higher rates to depositors than would otherwise be the case and therefore give them a competitive advantage over other deposit-taking institutions or enable them to charge a lower rate for mortgages. The report noted that the main justification for the arrangements is the administrative convenience to the Inland Revenue but nevertheless it was argued that they distorted competition between building societies and other deposit-taking institutions. It was noted that the Treasury had informed the Wilson Committee that they would be unlikely to favour such a system if they were starting afresh and the Inland Revenue have resisted the extension of similar arrangements to other institutions. The Wilson Committee also believed it to be wrong for non-taxpaying building society investors 'many of whom may be unaware of the true position, to subsidise the taxpaying depositor or the house-purchaser'. The Committee recommended that the income tax arrangements should be terminated and that some means should be found to allow non-taxpaying building society depositors to receive interest at the gross rate.

The government has shown no signs of acting on this recommendation. In any event, the sharp increase in the composite rate in relation to the basic rate thrown up by the 1978/9 statistical investigation removes, to a significant extent, the alleged advantages which building societies enjoy by virtue of the income tax arrangements. Indeed, it was this development which led to substantial discussion about the merits of the income tax arrangements within the building society industry.

Chapter 14

The Recommended Rate System

An increasingly important policy issue which the building society industry has had to face in recent years has been the system by which the Council of the Association recommends rates of interest which societies should pay to investors and charge to borrowers. The recommended rate system has been subject to considerable external criticism and there have also been increasing signs that societies themselves are not entirely happy with the way the system has operated. Pressure on the recommended rate system has also been increased by growing competition for both savings and mortgages on the part of the banks, trustee savings banks and national savings. This chapter examines the nature of the recommended rate system, the effects of the system and official policy towards the recommendation of interest rates.

The Development and Nature of the Recommended Rate System

Chapter 1 of this book noted the growth of competition between societies in the 1930s, culminating with the 'code of ethics' split in 1936. Competition between societies in the 1930s was influenced by the prevailing economic climate. The depression, causing as it did very low interest rates, meant that societies had a plentiful supply of mortgage funds and were competing to lend money. The nature of that competition was at times somewhat fierce and many in the industry wanted to see a more orderly system.

In 1939, the Council of The Building Societies Association began to recommend rates of interest to be charged to borrowers and offered to investors. The recommendations have never been binding on societies but in practice the larger societies have tended to follow the recommendations as have most of the smaller ones although a significant number have chosen to operate on higher rates. The manner in which rates of interest are set by the Council was described in detail in Chapter 5 and at this stage it is sufficient to say merely that the Council's recommendations have tended to lag behind market rates and moreover that they have been generally below market rates. The rates of interest recommended by the Council for ordinary shares and new mortgages since 1939 are shown in Table 14.1

The Council of the Association normally meets monthly and thus the opportunities to change rates are somewhat limited. This leads to tremendous pressure at times of a possibility of changes in rates with discussions having to take place under the glare of publicity.

It has been noted that a number of smaller societies elect to operate on rates above the recommended rates and this has been a long-accepted part

Table 14.1   BSA Recommended Interest Rates, 1939–81

Year	Month of recommendation	Ordinary shares		New mortgages	
		Effective date	Rate %	Effective date	Rate %
1939	September				5.50
	November		3.50		
	December				5.00
1945	September				4.00
1951	April		2.25		
1952	March	April	2.50		4.50
1955	July	September	3.00		5.00
	November				5.25
1956	April			May	5.50
	July	October	3.50		6.00
1959	May	July	3.25	July	5.50
1960	May	July	3.50		6.00
1961	May	October	3.75		6.50
1963	January	April	3.50	February	6.00
1965	January	February	3.75	February	6.75
	June	July	4.00		
1966	May				7.125
	December	January 1967	4.25		
1968	April	May	4.50	May	7.625
1969	March	April	5.00	April	8.50
1971	October	January 1972	4.75	November	8.00
1972	September	October	5.25		8.50
1973	January	February	5.60		
	March	April	6.30		
	April	May	6.75		9.50
	August				10.00
	September	October	7.50		11.00
1975	April	June	7.00		
1976	April	May	6.50		10.50
	October	November	7.80		12.25
1977	April	May	7.00		11.25
	June	July	6.70		10.50
	September	November	6.00		9.50
1978	January	February	5.50		8.50
	June	July	6.70		9.75
	November	December	8.00		11.75
1979	July	August	8.75	January 1980	12.50
	November	December	10.50		15.00
1980	December	January 1981	9.25		14.00
1981	March	April	8.50		13.00
	October	November	9.75		15.00

Notes:
1 The effective dates for ordinary shares are the first of the months shown.
2 Normally, recommendations for new annuity loans apply immediately although on some occasions a date has been specified. No firm dates are set with respect to existing loans. Rates of interest on existing loans are usually reduced on the first of the month following the recommendation or on the first of the following month. Rates of interest can only be increased in accordance with the period of notice given in the mortgage deed. Ten years ago a three month period of notice was normal but now most mortgage deeds provide for one month's notice or no notice (in which case the rate will probably be increased on the first of the month following the recommendation).

of building society practice. Such societies have been able to grow very successfully as higher mortgage rates have not prevented loans being made in that there has been a permanent shortage of mortgage funds. However, recently the recommended rate system has come under increasing pressure and there have been attempts to tighten up the system.

In 1973 economic conditions turned against societies very quickly and there were no less than five BSA recommendations on interest rates. Several of these recommendations were precipitated by the actions of one or two large societies giving notice of their intention to increase rates. It was this factor, amongst others, which led to the Memorandum of Agreement between building societies and government. The Memorandum included as paragraph 5:

> The boards of directors of the 20 largest building societies, in recognition of the importance to existing and future owner-occupiers of the successful realisation of the objectives set out in the Memorandum, agree to support recommendations made or advice given by the Council in the light of reports given to the Council by the Joint Advisory Committee, subject only to the constraints imposed upon them by their obligation to manage their societies prudently in accordance with their responsibilites under the law and to the members and depositors in their society.

This clause is somewhat vague and there have been disagreements over what it actually means but the intention was that the largest societies should be bound to follow the recommendations made by the Council in respect of interest rates.

The recommended rate system came under pressure again early in 1977 when one large society gave notice of its intention to increase the ordinary share rate. The event was the culmination of a lengthy internal debate in the industry as to the merits or otherwise of term shares. Term shares had become increasingly popular since 1974 and were outside of the recommendations of the Association. The society concerned did not offer term shares and felt that the ordinary share rate was too low. A change in the economic environment enabled the society to withdraw its notice to increase rates and The Building Societies Association set up a committee to examine recommended rates. As a result, it was decided to recommend rates of interest on term shares and on subscription shares as well as on ordinary shares and this came into effect from April 1977.

The recommended rate system came under pressure again later in 1977 when several large societies decided not to reduce their rates for existing investors as quickly as the BSA Council had recommended.

For much of 1979, building society rates were not fully competitive and this led a number of societies to offer new forms of investment, in particular, shares offering a premium rate in exchange for a relatively short period of notice, term shares under which investors could continue to receive the premium rate after the term had expired and high rate shares subject to a penalty in the event of a withdrawal being made. Also, on the mortgage side, an increasing proportion of business was being done at rates above the BSA recommended mortgage rate. In 1974, 1975 and 1976, most societies introduced higher mortgage rates for loans of £15,000 or more. This £15,000 threshold was then a substantial figure but in real terms it was gradually reduced thereby causing an increasing proportion of loans to be above the recommended rate. Notwithstanding this weakening of the interest rate cartel, most societies continued to pay and charge on the bulk of their business the rates of interest recommended by the Council of the Association.

It is probably helpful to conclude this introductory section by setting out briefly how the recommended rate system works today. When the Council feels that a change in interest rates is necessary it recommends to societies a rate to be paid on ordinary shares and a base mortgage rate. Until October 1981 the Council also recommended rates for term shares, subscription shares, personal deposits and other less important accounts. However, some of these recommendations had been overtaken by events and for this reason the Council decided to restrict its recommendations to the two most important rates.

No building society is obliged to follow the rates of interest recommended by the Council although it has been argued that the Memorandum of Agreement obliges the largest twenty societies (now seventeen through mergers) to follow those recommendations. Against this view is the fact that the Memorandum of Agreement commits societies to support only recommendations made or advice given by the Council 'in the light of reports given to the Council by the Joint Advisory Committee'. In practice, the JAC has made no recommendations nor has it given advice to the Council on rates of interest.

The Building Societies Association operates a mechanism known as the interest rates undertaking which is frequently confused with the recommended rate system. Societies which are signatories to the undertaking agree to give the other signatories twenty-eight days' notice if they introduce a higher rate on any investment scheme. The undertaking can therefore be seen as an exchange of information and it is of course closely tied in with the recommended rate system. The intention is that if one large society gives notice of a significant change in its rates then there is an opportunity at an intervening Council meeting for the matter to be debated and possibly for the Council to make a recommendation.

It follows by definition that a price fixed through a cartel must be one other than that which would obtain in a free market and this has been the case with the BSA recommendations. Invariably the mortgage rate has been below a market clearing level with the result that there has been an unsatisfied demand for mortgage loans. It is this feature of the cartel which has attracted some criticism in recent years. On the other hand, it is the very same facet of the cartel, that is that it keeps the mortgage rate down, which has led to government acquiescence in its continuance and also to some building society justification for the system.

The Effects of the Recommended Rate System

It has been noted that one effect of the recommended rate system is to keep the mortgage rate below a market clearing level and hence to lead to excess demand. One criticism of the system is that this in itself is undesirable in an advanced industrial country where people expect to be able to buy those commodities which they require. The lack of readily available mortgages also causes problems for the housing market and in particular house-builders. There have been many periods in which the sale of a new house could not go through or, more likely, was delayed, because mortgage finance was not readily available. Also, in the secondhand market, the lack of mortgage finance on demand has led to chains breaking down and could increase the cost for some house-purchasers.

Because the majority of building societies have not charged a market clearing rate for mortgages, the way has been opened for some building societies and other financial institutions to enter the mortgage market in a significant way. Indeed, one of the most surprising aspects of the mortgage market in the post-war period has been the failure of savings banks and banks to exploit a profitable outlet for their funds. There have been occasions when the limited amount of lending done by the clearing banks has been at rates of interest perhaps 6 or 7 per cent above the building society recommended rate and the fact that the banks have been able to lend on good securities at such rates indicates just how far below the market clearing rate the building society rate has been at times. Some building societies had also exploited this position to make relatively high yielding loans which have enabled them to pay out higher rates to their investors and thereby to grow more rapidly than their competitors.

Critics of the recommended rate system have also argued that by stifling price competition it has encouraged non-price competition and they have pointed to the growth in the number of building society branches and also to the high level of advertising as examples of this. Indeed, economic theory would lead one to suggest that if price competition is restricted then non-price competition will take its place and this has been noticeable in other industries, in particular, the airline industry.

Several defences have been offered for the recommended rate system. Perhaps the most important is that the mortgage contract is quite different from other contracts which people enter into. Normally, someone purchasing a good knows what he is buying and pays out a sum of money there and then for it. In the case of a building society mortgage, the variable rate nature of the contract means that the purchaser (that is the borrower) cannot be at all certain of the price he is being asked to pay. He might take out a loan at, say, 10 per cent only to find that two months later that rate has been increased to 20 per cent. As economists know, a free market implies perfect knowledge and it is impossible for consumers of building society mortgages to have perfect knowledge if their rate of interest can be changed at virtually no notice and by any amount. The recommended rate system can therefore be seen as affording a measure of protection to borrowers and without it there seems little doubt that on occasions in the past the rate of interest to existing borrowers would have increased very significantly in short periods of time in response to market pressures.

A second justification for the recommended rate system is that it introduces stability into a market which affects millions of ordinary people. In the financial markets where institutions are the participants, rapid fluctuations in interest rates are an accepted part of operations. However, building societies deal with ordinary people – 20 million investors and 5 million borrowers – and many of their customers do not wish to see interest rates rising and falling by significant amounts in a short period of time. This is particularly true for borrowers, for many of whom the mortgage payment might represent a substantial proportion of their disposable income. The recommended rate system has, in fact, been remarkably successful in steering a middle course between the extreme fluctuations in interest rates.

Building societies reply to the criticism that the recommended rate system has increased non-price competition by pointing out that their management expenses compare very favourably with those of other financial institutions such as banks, unit trusts and trustee savings banks and that they have far fewer branch offices than do the clearing banks and that they have a considerably higher volume of deposits per branch than do the trustee savings banks.

Building societies are able to claim that the number of investors has increased in line with the growth of the number of branches in recent years and that newly-established branches can often become very profitable within a short time period.

At the end of the day, the arguments for and against the recommended rate system are finely balanced. Moreover, they are closely tied in with the issues discussed in the chapter on the Stow Report. If the BSA recommended rates are set at a market clearing level then, by definition, they will not be able to have the adverse consequences which their critics argue exist and indeed the recommended rates would become superfluous. The nearer BSA recommended rates are to market rates, the greater the fluctuation in those rates is likely to be and the less will be the opportunities for non-price competition. However, it does seem likely that events are overtaking the results of the intensive debate now going on as to the merits or otherwise of the recommended rate system. Societies have been increasingly going their own way in recent years and stronger competition from outside is forcing the industry as a whole to adopt a more competitive stance. There seems every likelihood that building societies will become more integrated into the rest of the financial system and thereby operate on rates of interest similar to those paid and offered by other institutuions.

The Development of Government Policy Towards the Recommended Rate System

In general, government has acquiesced in the recommended rate system, largely because of political preoccupation with keeping the mortgage rate down. This policy has led to government intervention in the form of an interest subsidy in 1973, a £500 million loan in 1974 and severe pressure on societies at other times. The government has considered, for reasons which are not entirely clear, that a rise in mortgage rates has a profound political impact whereas a rise in investment rates has no such impact. Recent experience suggests that in fact the political problems caused by rising mortgage rates are largely a result of the publicity created by the government itself and on those occasions when government has chosen to sit back and not comment on building society interest rates, large increases in the mortgage rate have been accepted with apparent ease. This was particularly noticeable in November 1979 when government chose not to comment on the rise in the BSA recommended mortgage rate to 15 per cent nor did it seek to influence that decision. The result was that the issue rapidly died down as a news event.

Government acquiescence in the recommended rate system can be illustrated by the fact that the recommended mortgage rate has been included in agreements between government and building societies. It was, for example, written into the agreements between the Ministry of Housing and Local Government (n(⁄ the Department of the Environment) and building societies participating in the house-purchase and housing scheme 1959. Also, the government has exempted building society rates of interest from restrictive practices legislation.

The Prices and Incomes Board report in 1966 did investigate the practice of recommending interest rates. It said that this practice 'tends to lead to the determination of margins between the investment and mortgage rates that are sufficient to allow the least efficient societies to survive and, at the same time, to give generous margins to the more efficient societies'. However, the Prices and Incomes Board did not advocate ending the recommended rate system, partly because this would call into question the practices of other financial institutions, in particular, the practice of the clearing banks in maintaining a fixed relationship between their rates and bank rate.

In 1967 the Prices and Incomes Board report on bank charges strongly recommended an increase in competition between the clearing banks and argued that there was no case for any agreement between the banks on their deposit rate and certain lending rates. In this report, the Board made a reference back to its earlier report on building society rates:

> Since we have recommended the dissolution of most of the collective agreements by the banks, we therefore also recommend that the recommendation by The Building Societies Association of a deposit and lending rate should cease. We would expect that as a result the rates would increasingly be determined by the more competitive as against the weaker societies.

No action was taken as a result of this recommendation.

The Labour government's Housing Policy Review also considered the recommended rate system. This noted that because societies are very similar, differences in interest rates offered for investments on similar terms would not last long even in the absence of recommended rates and the position with respect to the clearing banks was pointed to as an analogy. However, it was noted that with persisting unmet demand for mortgages there would be no inducement to charge lower mortgage rates in order to get a larger share of business and the ending of recommended rates would lead to increased competition via enhanced rates offered to investors.

It was noted that market clearing interest rates had their attraction for the potential purchaser in that an expensive loan was better than no loan at all. However, it was considered that market clearing rates would pose very serious problems for housing policy through the effect on marginal first-time buyers. It added that market clearing related to people actually in the market for buying a house and that these were only a fraction of all building society borrowers. The Green Paper made no recommendation on recommended rates but clearly it was in sympathy with the system.

The Bank of England has tended to take a somewhat stronger line against the recommended rate system than has the government and this was exemplified in a speech made by the Governor of the Bank of England to The Building Societies Association annual conference in 1978. The Governor's comments are set out below in full.

Recommended rates and competition

The other main aspect of competition is internal competition amongst societies themselves. As I see it, this is determined by the recommended rate agreement, in combination now with the guideline system. In most industrial or service sectors we might wonder whether such a system would not discourage efficiency and innovation and perhaps encourage competition of the wrong sort, for example in an unnecessary expenditure on outlets or branches.

It is, I think, difficult to judge whether this has happened in your case. It is a matter of record that the number of building society branches has doubled since 1969, but there have, of course, been more mortgages to service and more money to gather in. The number of share and deposit accounts has more than doubled, and the number of mortgage advances increased by about one-third. Your very success in these spheres must be an important part of the defence against doubts about efficiency.

No doubt those branches earn their keep but it is not altogether surprising that outsiders sometimes wonder about the extent to which some of them do so only because the margin between borrowing and lending rates is fixed under present arrangements to ensure such an outcome.

Such scepticism is bound to arise in situations where the traditional objective test of efficiency – profit – is absent or in some way trammelled. It is therefore, I believe, important that careful consideration be given to the question whether alternative arrangements might not have beneficial effects.

It has been argued, for example, that if the fixing of borrowing and lending rates according to their own best judgment were to rest more firmly with the directors of each building society there would be found some scope for cutting costs and margins, with resulting benefits to the successful society and to both its investors and its borrowers.

The effects of competition

In considering such a substantial change, however, it would be essential to think through the consequences thoroughly. Some would argue that the cost of mortgages would rise. This might be so, although whether temporarily while adjustments were taking place, or permanently might very much depend on the extent to which competition was genuinely unfettered.

Also, it is likely that keener competition would lead to amalgamations among societies, and these might well be desirable in some cases in any event – even though they may be difficult to achieve. The difficulties seem to stem not so much from the statutory procedure whereby a merger has to be approved, since the most onerous provisions can be waived by the Chief Registrar of Friendly Societies, but rather to the inhibitions societies themselves have against mergers because of the resulting loss of identity by one of the parties. What this points to is the need particularly to encourage mergers which would improve efficiency without losing the very valuable ingredients of flexibility and grass-roots contact that local societies are able to provide.

Increased competition within the movement, and indeed other possible changes adumbrated earlier, might well lead to fears of imprudent practices creeping in. Imprudence tends to be an unwelcome risk of freedom and innovation. The answer is not, in my judgment, to stifle freedom and innovation, but to ensure that supervisory arrangements are constantly examined for their adequacy and relevance.

The Wilson Committee Report devoted a chapter (8) to the recommended rate system. After describing how the recommended rate system worked, the chapter noted that in the past it has been defended by the BSA 'as the best way to keep the mortgage rate as low as possible and to maintain equity between their savers and borrowers'. The report commented that the system has increasingly come under pressure as it keeps the mortgage rate below the market clearing level and noted the argument that the recommended rate system produces a margin larger than the most efficient societies need. In this respect, it examined administrative expenses and branch expansion. However, the comment of the Chief Registrar of Friendly Societies that costs of societies are generally not excessive was mentioned.

The report accepted that each new branch tended to become profitable but argued that even if this was the case there was no guarantee that the whole branch network would be cost-effective and that a new branch might draw funds from another branch of the same society as well as from competing societies. After noting that there are twenty societies in the UK which try to offer the same facilities on a national basis, it was argued that this must imply some waste of resources and that greater competition between societies would cause them to examine the viability of their branch networks with some care.

The Wilson Committee drew an analogy between the recommended rate system and the pre-1971 clearing bank cartel. It was argued that although the cartel had been approved of by government and the banks at the time, it was now recognised that it did have deleterious effects on their innovativeness and flexibility and that it was partly responsible for allowing the American banks to make such a strong entry into the British market.

The Wilson Committee tended to the view that the interest rate cartel produced doubtful benefits and, by encouraging non-price competition, was wasteful of resources. It argued that the only way of providing a competitive spur to societies was the ending of the recommended rate system.

The Wilson Committee suggested that by cutting down the margins, societies might be able to pay higher rates to their depositors without raising the mortgage rate. This is a somewhat surprising conclusion as almost every other commentator is agreed that abolition of the recommended rate system would lead to higher investment and mortgage rates and that there is very little scope for a reduction of margins in the industry as a whole.

The final paragraph of the Wilson Committee's chapter on the recommended rate system merits repeating in full:

> The recommended rate system has already come under pressure from within as the building societies have individually sought to increase their share of scarce funds by means such as term shares. Although the BSA have tried to contain this within an agreed framework, they have not had complete success. External pressure on the cartel results from the queue for mortgages and the expansion of the building societies' branch networks, both of which have become matters of public concern. We believe that these problems could be alleviated by greater competition among the societies. Whether the likely consequences of ending the interest rate cartel would be acceptable involves judgements about housing policy and social priorities which are clearly outside our remit. But we believe nevertheless that there are powerful arguments in favour of increasing competition among the building societies and to this end we recommend that the recommended rate system should be abolished.

Governments have shown no inclination to act on this recommendation of the Wilson Committee nor indeed on most of the other recommendations. However, there does seem to have been an increasing acceptance that greater competition between building societies themselves is inevitable and that this trend is likely to be accentuated by the growth of external competition.

The Consequences of Ending the Recommended Rate System

There seems little doubt that if the BSA Council ceased to recommend interest rates then, in a very short time, it would be the market that would establish building society rates of interest. This would mean that rates would be higher in relation to other rates than they have been in the past and that the market for mortgages would be cleared. The obvious beneficiaries from such a change would be those active in the housing market, both buyers and sellers. House-buyers would be able to borrow as much as they were willing and able to afford, subject only to the building society being satisfied that the risk was not excessive.

For building societies, one advantage of ending the recommended rate system would be to lessen the likelihood of other institutions taking a substantial share of the mortgage market. The point has been made that the reason why the banks have been able to lend at rates well above the building society rate is that the building society rate has itself been below a market clearing level. If the mortgage rate was at or near a market clearing level the banks would be less able to make significant inroads into the market.

If building society rates reach a market clearing level then the mortgage market would be integrated more generally into the financial markets and this might open the way for a secondary market in mortgages as exists in other countries and also for the possibility of mortgage loans being transferred when houses are sold, again a common practice in other countries.

The ending of the recommended rate system would also benefit building society investors in that they would receive higher rates of interest relative to those offered by other institutions. However, quite possibly the ending of the cartel might lead to a reconsideration of the amount which building societies pay for some types of money, in particular, small amounts withdrawable on demand. There are many in the industry who believe that at present too high a rate is paid on such deposits.

There are always dangers in moving from a state of no competition to one of free competition and these would be evident if the BSA recommended rate system broke down. Those societies that currently prosper by operating on higher interest rates than the normal would immediately be placed in difficulty if all creditworthy potential house-buyers could obtain loans at the normal rate from one of the more established societies. The danger would exist that the less efficient societies might indulge in risky lending and some might even have to face existing loans being refinanced at lower rates of interest. Such a situation would lead to a considerable rationalisation of the industry with more efficient societies growing rapidly and the less efficient ones going out of business.

It is far from easy to speculate on the political consequences of ending the recommended rate system. As the Wilson Committee pointed out, the cartel operated by the clearing banks was universally held to be a good thing until its abolition in 1971 since which time it has been universally recognised to be a bad thing. The ending of the cartel would, in the short term, mean higher mortgage rates and arguably this might not be politically acceptable. On the other hand, it can be argued with equal force that the political sensitivity of the mortgage rate stems partly from the existence of the recommended rate system. At present there is something called 'the mortgage rate' which can be changed on ten days of the year only. If the mortgage rate was set by market conditions and indeed if there was no one rate then quite possibly there would be less public and political sensitivity to changes in the rate.

The potential losers from ending the recommended rate system would be existing owner-occupiers and especially those who have no wish to move at some time in the future. In most other countries, mortgage rates are set at a market clearing level but in nearly all of those countries the rates are fixed and the borrower therefore knows what he is undertaking the moment that he takes out his loan. It has been noted that the position of the existing borrower is one reason that societies give for maintaining the recommended rate system. Possibly, if a sufficiently free market could be established, existing borrowers would have a measure of protection in that if their society tries to raise their rates unduly they could refinance their loans at a lower rate of interest. However, the costs of so doing are quite considerable and many existing borrowers would still be vulnerable to unilateral action on the part of their society.

It is possible to devise means of protecting existing borrowers from sharp increases in the mortgage rate. There are any number of schemes which involve divorcing the rate charged on the mortgage account from the repayments actually made. However, all such schemes necessarily involve an increase in the size of the mortgage debt and experience shows that this is not acceptable to many borrowers, however irrational this view might be.

It remains to be seen if the recommended rate system will end and if so what the exact consequences will be. Certainly there has been greater competition between societies themselves and other financial institutions and the cartel is gradually being eroded.

Chapter 15

The European Community and Housing Finance

An Introduction to the European Community

The European Community or Common Market, as it is sometimes known, is a grouping of countries in Western Europe. The Community had six members when it was established in 1957 – France, West Germany, Italy, Belgium, the Netherlands and Luxembourg. Great Britain, Denmark and the Republic of Ireland joined the Community in 1973, and Greece became a member at the beginning of 1981. Portugal and Spain are seeking to join the Community at some time in the future and another potential member is Norway which had agreed to join the Community at the beginning of 1973 but whose government's decision was overturned by a referendum.

The origins of the European Community go back to the early 1950s when the European Coal and Steel Community was formed. This working relationship led to more general political co-operation and the Treaty of Rome, which brought into being the European Economic Community, was signed on 25 March 1957. The Treaty, like other treaties between sovereign states, had to be approved by the parliaments in each of the six members.

Looked at widely, the European Community is a political animal and the motives behind its foundation and progression are political rather than economic. The original linking together of the German and French steel industries was partly designed to minimise the prospects of a future war between the two countries. For Germany, the European Community was one of the avenues to political respectability following the Second World War. France has seen the Community as being a political counter-balance in the Western world to the United States and has also sought benefits for its agricultural industry. Detailed policy-making within the Community needs to be seen in the light of these overall objectives and to a considerable extent it is not detailed measures which are eventually agreed which are of significance but rather the discussion behind the agreements is intended to promote political and economic understanding.

The stated aims of the European Community are ambitious; in effect, to create a single market covering much of Western Europe. In practice, the Community remains very much a grouping of independent sovereign states which collaborate together on a systematic basis over a wide range of activities. The European Community is very different from federal states such as Canada, Australia and the United States. There has been little centralisation of important decision-taking and most major issues are still hammered out in detailed and lengthy negotiations between respective governments, all intent on preserving their domestic interests.

Effectively, the decision-taking body of the European Community is the Council of Ministers. Contrary to its name, this is not a specific group of people but, rather, the ministers depend on the subject under discussion. Thus, if transport is being discussed then the transport ministers of the various countries would comprise the Council of Ministers. The chairmanship of the Council rotates between the member states at six-monthly intervals and inevitably this lack of continuity, together with the strain imposed on the resources of the smaller member states, does not make for good decision taking.

The Commission is the European Community's civil service. It comprises staff whose job it is to research policy and to put forward proposals together with supporting staff and a large number of interpreters. The Commission is divided into directorates-general, with each covering a specific sphere such as agriculture or competition. The Commission is further sub-divided into directorates. Thus, Directorate-General XV is the one responsible for 'financial institutions and taxation' and, within this, Directorate A is responsible for financial institutions. There are fourteen commissioners, two from each of the larger countries and one from each of the smaller nations. They serve for a four-year term although they can be, and frequently are, re-appointed. The appointment of commissioners and senior Commission staff is done on an entirely national basis, something which might not seem to be in tune with the objectives of the Community. Thus, it is a rule that the commissioners and directors-general for each specific area must not be from the same country.

The European Parliament is a directly elected body with 434 members. However, to call it a parliament is perhaps something of a misnomer in that it has few powers and its rather nomadic existence of meeting in Luxembourg and Strasbourg has further served to reduce its influence. However, in time the Parliament could gain a much greater status.

The final major body of the European Community is the European Court of Justice which has an important role in interpreting Community legislation and in establishing case law.

The method of operation of the European Community is somewhat tortuous. Attempts to harmonise a policy will probably start with research being conducted by the Commission who will publish their ideas, as a Commission Staff Working Paper, at a much earlier stage than is common in most countries. Thus, a 'draft directive' might be published which would be more tentative than a 'White Paper' in Britain. The draft directive will be subject to detailed amendment and many years are likely to elapse before the Council finally adopts a directive and it becomes Community policy. Basically, directives require member states to bring their laws into line within the overall constraints of the directive but the method by which this is achieved remains a matter for the individual states.

The Need for Harmonisation of Housing Finance in the Common Market

Before discussing in detail the proposals which have been made to harmonise housing finance in the European Community, it is helpful to discuss at a theoretical level why there should be such harmonisation. This is a very important issue and one that is frequently neglected. Indeed, there has sometimes been a tendency for harmonisation to be seen as an objective in its own right rather than as a means to an end. The Commission is now extremely sensitive to this criticism and there is less evidence of harmonisation for its own sake. Basically, a common market implies an area in which there is free movement of people, capital and physical resources in response to economic forces. A reasonably free market already exists in respect of physical goods as tariffs between the states of the European Community have largely been abolished. Equally, following the abolition of exchange controls in Britain in 1979, there is now, to a significant extent, a free market of capital within the Community.

In the context of housing finance, the question that has to be asked is what steps have to be taken in order to ensure that people, capital and goods are not inhibited from moving across the frontiers of the Community because of the differing systems of housing finance. Immediately, this implies that it is not essential to have identical systems of housing finance in each country. Nor is it essential that housing finance institutions should operate across state borders. However, at this stage a wider issue must be brought in. Different systems of housing finance can have important competitive effects between the countries of a common market. Thus, if there is subsidised housing in one country but not in others this might influence people's willingness to move in response to economic forces. Equally, if housing finance is heavily subsidised it can distort competition between housing and other industries.

Taking the narrow issue first, it can be argued that the effective operation of a common market does not necessitate housing finance institutions to operate in more than one country. In a number of other countries such as the United States and Australia housing finance institutions can operate, for the most part, only in their state of origin and this does not stop the two countries concerned being common markets in every sense of the expression and indeed political unions. Even in some of the Community countries, such as West Germany, some financial institutions, for example, the public savings banks, are able to operate only within their respective states. Thus, while the ability of housing finance institutions to operate across national frontiers might be desirable, experience in other countries shows that it is not essential if a common market is to exist.

However, as has already been indicated, what matters is that people should not be inhibited from moving across national frontiers because of differences in housing finance systems. Thus, it would be quite improper if British building societies refused to lend to people moving to the UK from Germany or Italy and it would be equally improper if German savings banks did not lend to foreign nationals. In practice, such discrimination is not significant although the frequent requirement to have savings before one can borrow (contractually in Germany, customarily in Britain) does not make things easy for foreigners. However, the point should be made that many people who are likely to move across national frontiers may wish only to rent accommodation rather than buy, especially if they expect their move to be short-term. In this context, the Rent Acts, discouraging as they do the provision of market rented accommodation in Britain, can be seen to be a more important deterrent to the free movement of labour between Britain and the rest of the European Community than can the different nature of the housing finance systems.

Certainly, housing finance institutions can argue that they are at a disadvantage if they cannot help those of their existing customers who wish to move abroad and this is a valid point. However, it is open to such institutions to make co-operative arrangements with similar institutions in other countries which then might be able to overcome any such problems.

The question as to whether national housing finance systems can lead to wider distortions is a more crucial one and, perhaps for that reason, has hardly been touched on as yet. Certainly it is inconceivable that Britain would repeal its Rent Acts because these adversely affect the operation of the Common Market or that council rents could be doubled or that mortgage tax relief could be abolished. Yet in terms of the operation of a common market these are more significant factors than the lack of a common market in housing finance.

The need to have cross-frontier operations by housing finance institutions in the Common Market or the harmonisation of those systems is somewhat weaker than the need to have cross-frontier flows of industrial goods. Perhaps for this reason little progress has been made on harmonising housing finance or permitting financial institutions in the European Community countries to operate in other countries of the Community merely because of the existence of the Community.

Before turning to what has been happening in practice in the European Community, it is necessary at this stage to point out that the scope for integrating markets at the retail level is far less than integrating markets used by commercial enterprises. Governments may be less and less nationalistic but people tend to stick to the institutions they know in their respective countries and experience has shown that it is very difficult for foreign banks and other financial institutions to make inroads into the various national markets at the retail level. For example, the American banks have been very successful in securing a high proportion of wholesale banking in Britain but they have been far less successful at the retail level.

European Housing Finance Organisations

Research reveals that there is a wide diversity of housing finance systems in the European Community. Some countries, such as Denmark, rely almost exclusively on the mortgage bank system while Britain and the Republic of Ireland rely exclusively on the savings bank system. Germany and France offer a combination of the systems. Moreover, in most of the countries housing finance is provided either directly by more general financial institutions such as banks or by specialist subsidiaries of larger financial institutions. Britain, Ireland and Denmark are exceptions in that in those countries housing finance is almost entirely provided by specialist organisations.

Not only do national housing finance systems differ in the various countries of the European Community but there are also differences of equal, or probably greater, importance in the tax systems, incentives to save and the housing markets. These differences make it very difficult for specialist housing finance organisations to contemplate operating in other countries.

In West Germany, the Bausparkassen system depends on the federal government's tax incentives and the Bausparkassen would not be able to use such a system in Britain. British building societies have special tax arrangements with the Inland Revenue which make their investments less attractive to overseas investors. The many other differences that exist make it clear that complete harmonisation of housing finance systems is an impossible and, indeed, an unnecessary objective. Modifications to allow them to work side-by-side on a competitive basis pose major problems but a start has been made.

One great spin-off from the European Community has been the establishment of Communitywide trade associations. There are two associations within the Community to which housing finance organisations belong and Britain is strongly represented on both. They have played a major role in formulating Community action on housing finance.

The European Federation of Building Societies (EFBS) was founded in Brussels in 1962 by representatives of building society-type organisations in Rotterdam, Brussels, Paris and Bonn. Today, the Federation comprises the national associations or institutions of the most important countries belonging to the Community or which are associated with the Community. The Building Societies Association of Great Britain became a full member of the EFBS in June 1973, following Britain's accession to the Community. Currently, there are five hundred building societies or their European equivalents which are directly or indirectly represented in the Federation.

The primary aims of the Federation are:

(a) Collaboration amongst its members in relation to the European Community.
(b) The study of measures necessary to the development of the Community and the co-ordination of activities of the organisations with special regard to the problems of supervision, taxation and monetary control.
(c) The representation of interests of members in the bodies of the European Community.
(d) Studying of conditions under which competition among the various organisations will develop and co-operation with organisations or groups of organisations with comparable activities.

Like other European organisations, the EFBS has been particularly successful in promoting an increased level of understanding of housing finance between its members. To some extent, this is achieved through triennial congresses, the most recent of which was held in London in 1979.

The Commission's governing body is its Council of Management. In 1972 three permanent committees were established.

The work of the Marketing, Advertising and Competition Committee is centred on three areas:

(a) The exchange of information on the housing and housing finance markets.

(b) The studying of the conditions under which competition takes place in various countries.

(c) Involvement in the creation of Community policy on advertising and competition. In this context, the Committee has dealt with, for example, a 'preliminary draft directive on the activity of financial intermediary and auxiliary and on the canvassing and advertising of loan and deposit facilities for the public'.

The Economic Affairs Committee is primarily concerned with financial matters. It has studied existing operating ratios in the context of different housing finance systems and has also prepared a booklet setting out in English, French and German a glossary of terms used in housing finance. The Committee is also concerned with tax systems and the currency aspects of the proposed special directive on housing finance, which will be explained later in this chapter. Attention is currently being given to a draft directive on the annual accounts of banks, which could have application to housing finance.

The Legal Affairs Committee undertakes the scrutiny of the proposals for changes in the law which emerge from Brussels and which have some bearing on the operation of building society-type organisations. It discusses with the Commission any proposals which trouble the Committee. It is concerned both with the policy underlying the proposals and with their detail. Among the topics recently within its ambit are the legal aspects of the proposed second directive on housing finance, the proposal for a directive on doorstep selling, the draft directive on consumer credit, a working paper on the closure and dissolution of credit institutions, the Convention of Bankruptcy, Winding-Up, etc. and the harmonisation of the laws relating to guarantees and indemnities. It was also involved with the First Directive on Credit Insitutions mentioned below.

The second European organisation concerned with mortgage finance is the European Community Mortgage Federation (ECMF) which was formed in Brussels in 1967 and which was recognised by Royal Decree in 1971 as an International Association under Belgian law. Unlike the EFBS the ECMF involves all types of mortgage lenders and not just housing finance institutions. It comprises institutions from Belgium, Denmark, Germany, Great Britain, Greece, Italy and the Netherlands; Norway and Spain have observer status.

The ECMF has three objectives:

(a) To enquire into measures that could be adopted within the EEC to encourage mortgage lending and to disseminate the results of such enquiry, together with other information of interest in the field of mortgage lending in the countries of the EEC.

(b) To give expert advice to the institutions of the EEC on all questions of interest to mortgage lenders.

(c) Generally, to promote the interests within the EEC of mortgage lenders, whether professional or institutional.

The Federation has a permanent secretariat based in Brussels and carries out its work through a General Council, Executive Committee and two working parties.

The First EEC Directive on Credit Institutions

In 1972 the Commission took its first significant step towards harmonising financial systems when it published a 'draft directive for the co-ordination of the legal and administrative provisions for the taking up and exercise of the independent operator activities of credit institutions'. This was a very ambitious document seeking to establish at one stroke a single legal framework for all financial institutions in the Community. The framework would include common standards with respect to solvency and liquidity ratios. This objective was unrealistic and the draft directive died a rapid death.

A less rigid draft directive was published in 1974 and after considerable debate this became, on 12 December 1977, a first Council directive (no. 77/780/EEC) 'on the co-ordination of laws, regulations and the administrative provisions relating to the taking up and pursuit of the business of credit institutions'. This is a very general directive and is sometimes known as the 'umbrella directive' and covers all financial institutions, not just specialised housing finance institutions. The directive is largely concerned with conditions which must be met so as to enable a credit institution to begin operation and does not deal extensively with the supervision or method of operation of existing financial institutions. The objectives of the directive are listed as including the protection of savings and the creation of conditions for fair competition although in practice the directive does little to further these aims.

The directive applies generally to credit institutions although central banks and some other organisations (for example the National Savings Bank and the Agricultural Mortgage Corporation in the UK) are exempted. Member states are permitted to defer application of the directive where its immediate application would cause short-term technical problems. The deferment can be for a maximum of eight years and therefore it must be implemented in all countries by the end of 1985. In fact, some countries, for example West Germany, were in effect implementing the directive before it was approved and thus no further action was required on their part.

Article 3 of the directive obliges members to require new credit institutions to obtain authorisation before commencing business and to lay down the requirements for obtaining authorisation. Four conditions must be complied with before a credit institution can be granted authorisation:

(a) It must possess its separate own funds.
(b) It must possess adequate minimum own funds.
(c) There must be at least two persons who effectively direct its business.
(d) These two persons must be of good repute and have sufficient experience to perform such duties.

It should be noted that these requirements are not particularly onerous and would not pose a problem for any reputable financial institution except, perhaps, for very small ones. Moreover, the requirements would not, for the most part, apply to existing financial institutions although the directive does lay down conditions under which authorisation can be withdrawn. For example, if an existing institution fails to continue to meet the four principles set out above, its authorisation can be withdrawn and this might, for example, have implications for some building societies in Britain which cannot claim to have two persons effectively directing the business of the society.

Article 4 of the directive is particularly significant in that it provides that authorisation in a member state of an organisation whose head office is elsewhere cannot be denied simply because that type of organisation is unknown. Thus, the UK would not be allowed to refuse to authorise a Bausparkasse on the grounds that British law made no provision for this type of organisation. Article 6 of the directive requires that the competent authorities should establish ratios between the various assets and/or liabilities of the various credit institutions with a view to monitoring their solvency and liquidity and any other measures which may serve to ensure that savings are protected. Article 11 of the directive provides for an advisory committee of the competent authorities of the member countries to be set up.

It should be emphasised that this directive does not allow financial institutions not previously authorised to operate abroad to do so. More generally, the directive is a very modest measure but it is significant that no less than thirteen years will elapse between its initial inception and its complete implementation. This is an indication of the pace at which the harmonisation of financial institutions can be expected to proceed. The directive is seen as being the first step on the long path of full financial harmonisation under which the institutions would be supervised by their state of origin under an agreed set of observation ratios and be able to operate and establish branches in any other state of the Community.

Staff Papers on Housing Credit

So far as it can be discerned, the Commission's policy towards the harmonisation of housing credit rests on three principles:

(a) A gradual approach.
(b) Control being exercised by home countries.
(c) The maintenance of different systems which could operate alongside each other.

The first document from the Commission on this subject was a staff paper on co-ordination of the legal provisions relating to housing credit (XV/38/78, April 1978). Broadly speaking, this was a fairly ambitious document which concentrated on cross-frontier operations by housing credit institutions. It noted the problem that, in general, specialist mortgage institutions are not able to lend outside of their country of origin because of domestic legislation. The more general financial institutions are not of course under any such constraint. The paper considered whether such institutions could be defined either by reference to their activities or by a listing of the relevant institutions. One problem that the Commission immediately came up against was that there are no specialised institutions in Belgium or Luxembourg and, in Italy, the savings banks, while not being specialist, are by far the major providers of mortgage finance.

The document basically comprised a study of the obstacles to cross-frontier operation. The major ones listed were:

(a) Foreign exchange regulations.
(b) The categories of security which can be accepted.
(c) The exchange risk.
(d) The payment of housing subsidies through domestic institutions.
(e) Restrictions on the establishment of foreign subsidiaries or branches.

The staff paper proposed that there should be a special directive to remove, as far as possible, these obstacles. It suggested, for example, that there could be a simple declaration that the various securities accepted by specialist housing finance institutions should be accepted as being equal. This is an attractive approach but it poses major problems for institutions such as building societies for whom the concept of the British mortgage is of vital importance and is enshrined in building society legislation. It was also anticipated that a special directive might set out mechanisms for reducing the exchange risk and for making the necessary supervisory changes.

A second staff paper under title 'Freedom of Movement in the Housing Credit Sector', Second Commission Staff Paper (XV/118/79, October 1979), is somewhat less ambitious and is seen by the Commission as being complementary to the first staff paper. It concentrates largely on freedom of establishment. It suggested that the scope of the special directive should be restricted to institutions whose activity consists of the granting of loans secured by mortgage on residential property. The document accepted that at present it was not feasible to consider operations in foreign currencies. Significantly, the document also accepted that it would only be attractive for an institution to set up abroad if it could use its own domestic system. Thus, there would be little point in a British building society going to West Germany and operating the Bausparkasse system when West German Bausparkassen already do this effectively. Equally, there would seem little point in a German Bausparkasse coming to the UK and trying to operate in the same way as a British building society.

The paper recognised that there were four major problems with this approach:

(a) The compatibility of the various systems for the reasons outlined above.
(b) Supervision, for which it was proposed that there should be close co-operation between the member states.
(c) The structure of the capital market, for example, regulations governing the ownership of bonds (not particularly relevant for British building societies).
(d) Competitive distortions arising, for example, from the way in which monetary policy is implemented. Thus, one country might at any one time have a credit ceiling and it would be anomalous if domestic institutions were subject to this but not foreign institutions.

Discussion is continuing on these two staff papers and eventually is expected to lead to a draft directive. However, such a directive is unlikely to become a Council directive for a considerable time as clearly there are immense problems to be solved before each member nation of the European Community is in a position to allow its specialist housing finance institutions to operate in other countries.

Britain and the European Community

Britain chose not to join the European Economic Community at its inception in 1957, largely on political grounds. By 1961 there was a change of heart and Britain applied for membership of the Community. This application was, effectively, vetoed by General de Gaulle in 1963. In 1967 Britain re-applied and this time, albeit after lengthy negotiations which were held in abeyance on more than one occasion, the application was successful and on 1 January 1973 Britain became a full member of the Community. The Treaty of Accession sets out the terms on which Britain joined the Community and as far as British law is concerned, the relevant legislation was the European Communities Act 1972, the most important features of which were the recognition of the Institutions of the Community and the adoption of a Community method of law-making.

The Building Societies Association was very quick to take the initiative on European matters and as early as 1972 it formally requested the government that in the next building society legislation there should be a provision to allow societies to invest a certain proportion of assets in other countries of the Community.

Before dealing with the first Council directive and, more generally, the steps that have to be taken before building societies are able to operate abroad, it is essential first to examine what the constraints are at present and secondly why building societies should wish to operate abroad.

The obstacle to British building societies operating in the other countries of the European Community is entirely British law. The Building Societies Act 1962, the statute under which societies operate, envisages societies operating only in the United Kingdom and section 1, which confines their lending to loans made on the security of mortgage of freehold or leasehold estate, in itself is adequate to rule out lending in any other country of the Community with the exception of the Republic of Ireland which also has this type of tenure. It would be feasible for the British government if it so wished to amend building society law such that societies would be free to operate in any other country of the Community or indeed the world and there is no special need for this to be done within the context of the European Community. It is an interesting analogy that the Royal Bank of Canada and Citibank Savings, organisations from North America, both freely lend on mortgage in Great Britain without anybody mentioning the words 'common market'. However, the UK has a very liberal attitude with regard to the operations of foreign institutions; some EEC countries are less liberal and this poses difficulties.

Why then should British building societies wish to operate in the other countries of the European Community? The Building Societies Association has argued that as the United Kingdom is a full member of the European Community, societies should play a wider role in the Community as the Treaty of Rome intends. Four reasons are given to support this view:

(a) It is argued that building societies are at a competitive disadvantage by their inability to lend funds elsewhere in the Community. There are a number of Britons who work in the Community and societies are not able to assist them with house-purchase. Equally, there might be a number of

Europeans working in the UK who might save with a building society if they could be certain of obtaining a building society loan on their return home. The Association points out that societies cannot compete on equal terms with British banks or foreign credit institutions who are able to operate across national frontiers.

(b) Operation in the European Community would conform to an existing pattern of development which the building society concept has made acceptable.

(c) Wider EEC operations would be likely to encourage inflows of capital to the UK.

(d) Britain's trade is predominantly with the European Community and the financial markets logically should follow this trend.

The Association has lobbied hard for legislation to confer powers on societies to operate across EEC frontiers but the British government has not been enthusiastic in its support for societies. The main reasons for caution would seem to be as follows:

(a) Societies are seldom able to meet mortgage demand in Britain so the logic of allowing them to operate elsewhere is open to question.

(b) In practice, the number of Britons abroad who require building society finance to enable them to purchase homes is very small.

(c) Legislation to enable societies to operate in the European Community would have very far-reaching implications for organisations which have hitherto been purely domestic.

In support of its application, the Association commissioned study groups to examine the housing and financial markets in four countries of the Community – West Germany, Belgium, the Netherlands and France – and the reports of these working groups provide valuable information on the situation in those countries. These reports tended to show that the main obstacles to societies' operating elsewhere in the Community were not the legal constraints but rather were marketing constraints. Of all systems of housing finance, the British system is perhaps least easily transportable across national frontiers in that it depends entirely on the retail markets. It would be relatively easy for, for example, a German mortgage bank to set up in Britain because it knows that its bonds would sell given a market yield and there is an unmet demand for mortgage finance. However, societies do not use the capital markets but rather rely on obtaining funds from the retail sector which is already well catered for by savings institutions in Germany and France. The strength of the savings banks in these two countries in particular comes as something as a shock to those used to the British system.

In fact, progress in integrating British building societies into the European Community has been very slow. The only positive step which the government has been required to take has been to implement the first Council directive. It was noted that this directive allowed for a deferment period of up to eight years in the event of technical difficulties. On 26 May 1978, the then Minister of State at the Treasury indicated that the government had decided to defer the application of the directive to building societies and also to the trustee savings banks. The Minister commented:

Building societies are subject to prudential supervision by the Chief Registrar of Friendly Societies under the Building Societies Acts. Substantive amendments to those Acts would be required to comply with the directive. The Government intend to bring the necessary legislation forward as soon as it is practicable to do so having regard to the pressures on the Parliamentary timetable. Consultations on the form of the legislation are in progress with The Building Societies Association.

The Association regretted this announcement by the government although it was not entirely unexpected.

Chapter 12 noted that primary building society legislation was expected in the 1980/81 session of Parliament and it was hoped that this legislation would include implementation of the first Council directive and also, and far more significantly, powers to enable societies to operate in the other countries of the European Community. However, on 8 August 1980, the Financial Secretary to the Treasury, Mr Nigel Lawson, announced that the Government intended to apply to building societies the first European directive by means of regulations to be made in the 1980/81 session of Parliament under the European Communities Act 1972. He went on to indicate that the government had no immediate plans for primary legislation. This statement itself is significant in that it seems to contradict the statement made on 26 May 1978 by the then Minister of State at the Treasury, who indicated that substantive amendments to the Building Societies Act would be required to comply with the directive.

The directive was duly applied to societies by the Building Societies (Authorisation) Regulations 1981 which came into effect on 1 December 1981. This requires societies seeking authorisation to satisfy two conditions:

(a) The business should effectively be directed by two individuals.
(b) The society should have a combination of deferred shares and reserves of the greater of £50,000 or the old sliding scale for reserves.

All existing societies are deemed to be authorised but if, after eighteen months, a society does not meet the two requirements then authorisation can be withdrawn.

Amending the Building Societies Acts to enable societies to operate in the other countries of the European Community is a reasonably simple matter. The Association's working group on Germany suggested that the Acts would need to be amended to give societies power:

(a) to raise funds in European currencies;
(b) to lend in European currencies;
(c) to recognise European land charges as equivalent to a mortgage;
(d) possibly to allow lending on second mortgage;
(e) to allow liquid funds to be held in European banks;
(f) to allow surplus funds to be invested in suitable European investments;
(g) to provide for operation, membership, voting rights, etc.

There would also be a need to legislate on various incidental matters arising from the essentially domestic nature of the present building society law.

However, as has already been indicated, the main obstacle to cross-frontier operations by national housing finance institutions is not so much the legal obstacles but rather more practical marketing and economic problems. The government might be satisfied that it could amend building society law so as to make good law but its concern is probably more with prudential aspects of operations abroad. One possibility would be for societies above a certain size to be permitted to operate elsewhere in the European Community. In any event, it is clear that significant progress on this subject is a very long way off.

The Likely Progress of the Harmonisation of Housing Finance

This chapter has illustrated the immense difficulties of harmonising housing finance systems or allowing specialist housing finance organisations to operate across national frontiers. Not only are the difficulties tremendous but the benefits, while being significant, are arguably not substantial. It seems probable that the progress in allowing institutions such as building societies to operate abroad will be slow, not because of any lack of will at the Community level but simply because domestic supervisory bodies will need to be wholly satisfied that cross-frontier operations can safely be allowed. Meanwhile, the substantial increase in understanding of the various systems is undoubtedly beneficial and does open the way for substantive progress in due course.

In the absence of more radical measures, there is one useful avenue that can be taken to promote the objectives of the European Community in terms of housing finance and that is the establishment of links, formal or informal, between the specialist housing finance organisations. The point has been made that what it is important for a common market to achieve is that people should not be hindered if they wish to move across national frontiers. This could be achieved by a British building society's being willing to lend in West Germany but it could also be achieved by a co-operative arrangement between, say, a building society and a German savings bank under which each would treat each other's members as being their own. Thus, if a borrower of a particular building society in Britain wished to buy a house in West Germany the society would, through its German counterpart, make the necessary arrangements. It would of course be necessary for the institutions to understand each other's systems and to a significant extent this can be achieved by, for example, the exchange of staff for short periods and by the exchange of information. British law effectively prevents a formal link between a building society and a foreign institution but there is nothing to stop an informal link and indeed some societies have already taken preliminary steps in this direction.

To the extent that national organisations make mortgage loans in other countries then one expects that the major progress will be made not by the specialist organisations but rather by the general banks which already operate on an international basis and which are therefore more able to take on an additional role. If the banks are not able to make loans in other countries directly then their existing business contacts should enable them to assist their customers to obtain their requirements.

This is a rather pessimistic conclusion as far as British building societies are concerned because notwithstanding their huge size in relation to other specialist and indeed general financial institutions, they are not very well placed to lead the way in terms of establishing a common market in housing finance. This is unfortunate in many ways because societies have shown their huge commitment to the concept of the European Community by promoting understanding and conducting research into other European countries.

Chapter 16

Building Societies: The Future

This book is being published at a time when the building society industry is undergoing considerable change. The post-war period has seen the industry grow uninterruptedly and moreover societies have faced little competition either from other societies or from competing institutions. This final chapter of the book rehearses the reasons for the success of building societies in the post-war period, examines why the nature of the industry is changing and assesses the impact of the new competitive environment.

The Development of Building Societies in the Post-War Period

Building societies have enjoyed immense success in the post-war period, because they have efficiently taken advantage of favourable market opportunities which have presented themselves. Societies have been fortunate to be operating in two large and growing markets and that their natural competitors have not competed.

On the housing side owner-occupation is the only tenure which is able to give most people the choice that they desire in their housing. This is not necessarily because of the innate qualities of owner-occupation but rather because the Rent Acts have virtually ended the supply of private rented accommodation on to the market and because local authority housing is allocated by administrative means rather than by the market mechanism. Furthermore, the tax advantages which owner-occupation has enjoyed has meant there has been an investment demand for housing as well as a stimulated consumption demand. Also, the tax advantages to be gained by holders of mortgage loans, as distinct from owner-occupiers as such, have enhanced the demand for mortgage finance in relation to the total demand for owner-occupied housing. People have been consistently advised that they should buy the most expensive house they can afford and, whatever house price they do pay, they should take out the largest possible mortgage.

Thus societies have faced an attractive market for housing loans but what has probably been more important is that their natural competitors have not competed in this market. In most countries savings banks are major providers of housing finance either directly or through their involvement in related organisations. In Britain, the savings banks have been restrained by government controls and not only are they very much smaller than their counterparts in other countries but until recently they had effectively operated only on the liability side of the balance sheet, handing over all the savings they attracted to government.

The clearing banks have not been significantly involved in the mortgage market partly because their philosophy in the post-war period has been geared more towards the corporate customer but also, to be fair to the banks, because they have been subject to an array of direct controls either on their lending or on their deposit taking activities. This has prevented them from making any significant inroads into the mortgage market regardless of their philosophy.

Similarly on the savings side of the business, societies have largely had a growing market to themselves. In the post-war period national savings has taken a steadily declining market share because poor products have been marketed badly. Even now, when the government is aggressively using national savings to fund the public sector borrowing requirement, it remains the fact that the National Savings Bank is, for administrative reasons, able to pay interest only on balances held for a complete calendar month in the investment account and that the Department for National Savings has not been able to produce an instrument which gives investors a regular income.

The banks have not sought to attract personal savings for a variety of reasons including the points already mentioned, that is that they have not been primarily interested in the personal market and they have been inhibited in their deposit taking activities by government regulation, especially the corset. However, the banks do have another motive for not seeking to attract savings. They hold a substantial amount, some £15,000 million at the end of 1980, in current accounts which have no interest cost. By aggressively marketing savings products, they run the risk that money in current accounts could be transferred into high cost accounts with a consequential effect on profitability.

The Consequences of the Old Competitive Environment

Building societies efficiently responded to the competitive environment which they faced. They expanded their operations such that in 1977 and 1978 they accounted for 95 per cent of the large and growing mortgage market, nearly 50 per cent of the personal sector liquid funds market and perhaps 60 per cent or even 70 per cent of what might be described as the genuine savings of individuals.

Moreover, societies have found it beneficial to restrict interest rate competition between themselves, this being achieved by the recommended rates system operated by The Building Societies Association, assisted by government pressure to hold the mortgage rate down and keep societies as firmly as possible under government control. One consequence of the cartel has been a persistent shortage of mortgage funds in relation to demand and hence societies have not had to market their mortgage products. Also, the cartel has contributed to the growth of non-price competition and it has meant that there has been no necessary correlation between the efficiency of a society and its success, whether this be measured by its growth rate or by its profit rate.

To summarise, by the late 1970s the building society industry had adapted well to provide 90 per cent of mortgage finance and to an ever-expanding mortgage market and taking half of personal savings. Moreover, this was achieved in a way which depended on minimal competition in respect to interest rates between societies. It is from this starting point that this industry has to face a new competitive environment.

Reasons for the Change in the Competitive Environment

The competitive environment is changing for a number of reasons. It is significant that these developments are occurring not only in Britain but also in the other English speaking countries, the USA, Australia and South Africa in particular. In all of these countries there has tended to be a demarcation between general financial institutions, that is banks, and specialist housing finance institutions such as building societies and savings and loan associations in the USA. A number of longer term trends have led to the breaking down of the lines of demarcation including:

(a) Technological advance which has made it easier for small institutions to offer a money transmission service in one form or another and to this extent the specialist institutions have encroached on the markets of the general banks.

(b) People have become accustomed to doing their shopping in a supermarket rather than in a number of small stores and there seems to be a measure of consumer preference for obtaining all financial requirements from one institution rather than having to deal with several. This puts a premium on being able to offer a range of financial services rather than just one.

(c) Traditionally the people running building societies and banks have been prepared to keep out of each other's areas but a new breed of managers in both types of institution is less prepared to observe such conventions and is intent on increasing market share regardless of who might be hurt in the process.

The breaking down of the lines of demarcation is most evident in the United States where the Depository Institutions Deregulation and Monetary Control Act 1980 effectively removed the remaining distinctions between banks and the specialist housing finance organisations, savings and loan associations. In Australia the recent report of the Campbell Inquiry into the financial system advocated a substantial freeing of the various regulations affecting the financial institutions and this again is expected to lead to greater competition between banks and building societies. Similar developments are also expected in South Africa.

In Britain the authorities have been aiming for a more competitive financial market and this has coincided with the wish of the banks to regain market share which they have lost to building societies.

The financial system, and in particular the banking system, was subject to controls throughout most of the 1960s and 1970s. In the 1970s these controls became more important because of the general move towards acceptance of monetarist philosophy, that is that the only effective way to control the economy is to control the money supply. Initially and naively governments assumed that money could be equated with bank deposits and therefore if the growth of bank deposits could be controlled, or alternatively if bank lending could be controlled (the effect of the two is identical), then the money supply would also be controlled. The main effect of this action was, not surprisingly, the development of alternative forms of money which circumvented the banks and therefore were not counted in the official statistics but nevertheless had the same economic effect as an increase in the money supply. Gradually it was realised that the only effective way to control the money supply, in the economic as opposed to the statistical sense, was through the market mechanism – that is, given a certain size of public sector borrowing requirement, through using interest rates – and this affects building societies as well as banks. The government also came to the view that the controls which had been imposed on the banking system were unfair on the banks and in particular had inhibited them from competing with building societies and had contributed to the somewhat lethargic state of the banking industry.

The first step towards a reform of the system was the introduction of the Competition and Credit Control regulations in 1971 but the government lost its nerve and reintroduced direct controls from 1973, most notably the corset which penalised the banks if their interest bearing deposits grew at more than a specified (low) rate. The corset was finally abolished in June 1980 and the government is now implementing its monetary policy much more through the market.

The new freedom which the banks now have has enabled them to take action to regain market share which they lost to building societies and to exploit their major strength in the retail financial markets, that is their ability to offer a complete range of financial services to the individual. Moreover the banks, through the protection of their own cartel in the 1960s, over expanded their branch networks and in order to make branches profitable it is necessary to generate more business through them and again this can be achieved more easily through the personal customer than through the corporate borrower.

Not only is the government stimulating competition between private sector financial institutions but simultaneously it has chosen to compete aggressively itself for retail savings. In 1979 the government took a decision to increase the use of national savings to fund the public sector borrowing requirement and this policy was reinforced in 1980 and 1981. The government has established targets for national savings, £3.5 billion in 1981, and has ensured that these are met by introducing more attractive products or by increasing the limits on holdings of those products. There is no way in which the private sector as a whole can compete against national savings because of the tax-free nature of the various national savings products.

The New Competitive Environment

A new and radically different competitive environment is evolving for building societies. It is an environment in which the banks and national savings, and also the trustee savings banks which are gradually moving into the private sector, are competing aggressively for savings and where the banks are also seeking to take a substantial share of the mortgage market. This change may also coincide with a desire on the part of the government to reduce the attractiveness of house purchase and particularly of mortgage finance. It is probably generally accepted by housing experts at least that the effect of subsidies has been deleterious and it is for political reasons that more radical action has not been taken to reduce housing subsidies. However, in 1974 the government introduced a £25,000 ceiling for mortgage loans qualifying for tax relief and this ceiling is beginning to bite more and more; if it is maintained it will have the effect of eroding tax relief substantially in real terms and therefore reducing the attractiveness both of house purchase and, more importantly for building societies, of mortgage finance.

It therefore seems that the demand for mortgage finance will not rise as rapidly in the future as it has in the past and this in turn means that building societies will not be able to grow as rapidly unless they move into new fields. Moreover the point has been made that building societies now face substantial competition for mortgage business from banks and, to a lesser extent, from savings banks. There are differing views as to the extent to which the banks are committed to the mortgage market. Some see the present high level of bank lending (in the second half of 1981 they were accounting for 40 per cent of the market) as a temporary aberration and that when the demand for industrial finance revives, then the banks will concentrate their lending in this area. Some also argue that bank lending is unprofitable.

There are no good grounds for accepting these arguments. Banks, unlike building societies, are not constrained by the need to raise funds when making loans. Every bank loan creates a deposit which the banks are then able to attract back. In the absence of government controls, banks are free to lend as much as they wish as long as they are satisfied that their lending activities are profitable. It follows that there is no reason why an increase in demand for finance from the corporate sector should lead to any reduction in the banks' ability to lend to the personal sector.

The question of bank profitability is more difficult. Certainly the banks have very high overheads, but these are incurred through the necessity to maintain an expensive branch network and to operate a money transmission service. Indeed the banks calculate that to operate a current account each year costs approximately 10 per cent of average current account balances. This compares with a cost of little more than 1 per cent for operating building society accounts. However, there is no reason why the banks should apply these costs to their mortgage lending functions. If banks wish to make loans on mortgage, then they have to raise additional finance to support these loans and that is done on the wholesale money markets. The cost of raising such funds is relatively modest and it is possible for bank mortgage rates to be only a little above wholesale money market rates for bank lending on mortgage to be profitable.

Both publicly and privately, the banks have indicated that they are in the mortgage market to stay because they regard it as essential for them to offer a complete range of financial services to the individual. Building societies can, therefore, expect to continue to face strong competition for mortgage business.

A few figures can illustrate how serious the position could be for building societies. Societies' mortgage balances have been growing at approximately 16 per cent a year in recent years. If the demand for mortgage finance slows down because of the limitation on tax relief, and the reduced attractiveness of housing as an investment, then possibly the rate of increase of balances could fall to, say, 12 per cent. If the banks are intent on gaining a significant share of the market, then possibly societies might need to fight very hard in order for their balances to rise by as much as 8 per cent a year.

It is less certain whether societies will continue to face strong competition on the savings side of their business from national savings. Certainly in the short term there is little likelihood that the Government will reduce the extent to which it relies on national savings, but in due course the market may well be exhausted and government will have to resort to more traditional means, that is the gilt market, to fund its borrowing requirement. However, history does tend to show that when government finds it can raise finance in a certain way, then it is unlikely to stop using that method, even though other avenues might be slighly more economical.

The banks are also likely to compete more strongly for savings, again as part of their wish to provide a complete financial package to individuals. One factor which is inhibiting them in this respect is that they hold a substantial volume of current account balances which are interest free. Any aggressive advertising of the savings service could lead to balances being transferred from interest free current accounts to high yielding savings accounts. The obvious way for the banks to overcome this problem is to put their current accounts on a proper footing, that is to pay interest on balances and to levy a proper scale of charges. Some banks are beginning to move in this direction and it seems likely that, within a few years, banks will offer an interest bearing cheque book account. This could be very competitive with the traditional building society ordinary share account and, if combined with strong national savings competition, could mean that building societies will need to fight substantially harder in order to maintain a high inflow of funds. However, if, as has been suggested, the demand for mortgage finance rises less rapidly, then building societies will have less need to raise a substantial volume of funds.

The Consequences of Greater Competition

The point has been made that not only are building societies having to face considerably greater external competition, but they are also competing more aggressively between themselves. To some extent, this has resulted from external competition and indeed traditional economic theory suggests that where there is external pressure on a cartel, then that could contribute to the cartel breaking down. However, there is also no doubt that there have been separate internal strains on the cartel. In particular, the more efficient societies no longer wish to be as constrained by the need to accommodate less efficient societies, whatever their size.

The transition from an industry in which there is little competition to one where there is strong internal and external competition tends to be beneficial for consumers but very painful for the organisations concerned. This makes it particularly difficult for the organisations, because they are not able to attract considerable public or governmental sympathy. Thus, government and the public are primarily concerned about the existence of savings products and mortgage finance and whether these products are provided by banks or building societies is not really material.

The first consequence of greater competition is that the importance of efficiency will increase. In the past, some societies which have done very well have not been efficient and it has been possible for any society to do well in terms of growth and profitability by operating above the BSA recommended rates. By the end of 1981 the position had been reached when there was little mortgage business, or at least little good mortgage business, to be had at a rate above the BSA recommended rate. However, some societies have to charge a higher rate because they have high cost savings products or high management expenses. By the beginning of 1982, profit margins were no longer solely the prerogative of building societies, either individually or collectively, and those societies which are able to obtain their money more cheaply than others or which have lower management expenses and also those which are able to lend, given that there is now competition for mortgage business, are likely to be the most successful.

It does not necessarily follow that the large societies will do best in the new environment and that the small ones will go out of business. Rather what seems important is market penetration. The five largest societies have nation-wide coverage, are household names and are able to make maximum use of national advertising. Smaller societies which confine their operations to a fairly tight geographical market are able to operate in a broadly similar way, although they cannot take advantage of the huge economies of scale available to the big societies. Those societies which have relatively spread out branch networks but no substantial market penetration may well find it more difficult to compete.

It follows, and again the experience of other industries supports this, that the pace of mergers within the building society industry will increase. Large societies may well try to get together to form very large societies in a position to compete with the five largest. Smaller societies may seek to merge in order to strengthen market penetration in relatively small areas. Already by the end of 1981, the pace of mergers in the industry was beginning to increase and it is understood that several fairly large societies were actively looking for merger partners.

In other industries such a situation would be likely to lead to outside organisations making takeover bids. It is understood that some American financial institutions, in particular, would like to gain control of building societies as an entry into the lucrative UK retail financial market. However, the peculiar nature of building society law prevents such takeovers.

The new competitive environment also has implications for the number of building society branches. In recent years, branches have been growing by about 10 per cent a year but now the pace of expansion is slowing down and some societies may even have to contemplate closing down branches. Again, this presents problems for building societies, partly because a building society branch has to have special office user planning permission and in the past some societies have paid a very high premium in order to obtain suitable branch premises. If the demand for building society branches suddenly falls, then the value of existing branches might well be affected.

Widening Societies' Activities

Building societies have always been vulnerable because they have had a limited range of products, that is basically a savings service and a mortgage service. The demand for the savings service is declining in relative terms because of competition from national savings and may decline further because of competition from the banks and savings banks. The demand for mortgage loans will rise less rapidly than in the past because tax relief is progressively being eroded and the building society share of the mortgage market over the next ten years will be less than in recent years because of bank competition. Building societies are not very well placed to respond to this competition by developing new lines of service but it seems that many will need to do so if they are to continue to survive as independent organisations. History tends to show that when a general institution, able to offer a package of services, competes with a specialist, then the specialist is likely to be the loser. For example, in retailing small specialist shops have gradually gone out of business as people have turned to department stores and supermarkets which may not be any cheaper for individual products but, because a complete range can be offered, the transaction costs are lower and convenience considerably increased.

Those societies that do not have substantial networks may be able to maintain a fairly profitable mortgage banking service. They can attract funds at market rates through advertising and possibly also on the wholesale money markets and can centralise lending functions. Those societies which have substantial branch networks will either need to slim them down or alternatively to develop more revenue producing business through those branches. One problem that societies have is that most branches are relatively small and are headed either by a relatively junior manager or a chief clerk. It follows that it is not easy to offer a full range of financial services and any services that are offered will probably need to be computerised. Societies generally are likely to develop into wider retail financial institutions. Some may be able to offer a cheque book service, possibly in conjunction with the banks, and most will need to consider the use of plastic cards and cash dispensers.

Conclusion

The 1960s and 1970s, more particularly, are likely to be seen as the golden age of building societies. Societies were faced with growing markets and little competition. They responded efficiently to the environment with which they were faced and enjoyed unprecedented growth and profitability. Such a situation is unrealistic to some extent and it was only a question of time before societies became subject to the pressures that influence most other industries.

What is, perhaps, surprising is the pace of change and the fact that all the elements of potential competition have appeared at much the same time. The freeing of the banking system has coincided with a change in philosophy on the part of the banks and the wish of the government to use national savings to fund its borrowing requirement. Government has also been less inclined to support owner-occupied housing and there has been a general wish to see housing subsidies fall and generally the priority given to housing has declined.

In the past, building societies faced a challenge of meeting a huge demand and this they responded to very well. Now the challenge is to survive in the face of greatly increased competition. This will lead to a very different building society industry with the most efficient societies probably doing very well but even they will have to fight very much harder to preserve market shares than has been the case in the past.

Bibliography

History

MG 2156.G7.

Ashworth, Sir Herbert, *The Building Society Story* (Franey, 1980).
Cleary, E. J., *The Building Society Movement* (Elek, 1965).
A Compendium of Building Society Statistics, Third edition (The Building Societies Association, 1980).
Price, S. J., *Building Societies: Their Origin and History* (Franey, 1958).

Law

The Building Societies Act 1962 (HMSO, 1962).
Guide to Building Society Finance, Second edition (The Building Societies Association, 1980).
Mills, J., Wurtzburg and Mills, *Building Society Law*, 14th edition (Stevens, 1976).
Thornton, C. E. I., and McBrien, J. P., *Building Society Law: Cases and Materials*, Second edition (Sweet & Maxwell, 1975).

The Building Societies Association

Boléat, M. J., *The Building Societies Association*, Second edition (The Building Societies Association, 1981).
Cleary, E. J., *The Building Society Movement* (Elek, 1965).
Price, S. J., *Building Societies: Their Origin and History* (Franey, 1958).
Report of the Council 1980–81 (The Building Societies Association, 1981).
Rules, Regulations and Bye-Laws of The Building Societies Association (The Building Societies Association, 1979).

The Chartered Building Societies Institute

Annual Report 1980–81 (The Chartered Building Societies Institute, 1981).
Butler, E. C. L., *History of the Building Societies Institute* (The Chartered Building Societies Institute, 1978).
Crerar, R. D., *Building Society Management* (The Chartered Building Societies Institute, 1980).

The Structure of the Building Society Industry

Boléat, M. J., *Building Society Branching* (The Building Societies Association, 1981).
Building Societies in 1980 (The Building Societies Association, 1981).
Building Society Branches: Development and Planning Issues (URPI Information Brief 80/3, 1980).

'Concentration in the building society industry', *BSA Bulletin*, October 1978, reprinted in *Studies in Building Society Activity 1974–79* (The Building Societies Association, 1980).

The Housing Monitoring Team, *The Structure and Functioning of Building Societies: A Head Office View* (Centre for Urban and Regional Studies, University of Birmingham, Research Memorandum no. 64, May 1978).

Building Societies and the Savings Market

'Building societies and the saving ratio', *BSA Bulletin*, no. 27, July 1981.
Building Societies and the Savings Market (The Building Societies Association, 1979).
Building Societies in 1980 (The Building Societies Association, 1981).
Committee to Review the Functioning of Financial Institutions Report, Cmnd 7937 (HMSO, 1980).
Evidence Submitted by The Building Societies Association to the Committee to Review the Functioning of Financial Institutions (The Building Societies Association, 1978).
'The growth of interest credited', *BSA Bulletin*, no. 27, July 1981.
Mortgage Finance in the 1980s (The Building Societies Association, 1980).
Studies in Building Society Activity 1974–79 (The Building Societies Association,1980).

Building Societies and the Housing Market

BMRB, *Housing Consumer Survey* (NEDO, 1977).
Building Societies and House-Purchase, 2nd edition (The Building Societies Association, 1980).
Co-operation Between Building Societies and Local Authorities (The Building Societies Association, 1978).
Cullingworth, J. B., *Essays on Housing Policy* (Allen & Unwin, 1979).
Housing and Construction Statistics.
Housing Policy Technical Volume, Cmnd 6851 (HMSO, 1977).
Murie, A., Niner, P., and Watson, C., *Housing Policy and The Housing System* (Allen & Unwin, 1976).
Studies in Building Society Activity 1974–79 (The Building Societies Association, 1980).
'Survey of building society mortgage lending, 1980', *BSA Bulletin*, April 1981.
The Housing Policy Review and the Role of Building Societies (The Building Societies Association, 1978).

The Financial Management of Building Societies

Annual Reports of the Chief Registrar of Friendly Societies.
Building Societies in 1980 (The Building Societies Association, 1981).
'Building society liquidity', *BSA Bulletin*, no. 22, April 1980.
'Building society reserves', *BSA Bulletin*, no. 24, October 1980.
Guide to Building Society Finance, Second edition (The Building Societies Association, 1980).
Rate of Interest on Building Society Mortgages, National Board for Prices and Incomes, Report no. 22, Cmnd 3136 (HMSO, 1966).
The Report of the Inquiry into Building Society Reserves and Liquidity to The Building Societies Association (The Building Societies Association, 1967).

'The effect of inflation on the management expense ratio of building societies', Evidence Submitted by The Building Societies Association to the Committee to Review the Functioning of Financial Institutions, reprinted in *Studies in Building Society Activity 1974–79* (The Building Societies Association, 1980).

Williams, L. E. H., *Building Society Accounts* (The Building Societies Institute, 1978).

Rates of Interest and Levels of Activity

Boléat, M. J., 'The British building society system and the European Community', in *Die Internationalisierung der Wohnungsbau Finanzierung* (Fritz Knapp, 1980).

Building Societies in 1980 (The Building Societies Association, 1981).

'Building society liquidity', *BSA Bulletin*, no. 22, April 1980.

Evidence Submitted by The Building Societies Association to the Committee to Review the Functioning of Financial Institutions (The Building Societies Association, 1978).

Building Societies and Housing Policy

Appraisal of the financial effects of council house sales (Department of the Environment, Scottish Development Department, Welsh Office, 1980).

Ashworth, Sir Herbert, *The Building Society Story* (Franey, 1980).

Boléat, M. J., *The Building Societies Association*, 2nd edition (The Building Societies Association, 1981).

House of Commons Environment Committee, 1979–80, *Council House Sales*, Minutes of Evidence, Tuesday, 13 May 1980, The Building Societies Association (HMSO, 1980).

House of Commons, Second Report from the Environment Committee, Session 1980–81, *Council House Sales*, vol. 1, Report (HMSO, 1981).

Housing Policy, Cmnd 6851 (HMSO, 1977).

Housing Policy Technical Volume (three parts), Cmnd 6851 (HMSO, 1977).

The Housing Policy Review and the Role of Building Societies (The Building Societies Association, 1978).

Murie, A., *The Sale of Council Houses* (University of Birmingham, Centre for Urban and Regional Studies, Occasional Paper no. 35, 1976).

Smith, M. E., *Guide to Housing*, 2nd edition (The Housing Centre Trust, 1977).

The Determination and Control of House Prices

Ashmore, G., *The Owner-Occupied Housing Market Since 1970* (University of Birmingham Centre for Urban and Regional Studies, Research Memorandum no. 41, April 1975).

Boléat, M. J., *The Building Societies Association*, 2nd edition (The Building Societies Association, 1981).

The Determination and Control of House Prices, papers and proceedings of a conference organised by The Building Societies Association on 28 January 1981 (The Building Societies Association, 1981).

The Guideline System, a Report by the Technical Sub-Committee of the Joint Advisory Committee on Building Society Mortgage Finance (Department of the Environment and The Building Societies Association, 1980).

'House prices and earnings', *BSA Bulletin*, no. 27, July 1981.

Housing Policy Technical Volume, Cmnd 6851 (HMSO, 1977).

Mayes, D. G., *The Property Boom: The Effect of Building Society Behaviour on House Prices* (Martin Robertson, 1979).

Whitehead, C. M. E., 'House prices – what determines them and can they be controlled?', *CES Review*, May 1978.

Whitehead, C. M. E., 'What should be done with the guideline?', *CES Review*, September 1979.

Co-operation Between Building Societies and Local Authorities

'Building society and local authority lending for house purchase', *BSA Bulletin*, January 1979, reprinted in *Studies in Building Society Activity 1974–79* (The Building Societies Association, 1980).

'The building society support scheme for local authorities', *BSA Bulletin*, July 1978, reprinted in *Studies in Building Society Activity 1974–79* (The Building Societies Association, 1980).

Co-operation Between Building Societies and Local Authorities (The Building Societies Association, 1978).

Housing Policy Technical Volume, Cmnd 6851 (HMSO, 1977)

Sources of Funds and the Stow Report

'The building societies in a changing financial environment', speech by the Governor of the Bank of England to BSA Annual Conference, May 1978, reprinted in *Bank of England Quarterly Bulletin*, June 1978 and *The Building Societies Gazette*, Conference Issue, 1978.

Housing Policy Technical Volume, Cmnd 6851 (HMSO, 1977).

Mortgage Finance in the 1980s (The Stow Report) (The Building Societies Association, 1980).

Report of the Working Group on Marketable Securities (The Building Societies Association, 1980).

Competition for Funds and the Wilson Report

Boléat, M. J., 'Competition between banks and building societies', *National Westminster Bank Review*, November 1980.

Committee to Review the Functioning of Financial Institutions Report and Appendices, Cmnd 7937 (HMSO, 1980).

Committee to Review the Functioning of Financial Institutions, Second Stage Evidence, Volume 3, Building Societies Association, Committee of London Clearing Bankers (HMSO, 1979).

Evidence Submitted by The Building Societies Association to the Committee to Review the Functioning of Financial Institutions (The Building Societies Association, 1978).

The London Clearing Banks, Evidence by the Committee of London Clearing Bankers to the Committee to Review the Functioning of Financial Institutions (Committee of London Clearing Bankers, 1978).

'The effect of inflation on the management expense ratio of building societies', *BSA Bulletin*, April 1979, reprinted in *Studies in Building Society Activity, 1974–79* (The Building Societies Association, 1980).

Building Societies and Monetary Policy

Boléat, M. J., 'Banks and building societies – controls are not the answer', *The Banker*, July 1979.
'Building society shares and deposits and the money supply', *BSA Bulletin*, no.22, April 1980.
Committee to Review the Functioning of Financial Institutions, Second Stage Evidence, Volume 3, Building Societies Association, Committee of London Clearing Bankers (HMSO, 1979).
'Components of private sector liquidity', *Bank of England Quarterly Bulletin*, September 1979.
Congdon, T., 'Building societies are already within the framework of monetary control', *The Building Societies Gazette*, April 1979.
Johnson, C., 'Banks and building societies – when is competition unfair?', *The Banker*, July 1979.
Llewellyn, D. T., 'Do building societies take deposits away from banks?', *Lloyds Bank Review*, January 1979.
Monetary Control, Cmnd 7858 (HMSO, March 1980).
Rose, H., *The Competition for Deposits and the Impact of Monetary Policy* (Institute of Bankers, 1979).
'The building societies in a changing financial environment', speech by the Governor of the Bank of England to BSA Annual Conference, May 1978, reprinted in *Bank of England Quarterly Bulletin*, June 1978 and *The Building Societies Gazette*, Conference Issue, 1978.
Turnbull, S. P., 'Building societies and monetary policies – equality in misery', *The Building Societies Gazette*, September 1979.

Prudential Supervision

Annual reports of the Chief Registrar of Friendly Societies.
Brading, K., 'Government postpone plans for a new building societies bill', *The Building Societies Gazette*, September 1980.
Brading, K., 'Chief Registrar speculates on changing government views about new legislation', *The Building Societies Gazette*, December 1980.
Burton, S., 'BSA plans to change the law on mergers and members' rights', *The Building Societies Gazette*, December 1980.
Chief Registrar of Friendly Societies, 'Supervision of building societies', Evidence Submitted to the Committee to Review the Functioning of Financial Institutions, November 1980.
Committee to Review the Functioning of Financial Institutions, Report, Cmnd 7937 (HMSO, 1980).
National Board for Prices and Incomes, *Rate of Interest on Building Society Mortgages*, Report no. 22, Cmnd 3136 (HMSO, 1966).
Registry of Friendly Societies, *Grays Building Society*, Investigation Under Section 110 of the Building Societies Act, 1962, Cmnd 7557, (HMSO, 1979).
The Report of the Enquiry into Building Society Reserves and Liquidity to The Building Societies Association (The Building Societies Association, 1967).
'A voluntary investors' protection scheme might offer 75 per cent compensation', Report of the Annual Conference of The Building Societies Association 1979, *The Building Societies Gazette*, Conference Issue, 1979.

The Income Tax Arrangements

Committee to Review the Functioning of Financial Institutions Report and Appendices, Cmnd 7937 (HMSO,1980).
Evidence Submitted by The Building Societies Association to the Committee to Review the Functioning of Financial Institutions (The Building Societies Association, 1978).
Guide to Building Society Taxation, Third edition (The Building Societies Association, 1981).
Price, S. J., *Building Societies: Their Origin and History* (Franey, 1958).
'The taxation of building society interest', *BSA Bulletin*, no. 17, January 1979, reprinted in *Studies in Building Society Activity 1974–79* (The Building Societies Association, 1980).

The Recommended Rate System

Committee to Review the Functioning of Financial Institutions, Report, Cmnd 7937 (HMSO, 1980).
Evidence Submitted by The Building Societies Association to the Committee to Review the Functioning of Financial Institutions (The Building Societies Association, 1978).
Evidence Submitted to the National Board for Prices and Incomes (The Building Societies Association, 1966).
Gough, T. J. and Taylor, T. W., *The Building Society Price Cartel*, Hobart Paper no. 83 (IEA, 1979).
Housing Policy, Technical Volume Part II, Cmnd 6851 (HMSO, 1977).
Mortgage Finance in the 1980s (The Building Societies Association, 1980).
National Board for Prices and Incomes, *Bank Charges*, Report no. 34, Cmnd 3292 (HMSO, May 1967).
National Board for Prices and Incomes, *Rate of Interest on Building Society Mortgages*, Report no. 22, Cmnd 3136 (HMSO, November 1966).

The European Community and Housing Finance

Boléat, M. J., 'The British building societies and the European Community' in Mulhaupt, L., and Wielens, H. (eds.), *Die Internationalisierung der Wohnungsbau Finanzierung* (Fritz Knapp, 1980).
British Building Societies in Europe, Papers given at a seminar held in London on 20 November 1980 (The Building Societies Association, 1981).
Building Societies and the European Community, Netherlands Research Group, Volume 1: Report (The Building Societies Association, 1979).
Building Societies and the European Community, Report of Working Group B, West Germany (The Building Societies Association, 1978).
Co-ordination of the Legal Provisions on Housing Credit, Commission Staff Paper, XV/38/78 – EN (Commission of the European Communities, 1978).
Fielding S. L., 'When ignorance is not bliss', *CBSI Journal*, February 1981.
'First Council Directive of 12 December 1977 on the co-ordination of laws, regulations and administrative provisions relating to the taking up and pursuit of the business of credit institutions', *Official Journal of the European Communities*, no. L 322/30 (Commission of the European Communities, 17 December 1977).

Freedom of Movement in the Housing Credit Sector, Second Commission Staff Paper, XV/118/79 – EN (Commission of the European Communities, 1979).

Osborn, F. M., 'British building societies' important role in two European associations', *The Building Societies Gazette*, May 1979.

Osborn, F. M., 'Building societies must discuss the form of UK Legislation on Europe', *The Building Societies Gazette*, July 1979.

Simpson, J. and Pitt, E., 'Housing finance and the law', *Habitat Europe* (Abbey National Building Society, Spring 1980).

Index